Medical Science
& the Law

Medical Science & the Law

Edited by Paula Goulden and Benjamin Naitove

Facts On File Publications
New York, New York ● Bicester, England

Medical Science & the Law

ISBN 0-87196-818-5

Printed in the United States of America

10 9 8 7 6 5 4 3 2 1

Table of Contents

PREFACE	vii
INTRODUCTION	1
ABORTION	3
Basics of the Controversy	3
State Legislative Controversy Prior to Supreme Court Decision	4
Supreme Court Ruling	12
1973 Supreme Court Ruling Upholds Abortion Rights	14
Attempts to Restrict *Roe v. Wade*	17
Further Court Action	18
Government Funding of Abortions Is Issue in Confirmation	19
House Votes to Further Restrict Funds for Abortions	24
Medicaid Abortion Funding Limits Upheld by Supreme Court	29
Right-to-Life Proposals to Amend the Constitution	32
Other State Court Decisions and Legislation	38
Other Supreme Court Decisions	43
Supreme Court Curbs State, Local Limits on Abortion	46
Other Congressional Action	49
Political Platforms	53
1976	53
Excerpts from Republican Party Platform	55
Religious Views	56
Other Public Views	60
CONTRACEPTION	67
Public Policy & Controversy	67
Population Policy and Birth Rate	72
Religious Views	75
The Pill	76
Birth Control Danger	81
Sterilization	83
BIRTH ISSUES	89
Wrongful Birth/Wrongful Life	89

CONTENTS

Preconception Injury 91
Surrogate Mothers 92
DEATH & DYING 93
Introduction 93
Definition of Death 93
Choosing Death 96
 Decision-Making for Terminally Ill Incompetents 102
Euthanasia 108
 Defective Neonates 110
SCIENCE & TECHNOLOGY 113
Introduction 113
Genetic Research 113
 Patenting Life 122
Test-Tube Babies 123
Artificial Hearts 126
EXPERIMENTING ON HUMAN SUBJECTS 129
Ethical and Legal Problems 129
Controversial Experiments 136
DRUGS 143
Introduction 143
Product Liability 143
 DES 143
 Other Product Liability Issues 147
 Other Access Issues 158
Cost-Benefit Standards 159
ETHICAL ISSUES AND HEALTH CARE 165
Informed Consent 165
Medical Ethics 170
Unnecessary Surgery 172
Health Costs and Scarce Resources 180
THE INSANITY DEFENSE 185
INDEX 191

Preface

A wit once defined law as "that which lags." If this is so, then medical science may properly be described as "that which advances." Medical science has both simplified our lives and made them more complicated by presenting new options for how we may live and die. As these new choices become available, the law has tried to keep pace in order to channel these decisions into socially acceptable forms. In this process, frequent conflicts have developed among physicians, lawyers and various political groups.

Traditionally, the law reserved to the government the power to decide life and death issues. The Judicial branch could condemn to death, and the Executive branch could pardon. No private person was allowed such power. However, as the Massachusetts Supreme Judicial Court recognized in the *Saikewicz* case, "advances in medical science have given doctors greater control over the time and nature of death." In addition, legal doctrines which have been developing independently since the early years of this century—such as the constitutional "right" to privacy—have given individuals more of a voice in the manner of their lives, deaths and medical treatment.

The law attempts to redefine, in light of new options, how life and death decisions may be made, who may make them, and the standards according to which they should be made. In the process, issues raised by medical choices have become the focus of political controversy. As courts resolve these conflicts inconsistently, or in a manner not to the liking of some, legislative solutions are proposed in attempts to override or reconcile judicial resolutions. Thus the interface of medical science and the law has been, and will continue to be, a field of great controversy.

Many issues recur throughout the topics covered in this volume. Not only is informed consent by patients an ethical issue in medical treatment generally, it is the source of legal controversy in cases that involve sterilization, the right to refuse treatment, products liability and access to new drugs. Likewise, privacy issues arise in abortion, contraception, sterilization, access to new drugs and right to refuse treatment cases.

This volume is based largely on weekly reports on world affairs by Facts on File, with cases and public reports included to complete coverage of the field. We have tried to cover all areas completely and without bias, in order to make this volume an accurate reference tool that will be useful to lay persons as well as to medical and legal professionals.

Paula F. Goulden
Benjamin J. Naitove

Introduction

The connection between medicine and law began to be defined as early as the third millenium B.C. in Egypt and Mesopotamia. In Egypt, it is said, this connection was personified by Imhotep (*circa* 2980–2900 B.C.), who was believed to have served simultaneously as chief justice and personal physician to Pharoah Zoser. Sumerian laws of the late third millennium and early second millenium B.C. were believed to have included ordinances of the payment of physicians and on punishment for unsuccessful medical treatment. These laws presumably were the inspiration for similar legislation in Hammurabi's Code of Laws (*circa* 1700 B.C.). Rome's *leges duodecim tabularum* (449 B.C.) provided that the fetus *in utero* had the same rights as a child already born to inherit its father's estate, and it gave the *pater familias* (the chief of a clan) the right to decide whether it was necessary to kill a seriously deformed child.

The Greek physician Hippocrates of Cos (*circa* 460–377 B.C.) is generally regarded as the "father of medicine." Hippocrates and his school produced major works on medical practice and medical law, and the so-called Hippocratic Oath is still the basic ethical guide for the medical profession.

The graduating physician, on taking the Hippocratic Oath, swears; ". . . I will prescribe regimen for the good of my patients according to my ability and my judgment and never do harm to anyone. To please no one will I prescribe a deadly drug, nor give advice which may cause his death. Nor will I give a woman a pessary to procure abortion. . . . In every house where I come I will enter only for the good of my patients, keeping myself far from all intentional ill-doing. . . . All that may come to my knowledge in the exercise of my profession or outside of my profession or in daily commerce with men, which ought not to be spread abroad, I will keep secret and will never reveal. . . ."

Religious qualms about abortion and birth control have played a major role in modern laws prohibiting or controlling such practices. Religion has also been one of the important factors in controversy involving the propriety of some modern scientific experimentation, especially in regard to research on human reproduction. But other considerations have also become increasingly important in the issue of how far medical science should—or should not—go.

Walter F. Mondale, then a Democratic Senator from Minnesota, pointed out to the U.S. Senate March 24, 1971 that it had become necessary "to consider and study the ethical, social and legal implications of advances in biomedical science and technology." Among developments motivating this concern, he said, were such breakthroughs as heart transplants, "test-tube fertilization of a human egg" and the prediction by Dr. James D. Watson "that we will soon see the day when a baby will be conceived in a test tube and placed in a woman who will bear the child."

1

Sen. Edward M. Kennedy (D, Mass.) discussed the issue in the Senate Aug. 1, 1972. "Advances in modern medical sciences have lengthened the span and changed the quality and very meaning of human life," he said. "But at the same time, these advances have opened a Pandora's box of ethical, social and legal issues in areas such as heart transplants, artificial kidneys, test-tube babies, genetic intervention, behavior modification and experiments on human beings."

The problems brought up by Mondale and Kennedy are part of a many-sided topic that in recent years has been dubbed "bioethics." This "life and death" subject is much involved with the "right to life," a term used in opposition to abortion. But it is equally concerned with "the right to die" or "death with dignity," expressions that question the medical profession's right to prolong life by extraordinary means after all hope for recovery—or even for consciousness or lucidity—has gone. Bioethics is also involved in the controversies over medical, surgical and psychological experiments with living human beings, in the disputes over birth control and in the issue of recombinant DNA research, in which genetic material is transferred from one organism to another.

These issues are the subject of this book, which is intended to serve as a record of the "life and death" topics as controversy over them gathered momentum during the 1970s. The material that follows is based principally on the account presented by FACTS ON FILE in its weekly reports on world affairs. A conscientious effort was made to record all events without bias and to make this volume a balanced and accurate reference tool.

Abortion

Basics of the Controversy

The controversy over abortion in the U.S. is largely viewed, rightly or wrongly, as a dispute between a religious viewpoint that insists on completely prohibiting the practice and a secular stand that abortion should be a private matter left to the option of women desiring abortions and their physicians. Although opponents of abortion include Protestants and Jews (and probably atheists as well), the general view appears to be that Roman Catholics and Evangelical Christians comprise the principal force working for a ban on abortion. The opinion prevails despite frequent statements by Catholic political figures that they will obey the law—regardless of whether it is pro- or anti-abortion.

Strong anti-abortion laws had been the rule throughout the U.S. until the end of the 1960s, and it was said by authorities as late as the middle-1960s that there was little chance of change. But, as Prof. Gilbert Geis of the University of California noted in "Not the Law's Business?" (a monograph produced in 1972 for the National Institute of Mental Health), "the rapidity of alterations in public attitudes and official policies in regard to abortion has been extraordinary." By 1970 Hawaii had enacted a law permitting "abortion on demand," and other states seemed ready to follow.

"The enhanced vigor . . . of the feminist movement played a very large role in the change," Geis asserted. Other factors, he said, included "Malthusian fears of over-population disaster," the increased ease of birth control methods and "the declining hold of theological orthodoxy on the minds and allegiances of Americans."

According to Geis, "it was a single sensational case, however, which thrust the abortion issue into public awareness. The case—that of Sherri Finkbine . . . —involved the use by a pregnant woman of a drug, thalidomide, that appeared 'likely' to cause her to give birth to a deformed child. Once the issue had been raised, it was but a short polemical jump from matters of physical deformity to those of psychic aberration, and from concern with the baby's well-being to concern with the mother's. Inevitably . . . the fundamental question appeared: Should the state have any right at all to dictate that the pregnant woman had to carry her child to term?"

(Mrs. Finkbine ultimately had an abortion in Sweden, where the fetus was found to be deformed.)

In 1973, the United States Supreme Court legalized abortion in a landmark case, *Roe v. Wade*. The Court declared all state and local laws which prohibit abortion during the first trimester of pregnancy unconstitutional, while permitting state and local governments more latitude to restrict abortion during the second trimester and prohibit it entirely during the third trimester. The basis of the Court's opinion was recognition of constitutional protection against government interference in a woman's right to privacy in matters that pertain to childbearing. The Court balanced the woman's interest in privacy against the state's interest in protecting the lives of the mother and the unborn child, and ruled that the woman's privacy rights were paramount during the first trimester—when abortion is safe and the fetus is not yet viable—but that the state's interest becomes controlling during the second trimester, when abortion procedures are less safe for the mother and the fetus may be able to survive outside the mother's womb.

The Court's recognition of a woman's constitutional right to privacy in deciding whether or not to carry a pregnancy to term was based on a long line of previous Supreme Court decisions in which the Court accorded expanding constitutional recognition to the "right" of privacy in making decisions which pertain to the home and family.

Definition. A "discursive" definition of the term "abortion" was prepared by the staff of the U.S. House Commerce Committee's Subcommittee on Health & the Environment. The definition:

abortion—termination of a pregnancy before the fetus has attained viability, i.e. become capable of independent extrauterine life. Viability is usually defined in terms of the duration of pregnancy, weight of the fetus, and/or, occasionally, the length of the fetus. A recent inquiry by WHO [World Health Organization] revealed considerable variation in the definitions used in different countries. It has traditionally been assumed that viability is attained at 28 weeks of gestation, corresponding to a fetal weight of approximately 1000 g. This definition is based on the observation that infants below this weight have little chance of survival, while the mortality of infants above 1000 g. declines rapidly. A variety of different types of abortions is distinguished: early—less than 12 completed weeks of gestation; late—more than 12 weeks; induced—caused by deliberate action undertaken with the intention of terminating pregnancy; sponta-neous—all abortions other than induced ones, even if externally caused, for instance by trauma or treatment of an independent condition; therapeutic—caused for the treatment of the pregnant woman.

State Legislative Controversy Prior to Supreme Court Decision

Hawaii legislature legalizes abortions. The upper house of the Hawaii State Legislature Feb. 25, 1970 adopted a bill that would legalize abortions in Hawaii performed by licensed physicians or osteopaths in a hospital sanctioned by the state or the federal government. Gov. John A. Burns let the bill become law March 11 without signing it.

The new measure repealed Hawaii's 101-year-old statute that permitted abortions only if the woman's life was in danger. Under the new law, any woman who had lived in Hawaii for at least 90 days would be allowed to have an abortion within the first four or five months of her pregnancy simply because she did not wish to have a baby.

The eligibility clause permitting the operation only within the first four or five months of pregnancy was inserted after the Roman Catholic Church had waged a long struggle to block the passage of the new bill. The requirement was viewed by some Hawaii legislators as a compromise measure to secure the bill's passage.

The residency requirement was included after Hawaii's House of Representatives voted down the same bill which lacked any residency clause. The requirement was written in after a conference committee between members of both Houses.

State Sen. Vincent H. Yano, who played a key role in having the bill adopted, indicated that he and Gov. Burns agreed that any abortion should be left up to the indi-

4

vidual mother and her physician. Opponents of the measure argued that the new law could create "an abortion mill" in Honolulu.

Administrators of hospitals in Hawaii reported a considerable rise in the number of abortion operations March 22.

At the Kapiolani Maternity and Gynecological Hospital in Honolulu, officials reported 46 abortions were performed in the first full week since the new law went into effect. Kapiolani administrators said this compared with a total of 70 abortions (under regulations of the old law) in a one-year period from 1968–1969. At Queen's Medical Center, the largest in Hawaii, 13 abortions were performed in the first week. This compared with the hospital's previous rate of about two a month.

Richard Davi, the chief administrator at Kapiolani, said the hospital could perform only 32 abortions a week because "we have so many other surgical cases to handle." Davi said that most of the women who had applied for abortions at Kapiolani appeared to be very young.

N.Y. also legalizes abortions. New York Gov. Nelson A. Rockefeller April 11, 1970 signed into law a controversial abortion reform bill that increased a woman's control over the medical termination of her pregnancy.

Under the new law, a woman and her physician could decide to terminate a pregnancy for any reason at any time up to the 24th week of pregnancy. After the 24th week an abortion could be performed only if the pregnancy jeopardized the woman's life. Under New York's old law, in effect since 1830, an abortion was permissible only to save a woman's life. The new law took effect July 1.

Stormy and emotional debate over the reform bill dominated nearly the entire session of the State Legislature. The State Senate voted March 18, 31–26, to replace the state's old law with what would have been the most liberal abortion reform bill ever passed in the U.S. Under the Senate version, there were no time limits on abortions, no resi-

dency requirements nor any provisions specifying how many times a woman could obtain an abortion. State assemblymen in the lower house predicted that the Senate version would not pass the Assembly unless some of those restrictions were written into the bill.

The Assembly March 30 rejected the Senate version of the bill, 71–73, three votes short of the 76 required for passage.

The bill was saved, however, when a Republican congresswoman in the early morning hours March 31 used a parliamentary maneuver to erase the unfavorable vote and table the bill for further discussion.

After a last-minute switch during a new roll call April 9, the Assembly passed a bill, 76–73, that would have removed all but one restriction on abortions in New York. The one provision written into the bill by the Assembly provided that an abortion could be performed for any reason up to the 24th week of pregnancy and after that only to save a woman's life. During the vote, Assemblyman George M. Michaels, an upstate Democrat, interrupted the roll call to announce that he was changing his "no" vote to "yes." "I realize, Mr. Speaker, that I am terminating my political career, but I cannot in good conscience sit here and allow my vote to be the one that defeats this bill." (Michaels failed to obtain the endorsement of his party for re-election April 19.)

The Senate voted 31–26 April 10 to accept the Assembly's version of the reform bill. The archbishop of New York, Terence Cardinal Cooke, issued an unsuccessful plea to Gov. Rockefeller on behalf of the Roman Catholic bishops of the state to veto the bill.

The Vatican published a message from Pope Paul VI Oct. 12 denouncing legalized abortion and euthanasia (mercy killing) as barbarism.

The letter was intended for a meeting of the International Federation of Catholic Medical Associations in Washington, D.C.

Vatican sources said the Pope's indictment of legalized abortion as counter to "centuries of civilization" clearly alluded to the new abortion law adopted in New York. The Pope said that "mercy killing" without the patient's consent was murder, with his consent was suicide.

Drop in deaths ascribed to new law—A former New York City health official said Oct. 12, 1971 that the liberalized abortion law had cut the city's maternal death rate by more than half since its inception.

Dr. David Harris, a former New York deputy commissioner of health, attributed the current low rate of two deaths for every 10,000 live births to the new, safe abortions which made criminal abortions unnecessary. The rate was the lowest in the city's history.

Harris made his report to the American Public Health Association, meeting in Minneapolis.

Harris said that through the years, abortion—mostly criminal abortions—had been the single leading cause of maternity-related deaths, accounting for about a third of such deaths each year.

According to medical figures, there were 15 abortion-related deaths in New York City in the first year the law was in effect. One year before the liberalized law was adopted, 24 deaths were tied to abortion-related causes.

Rockefeller for tightening abortion law— Gov. Rockefeller said April 25, 1972 that he favored amending New York's new abortion law by shortening the period during which a woman could legally obtain an abortion.

Rockefeller's remarks came amid renewed efforts by some organizations, predominantly Roman Catholic groups, to have the state legislature repeal the liberalized abortion law.

Under the liberalized law, a woman was allowed to have a legal abortion for any reason up to the 24th week of pregnancy.

Rockefeller recommended that the law be amended to reduce the 24-week period for permissible abortions to a 16-week limit. He said he believed "a modification in the present law is desirable" and if the legislature adopted such an amendment, "I will give it my approval."

Rockefeller vetoes repeal bill—Resisting pressure intensified by President Richard M. Nixon's intercession on the side of antiabortion forces, Gov. Rockefeller May 13, 1972 vetoed a bill that would have repealed New York's liberalized abortion law.

Rockefeller said: "I can see no jusitfication now for repealing this reform and thus condemning hundreds of thousands of women to the dark age once again."

The repeal bill would have restored New York's old abortion law under which a woman could only obtain an abortion when her life was in jeopardy.

Rockefeller had been under pressure from the Roman Catholic Church and groups across the state which had organized under the "right-to-life" banner to sign the repeal bill.

The pressure was increased when the Archdiocese of New York released a letter from President Nixon to Archbishop Terence Cardinal Cooke expressing support for the campaign to repeal the liberalized law.

Rockefeller took note in his veto message that the state legislature was under heavy election-year pressure to repeal the reform law. He said he respected "the moral convictions of both sides" in the issue, but he addded that "personal vilification and political coercion" surrounding the issue "raised doubts" that the legislature's votes "represented the will of a majority of the people of New York State."

Nixon had projected himself into the legislative fight in New York over abortion legislation by sending a letter to Cardinal Cooke enunciating his support for the repeal effort.

The text of Nixon's letter was released by the Archdiocese of New York May 6.

In his letter, Nixon said "I would personally like to associate myself with the convictions you deeply feel and eloquently express." Nixon called the drive of the antiabortion forces "truly a noble endeavor."

Following disclosure of Nixon's letter, there was a rising tide of criticism over Nixon's decision to intervene in a local issue. Rockefeller, who had tried to head off the

6

repeal campaign by vowing that he would veto any antiabortion bill, was reported May 8 to be "very upset" over Nixon's letter. Rockefeller's office said "we are referring all calls [on Nixon's letter] to the White House on this."

The White House moved quickly to assuage emotions stirred by the President's letter.

John D. Ehrlichman, Nixon's top advisor on domestic affairs, said May 10 that the letter to Cooke was intended as private correspondence and was not meant to intentionally embarrass Rockefeller. Erlichman attributed the White House's decision to give the archdiocese permission to publicize the letter to "sloppy staff work."

N.Y. law upheld—The New York State Court of Appeals July 7, 1972 upheld the state's liberalized abortion law by rejecting an argument that fetuses were legal entities having constitutional rights.

That argument, made in a case brought by Prof. Robert M. Byrn of Fordham University, was dismissed by the court, 5–2.

Byrn had claimed that the law, enacted in 1970, violated the 14th Amendment of the Constitution, which held in part that no state shall "deprive any person of life, liberty or property without due process of law."

Judge Charles B. Breitel, writing for the majority, said "unborn children have never been recognized as persons in the whole sense." Acknowledging that some religions and philosophies might see a conceived child as a person, "it is not true, however, that the legal order necessarily corresponds to the natural order."

Wisconsin law invalid. A three-judge federal court ruled in Milwaukee March 6, 1970 that part of the Wisconsin law forbidding abortions was unconstitutional. According to the ruling, a woman could have an abortion on demand of an "unquickened" child. The judges defined unquickened to mean a fetus before the first recognizable states of movement. In effect, the court's ruling liberalized Wisconsin's laws on abortion despite the fact that a coalition of con-

servatives and Roman Catholics had twice before beaten down attempts by liberals in the state legislature to ease the statutes on abortions.

The main opposition to the court's ruling was reported to have come from Roman Catholics, who comprised nearly 38% of the state's population. They were in great part responsible for turning back an attempt by liberals in the legislature to have a liberalization of Wisconsin's abortion laws in January.

The Most Rev. William E. Cousins, archbishop of Milwaukee, said "our reaction [to the court's decision] must be one of disappointment and dismay." He said the ruling was "clearly against a generally acknowledged principle that a fetus has a right to life."

One of the community groups which opposed the court's ruling was the Wisconsin Citizens Concerned for the Unborn, a group that received strong backing from the Roman Catholic Church. The association denounced the decision as a "disaster" and demanded an immediate appeal.

State Rep. Kenneth Merkel, a member of the John Birch Society, said that the decision "was typical of the sickness that is contagious in our federal courts. . . ."

An appeal of the decision was dismissed by the Supreme Court on procedural grounds Oct. 12.

Vermont law voided after repeal effort loses. After bitter debate, Vermont's State Senate March 18, 1970 killed a bill that would have repealed the state's 124-year-old abortion statutes. The 20–10 vote came after the Senate March 17 voted 15–14 to give the measure preliminary approval.

Nearly two years later, however, the state Supreme Court ruled unanimously Jan. 14, 1972 that the old antiabortion law was unconstitutional.

The law, which was enacted in 1846, permitted a doctor to perform an abortion only if a woman's life was in danger.

The court upset a lower court decision which dismissed a request by a welfare recipient for a declaratory judgment to block prosecution if she obtained an abortion.

Michigan law unenforceable. Michigan State Judge Clarence A. Reid Jr. ruled March 31, 1970 that the state's abortion law was unenforceable because of its vagueness. Reid dismissed the charges against a Detroit physician and his wife who were charged with conspiracy to commit an illegal abortion. Reid said he found the language incorporated in the state law that permitted a physician to terminate a pregnancy only when "necessary to preserve life" so vague as to deny the accused due process of law under the 14th Amendment of the U.S. Constitution.

Michigan rejects liberalization—In the Nov. 7, 1972 elections, Michigan voters defeated a proposal to liberalize abortion. The vote followed an intensive campaign that the two sides agreed would have national implications.

Pro-abortion forces in Michigan had succeeded in getting the issue on the ballot by having 300,000 persons sign petitions calling on the voters to override legislative refusal to liberalize a tough abortion law on the books since 1846. In its last four sessions, the legislature had failed to reach agreement on abortion reform.

Under the proposed law, physicians licensed by the state could terminate pregnancies at the patient's request during the first 20 weeks of pregnancy in a hospital, state-owned clinic or similar facility. Existing law allowed abortions only when a woman's life was in danger.

Virginia enacts liberalized law. Gov. Linwood Holton of Virginia signed into law during the week of April 5, 1970 a new and liberalized state abortion bill that was approved during the opening weeks of the 1970 legislative session. The new law would allow therapeutic abortions if the continuation of the pregnancy was "likely to result in the death of the woman or substantially impair the mental or physical health of the woman." The new law also provided for abortions if pregnancy resulted from rape or incest. The

new law revised a 123-year-old statute that permitted abortions only if the life of the mother was endangered by continued pregnancy. The revision went into effect June 26.

Texas abortion law held invalid. A three-judge federal panel in Dallas declared Texas' abortion statutes unconstitutional June 17, 1970 on the ground that they abridged the right of women to choose whether they wanted to have children.

The three U.S. judges said in their decision that the fundamental right of a single woman or a married couple to choose whether to have children was protected by the Ninth through Fourteenth Amendments. The judges acted on a suit brought by a pregnant, unmarried woman, a married couple, and a physician facing two charges of criminal abortion.

Texas law held that any person instrumental in causing an abortion with the woman's consent could be jailed for two to five years. Murder charges could be filed, under the state's statute, when death occurred during an abortion attempt.

The judges ruled that the Texas laws were "overbroad" and "vague" and did not properly define for doctors what constituted criminal abortion liability.

N.J. law voided. A federal court in Trenton, N.J. Feb. 29, 1972 invalidated New Jersey's 122-year-old abortion law. The law was held unconstitutional on the grounds that it was vague and an invasion of privacy.

In a 2–1 decision, the court held that the wording of the law "provides not a glimmer of notice" as to what one could or could not do. The New Jersey statute had prohibited abortions performed "without lawful justification."

The court added that the application of the law had not been clear. Some courts had found that it allowed abortions only to save the life of the mother, while prosecutors had agreed not to take action against abortions needed to safeguard the mother's life or her health.

The court added that the law also "chills"

doctors' exercise of their constitutionally-guaranteed free speech rights and violated their 14th Amendment rights to "freely practice" the profession of their choice. On the issue of privacy, the court held that the constitutionally protected "right of privacy" extended to abortion and that the reasoning behind the laws prohibiting abortions was not "compelling enough" to justify the invasion of that right. In a key passage of the decision, the court said that "we hold that a woman has a constitutional right of privacy cognizable under the 9th and 14th Amendments to determine for herself whether to bear a child or to terminate a pregnancy in its early stages, free from unreasonable interference by the state."

Connecticut abortion laws upset. A panel of three federal judges in New Haven, Conn. struck down as unconstitutional April 18, 1972 Connecticut's 112-year-old statute prohibiting abortion.

In a 2-1 decision, the court held that the state could no longer prevent a woman from deciding "whether she will bear a child."

According to one report, Connecticut's abortion reformers interpreted the ruling to mean that the state would no longer be able to prohibit doctors from performing abortions, or preventing women from having abortions, or stop persons counseling in favor of abortion.

Under the stricken laws, abortions were permitted in Connecticut only to protect the life of the mother.

Judge J. Edward Lumbard, of the 2nd Circuit U.S. Court of Appeals, writing for the majority, said: "what was considered to be due process with respect to permissible abortions in 1860 is not due process in 1972."

Concurring with Lumbard was District Judge John O. Newman. The dissenter was District Judge T. Emmett Clarie.

The old law was replaced by a new one enacted in May.

The new law, which was stronger than the one it replaced, allowed an abortion only when the "physical" life of the mother was threatened. The law was worded in that manner to prevent physicians from performing abortions to preserve what doctors said was the mother's mental health.

But the new law was also struck down as unconstitutional. The three-judge U.S. court in Hartford ruled Sept. 20, 2-1, that the law abridged the rights of a woman "to privacy and personal choice in matters of sex and family life."

In the September ruling, Judges Newman and Lumbard rejected the state's contention that a fetus was a legal person entitled to constitutional rights. Judge Clarie objected that the majority view represented federal judicial intrusion into the legislative sphere.

The U.S. Supreme Court Oct. 16 granted Connecticut a stay of the ruling voiding the new law. The stay would keep the new law in force until the High Court decided on its constitutionality.

The court's 8–1 ruling, with Justice William O. Douglas dissenting, came two weeks after Justice Thurgood Marshall refused to grant the stay. After Marshall's ruling Oct. 3, Connecticut succeeded in having the full court take up the stay question.

Florida liberalization. Gov. Reubin Askew April 13, 1972 signed into law Florida's liberalized abortion bill.

Under the new statute, abortions would be permitted to protect a mother's life or health, in case of rape or incest or if it seemed certain that the mother would give birth to a retarded or deformed child.

California birth rate down. A University of California demographer said July 28, 1972 that California's five-year-old liberalized abortion law was curtailing the state's birth rate and also beginning to reduce the number of children on welfare.

Kingsley Davis said "the facts clearly show that rates are down for both legitimate and illegitimate births and among both blacks and whites." Davis, chairman of the International Population and Urban Research Center at the Berkeley campus, made his claims at a hearing on family planning and illegitimacy by a state social welfare board.

Davis told the board that California births

declined by 11.5% from 1970 to 1971. The nationwide birth rate dropped 6%. According to Davis, abortions in California rose in 1970 to 65,000, nearly quadruple the number in 1969.

Some of new California law ruled too vague—The California Supreme Court held Nov. 22 that certain requirements in the state's abortion law were too vague to enforce, clearing the way for women to obtain hospital abortions on demand.

Among the provisions ruled unconstitutionally vague was a requirement that abortions be approved by local hospital committees. The court also said the medical criteria for an abortion were unconstitutionally vague.

The court's 4–3 decision meant that a woman in the first 20 weeks of her pregnancy could obtain a legal abortion if it were performed by a licensed doctor in an accredited hospital. The judgment for an abortion would now rest solely with the woman and her doctor.

Pennsylvania abortion law vetoed. Pennsylvania Gov. Milton J. Shapp Nov. 30, 1972 vetoed an antiabortion bill that would have been among the nation's strictest. In vetoing the bill, Shapp termed it "so restrictive that it is unenforceable."

Under the bill, an abortion could be performed only when a panel of three hospital-based physicians decided that the continued pregnancy would endanger the life of the mother.

The bill was sent to Shapp's office Nov. 20 after the House of Representatives backed it, 127–50. Shortly after Shapp vetoed the bill, the House failed to override his action by 34 votes.

A three-judge federal panel ruled in Pittsburgh that Pennsylvania's medical assistance program for welfare recipients unconstitutionally discriminated against recipients who chose to have abortions, it was reported May 8, 1974.

The ruling voided state regulations requiring agreement by two doctors that a

woman's life would be endangered by giving birth, evidence of rape or incest, or evidence of potential infant deformity before a welfare recipient could receive state reimbursement for an abortion.

Alaska liberalization vetoed. Gov. Keith Miller of Alaska April 18, 1970 vetoed a bill that would have given Alaska a reform abortion law almost without restrictions. Miller, a Methodist, said his decision to veto the measure was based on "the right to life."

He also said he disagreed with those who said he should not allow his personal convictions to influence his decision. "Any man who does not follow his personal convictions in conducting state business," he said, "is not worthy of the office of governor." Miller based a third objection to the bill on what he termed the bill's serious legal deficiencies.

The measure, passed by both houses of the legislature the week of April 13, would have allowed abortions to be a matter between the mother and her physician while the fetus was incapable of sustaining life independent of the mother, generally regarded to be until the 26th week of pregnancy.

Maryland liberalization vetoed. Maryland Gov. Marvin Mandel May 26, 1970 vetoed a liberalized abortion bill that would have erased all state restrictions on abortions. The bill was sent to the governor's office after it passed the General Assembly March 31.

Mandel emphasized that he had vetoed the bill on legal rather than ethical grounds. He said he was particularly concerned that the bill contained no residency requirements, that an unmarried minor girl could have an abortion without parental consent, and that the bill failed to include any time limit on when an abortion could be performed.

Mandel's veto could not be overridden by the General Assembly because 1970 was an election year for the legislature. The state constitution provided that a new legislature could not overturn the veto of a previous administration.

The veto left in effect a law enacted in 1968 that permitted abortions up to the 26th week of pregnancy in cases involving rape or incest, where there was a likelihood of a deformed baby or when the pregnancy endangered the mental or physical health of the mother.

Minnesota law held valid. A Minnesota district court judge Nov. 20, 1970 upheld as constitutional the state's 77-year abortion law in a test case involving a physician's deliberate violation of the statute. The judge gave the defendant, a woman gynecologist, a suspended sentence for violating the law.

In handing down the verdict, Judge J. Jerome Plunkett praised Dr. Jane Hodgson for her "forthrightness and courage" in testing the statute. He also said that she could "take solace from the esteem" in which fellow physicians held her.

Dr. Hodgson, 55, was convicted Nov. 19 of violating the abortion law and Judge Plunkett sentenced her Nov. 20 to 30 days in jail but suspended it pending the outcome of an expected appeal.

Dr. Hodgson had admitted performing an abortion on a woman who had contracted German measles early in her pregnancy. (Medical evidence had shown that the illness increased the risk that a baby would be born deformed.) Under Minnesota law, an abortion was permitted only when the life of the mother was in danger.

Illinois ruling overturned. The Illinois Supreme Court Jan. 27, 1972 vacated a lower court ruling that would have permitted a 15-year-old girl who had threatened to kill herself the right to have an abortion.

By a 4–3 vote, the court threw out the ruling of a Cook County circuit court judge who said the girl could have an abortion because of her suicidal tendencies.

D.C. abortion law upheld. The Supreme Court, by a 5–2 vote April 21, 1971, upheld the constitutionality of a 70-year-old district of Columbia law that permitted abortions only to protect the life and health of the mother. It was the court's first decision on the constitutionality of abortion laws.

The opinion, by Justice Hugo L. Black,

reversed the November 1969 ruling of a U.S. judge who held that the D.C. statute was unconstitutionally vague.

The court held that the statute was not vague. But Black in his opinion used what was regarded as qualifying language that was expected to limit enforcement of the D.C. law and others like it.

Black said "health includes psychological as well as physical well-being," a distinction not made in the D.C. law. He also declared that in future abortion prosecutions the government would have to prove not only that an abortion took place, but that the woman's life or health was not in danger.

(Officials of an abortion clinic in Washington, indicating that the decision gave them considerable latitude to perform legal abortions, said April 21 that their clinic would continue to perform them.)

Black was joined by Chief Justice Burger and Justices Blackmun, Harlan and White. Justice Stewart dissented, declaring that if a licensed physician performed an abortion the law should accept that the woman's health made it necessary. In another dissent, Justice Douglas agreed with the federal judge who said that the law was unconstitutionally vague.

Justices Brennan and Marshall did not paticipate in the decision because they felt that the court lacked jurisdiction to hear the case upon direct appeal from a lower district court.

In the original case, Dr. Milan Vuitch, a Washington physician, was indicted under th D.C. anti-abortion statute. The law was declared unconstitutional and the indictment quashed by Federal District Judge Gerhard A. Gesell, who held that the law's language was too vague. Writing that the word health provided "no clear standard to guide either the doctor, the jury or the court," Gesell dismissed the case. The Justice Department appealed directly to the Supreme Court, charging that Vuitch operated an "abortion mill," without taking into account the patient's health.

11

Supreme Court Ruling

AMA liberalizes abortion stand. A liberalization of its stand on abortion was approved by the American Medical Association (AMA) at its 119th annual convention, held in Chicago in June 1970.

Over objections lodged by Roman Catholic doctors, the AMA voted for the first time in its 123-year history June 25 to allow doctors to perform abortions for social and economic as well as medical reasons. The AMA voted 103 to 73 to consider abortions ethical if the following conditions were met: (1) The physician was properly licensed to practice medicine; (2) the operation was performed in a hospital accredited by public health organizations; (3) two other physicians were consulted on the case.

After the vote, Dr. Gino Papola, president of the 6,000-member National Federation of Catholic Physicians, said he intended to resign from the AMA. He urged the nation's 35,000 other Catholic doctors to do the same.

The next annual AMA convention took place in Atlantic City, N.J. June 20–24, 1971. Addressing delegates June 21, Dr. Robert H. Barter reported that his panel on abortions had found they were "acceptably" safe when done in the first three months of pregnancy in an accredited hospital or clinic. The panel also found that in any abortion complications could arise that would make the operation in a doctor's office unwise.

Bar Association backs abortion. The issue of abortion was taken up by the American Bar Association's House of Delegates at the ABA midyear meeting held in New Orleans Feb. 7–8, 1972.

One of the surprises of the session Feb. 7 was the House of Delegates' approval of a uniform statute to permit women to obtain abortions "upon demand." The House of Delegates, traditionally a conservative body on social issues, approved the abortion proposal with only 30 dissenting votes.

The proposal had been drafted by the National Conference of Commissioners on Uniform State Laws, a legal group seeking to reduce disparities among state laws.

Under their proposal, abortions could be performed by physicians upon demand only within 20 weeks of the onset of pregnancy. After that, abortions would be permitted only to preserve the expectant mother's mental or physical health, or if the fetus was gravely deformed, or if the pregnancy was the result of incest or rape.

This proposal was more liberal than any of the abortion laws at that time on the books in all states except New York and Hawaii, where abortion on demand was in effect.

Nixon vs. unrestricted abortion. President Nixon said April 3, 1971 that he regarded abortion as "an unacceptable form of population control" and therefore had ordered the Defense Department to abandon its year-old liberalized abortion policy and to conform with state laws.

The directive which the President struck down had enabled the wives of servicemen to obtain abortions more easily than under state regulations, which were generally more restrictive. According to military sources, the wife of a serviceman could obtain an abortion on the recommendation of a military doctor and one consultant. Most states had a more difficult procedure.

In his statement, the President said that if a particular state restricted abortions, "the rules at the military base hospital are to correspond to that law."

Military officials had said that the liberalized abortion policy, which was ordered into effect July 31, 1970, was designed to standardize abortion procedures throughout the armed services and not necessarily to make it easier for servicemen's wives to obtain abortions.

Statistics released by the Defense Department Oct. 15 showed that abortions at military hospitals had dropped sharply after Nixon's statement.

In the first nine months of fiscal 1971— while the exemption was still in effect— abortions at military base hospitals averaged

423 a month. In the last three months of fiscal 1971 following the President's cancellation of the exemption, abortions averaged 121 a month.

Public for liberalization. A federal study made public Oct. 27, 1971 indicated that half the public was in favor of liberalized abortion law. Two years previously, survey data indicated that 85% of the nation opposed liberalizing the laws governing abortions.

The new statistics were released by the Commission on Population Growth and the American Future, for which the nationwide survey was made. Seventeen hundred adults were questioned for the survey.

One of the study's questions concerned the circumstances under which an abortion should be allowed. Of those questioned, 50% said the decision should be made by the persons involved and their doctor; 41% said abortions should be allowed only in certain circumstances; the remaining 9% had no opinion.

Similar responses were recorded for a second question; "Do you think abortions should be permitted where the parents already have all the children they want?"

Among the other findings reported by the commission were:

Nearly 80% of those interviewed said they favored voluntary sterilization. In a 1966 survey 64% approved of it.

More than half thought the government should try to slow down population growth and to promote the development of smaller cities to better distribute the population.

More than half thought people should limit the size of their family even if they could afford more children.

64% back liberalized abortion laws—A Gallup Poll published Aug. 24, 1972 showed that 64% of the U.S. public favored full liberalization of abortion laws.

According to the latest poll, 56% of Roman Catholics now believed that abortion should be a matter for decision solely between a woman and her doctor.

The Gallup survey also showed that 73%

of those questioned believed that birth control services and information should be made available to teenagers.

The Gallup findings were based on personal interviews in June with 1,574 persons.

Abortion use widespread. A report prepared by the United Nations' Population Division, made public March 19, 1972 indicated that abortion might be the commonest form of birth control in the world.

The report said that "as the evidence accumulates many have come to feel that abortion may be the single most widely used method of birth control in the world today. It appears to be common in many countries, whether legalized or not."

The 162-page report noted: "In the countries where data of good quality have been analyzed, the death rates among women undergoing legal abortions have been very low."

Liberalized abortion laws urged. The Commission on Population Growth and the American Future, whose members were appointed by President Nixon to look into population growth problems, formally recommended March 16, 1972 that all states liberalize their abortion laws and permit women to obtain abortions on request.

The commission called for the government to fund abortion services and urged that health insurance plans be tailored to cover the cost of abortions.

While the commission had been set up to study population growth, it based its latest recommendations entirely on other grounds.

For the most part, the panel based its report on the view that "all Americans regardless of age, marital status or income should be entitled to avoid unwanted births."

The panel also assailed the "various prohibitions against abortion throughout the U.S.," asserting that they "stand as obstacles to the exercise of individual freedom: the freedom of women to make difficult moral choices based on their personal values, the freedom of women to control their own fertility, and finally, freedom from the burdens of unwanted childbearing."

The commission also linked a reduction in the number of illegal abortions to a decrease in maternal mortality and a decline in illegitimacy.

Using New York as a guidepost, where one of the nation's most liberal abortion laws was in effect, the commission pointed out that the maternal mortality ratios there dropped by two-thirds the year after abortion became available on request.

The panel noted that in 1971, New York City experienced the lowest ratio of maternal deaths since the city started keeping records.

According to the commission, the liberalized New York abortion law also exerted a downward influence on the city's illegitimacy rate.

Nixon rejects panel's proposals—President Nixon May 5 formally rejected the commission's proposals that all states greatly liberalize their abortion laws and make available contraceptive devices for teenagers.

In a written statement, Nixon said that the panel's report notwithstanding, he still regarded abortion as "an unacceptable means of population control." He added that he did not support what he called "unrestricted abortion policies."

Nixon also rejected the panel's proposal for states to make contraceptive devices and other family planning services widely available to minors. He said "such measures would do nothing to preserve and strengthen close family relations."

Mail running against abortion—The Commission on Population Growth and the American Future disclosed May 10 that mail it was receiving was running at the rate of 5–1 against a proposal that states liberalize their abortion laws.

According to a United Press International report, some of the opposition to the panel's proposal appeared to be organized. Some expressed their disapproval on form letters. Others sent antiabortion letters they said had been distributed in churches.

Bishops condemn panel proposal—Calling abortion an "unspeakable" crime, 240 of the nation's Roman Catholic bishops April 13 condemned the commission's recommendation that abortion laws be liberalized.

The bishops also rejected the panel's suggestion that the quality of American life would be enhanced by diminished population growth.

The bishops said the use of abortions to eliminate unwanted children rested on "an immoral and dangerous principle." The bishops added: "experience has already taught us that our social problems" would not be solved "merely by a population decrease, but require a change of heart and a reordering of priorities for the entire nation."

The bishops reiterated their stand against abortions at the end of their 3-day spring meeting in Atlanta. No vote or stand was taken, outside of the abortion action.

1973 Supreme Court Ruling Upholds Abortion Rights

Roe v. Wade

State bans voided. In a landmark decision handed down Jan. 22, 1973, the Supreme Court ruled, 7–2, that a state may not prevent a woman from having an abortion during the first six months of pregnancy. The ruling invalidated abortion laws in Texas and Georgia and, by implication, did likewise to laws in 44 other states.

Writing for the majority, Justice Harry A. Blackmun based the ruling on a constitutional right to privacy but rejected the plaintiffs' plea for abortion on demand. Justices Byron R. White and William H. Rehnquist, President Nixon's most recent appointee, dissented, charging that the majority had used "raw judicial power" in deciding a controversial legislative issue according to its own preferences.

The decision was criticized by Roman Catholic leaders, and praised by family planning and women's liberation spokesmen.

Blackmun denied the contention of Texas and Georgia that the unborn fetus was a "person" endowed with due process rights under the 14th Amendment, and noted that most restrictive abortion laws had not been imposed until the second half of the 19th century.

On the other hand, the opinion said, "the 14th Amendment's concept of personal liberty and restrictions upon state action" guaranteed a privacy right that included "a woman's decision whether or not to terminate her pregnancy." By interfering with the decision, the state could harm the pregnant woman medically or psychologically, or could "force upon the woman a distressful life and future" and bring "a child into a family already unable, psychologically and otherwise, to care for it."

But Blackmun specifically denied that the woman's right was absolute, since "a state may properly assert important interests in safeguarding health, in maintaining medical standards and in protecting potential life." After the first three months of pregnancy, during which time "mortality in abortion is less than mortality in normal childbirth," the state may intervene to protect the health of the woman, by licensing and procedural rules. However, the court barred state residency laws, or procedural obstacles, such as requirements that the woman's physician obtain the approval of committees of doctors.

In the last 10 weeks of pregnancy, Blackmun ruled, when the fetus "presumably has the capability of meaningful life outside the mother's womb," the state "may go so far as to proscribe abortion during that period except when it is necessary to preserve the life or health of the mother."

The Texas law, like those of 30 other states, had barred all abortions except when the woman's life was in danger. The Georgia statute, passed in 1972, based on the American Law Institute model penal code and similar to laws in 14 other states, allowed abortions when a doctor concluded that a woman's life or health was in danger, that the fetus might be born deformed or that the pregnancy had resulted from rape. Both states had been sued by pregnant women seeking abortions.

Blackmun, in reading the decision to the court, noted that most state legislatures were in session, and could write new laws in accordance with the ruling. Only New York, Alaska, Hawaii and Washington had abortion laws liberal enough to meet the court's criteria.

In a dissent supported by Rehnquist, White said the ruling meant "the people and the legislatures of the 50 states are constitutionally disentitled to weigh the relative importance of the continued existence and development of the fetus on the one hand against a spectrum of possible impacts on the mother," which White characterized as "convenience, family planning, economics, dislike of children, the embarrassment of illegitimacy, etc." White said the court was "interposing a constitutional barrier to state efforts to protect human life" while "investing mothers and doctors with the constitutionally protected right to exterminate it."

Although President Nixon had publicly opposed liberalized abortion, three of his four court appointees—Blackmun, Chief Justice Warren E. Burger and Justice Lewis F. Powell Jr.—voted to upset the Texas and Georgia laws. Nixon's directive regarding abortions in military hospitals did not appear to be affected by the ruling, which did not impose a governmental responsibility to perform requested abortions.

Roman Catholic cardinals Terence Cooke of New York and John Krol of Philadelphia issued statements denouncing the ruling. Cooke said he hoped opponents of abortion would "do all in their power to reverse this injustice."

Dr. Alan F. Guttmacher, president of

Planned Parenthood, Inc. welcomed the ruling but said "the three-month limit on unregulated abortions" imposed hardships "on the young and the poor who most often need an abortion after the 12th week." He said genetic defects in a fetus may not become apparent until late in a pregnancy. Officials of Zero Population Growth asked opponents of abortion "to work hard with us to improve access to contraception, thus eliminating the need for most abortions."

The court Feb. 26 unanimously refused to reconsider its Jan. 22 ruling, and it dismissed, without granting a hearing, a suit arguing that fetuses had a right to life. It held that the suit involved no "substantial federal question."

Controversy over decision. The Supreme Court decision was debated widely by advocates and opponents of liberalized abortion. One of the exchanges of opinion took place in the U.S. House of Representatives July 16, 1973.

Rep. Angelo D. Roncallo (R, N.Y.) warned that the abortion decision "has given added impetus to "segments of our society" prepared to dispose of "human life . . . if it is unwanted or somehow differs from an ill-defined norm." He held that "this demeaning, strictly pragmatic approach to life as a direct result of the Supreme Court decision can be measured. . . . [A]t a recent meeting of the American Medical Association, Dr. Joseph P. Donnelly noted that there were more abortions last year in New York City than live births." He continued:

As an Episcopal priest, the Reverend Charles Patrick Carroll, so correctly told the AMA's Conference on Medicine and Religion:

Medicine right now is without an ethic. The moment that you do what the patient demands, you open yourself to do what the state demands. If you can take life so glibly in the first two trimesters, what is to prevent you, please tell me, from taking it at any point in the spectrum? . . .

The abortion culture that has grown in the United States since the Supreme Court decision extends far beyond the abortion issue itself. All human life is being threatened by this pragmatic approach to research and medicine. In their never-ending quest for data, regardless of its significance, regardless of its availability through other means, researchers are filling their journals and computers without consideration for the humanity of their unwitting subjects.
. . .

Rep. Bella Abzug (D, N.Y.), Supporting the Supreme Court decision, held that the remarks made by those opposing it "reflect a view that one does not have to recognize the fundamental constitutional right of privacy of a woman over her body and over her decisions." She said:

The Supreme Court decision, by eliminating abortions from the criminal statutes, will now make it possible for abortions to be performed under safe medical conditions and not in the back alleys of the past which have crippled and taken the lives of many women. . . .

You are entitled to your personal religious and moral views but they are irrelevant to this Supreme Court decision.

For example, one has a right to free speech. I am sure the Members will recognize that. They may not like what one is saying when one is expressing that right of free speech. But if it is a valid exercise of free speech one cannot interfere with that right. Your remedy is to have the free choice not to listen.

The same thing goes with the subject of abortion. You cannot choose whether or not you want an abortion because you all happen to be men. But there are women in this country who may choose not to have abortions, and indeed that is their right. Nothing in this decision coerces abortion. But those who object to abortion have no right to prevent others from exercising their valid constitutional right to have an abortion. Their remedy is to have the free choice not to have an abortion.

Rep. William J. Keating (R. Ohio) asserted that "the basic right to life has been challenged by the court." He added:

Today we stand on the threshold of deciding whether or not we tolerate a new morality where the guarantees of the Declaration of Independence, the 14th amendment to the Constitution, and the previous traditions of our Judeo-Christian heritage do not apply to all human life.

When, for example, the Court states that the unborn are not recognized by the law as "persons in the whole sense," and when, further, it uses as a precondition for legal protection the test whether one has the capability of meaningful life, one begins to question what the logical next step will be to this type of logic . . .

What we have witnessed with the cases of sterilization in Alabama, with the Supreme Court decision on abortion, and with the increased discussion of euthanasia is the Federal Government determining who shall have the right to life and the right to give life and who shall not have these rights. . . .

Attempts to Restrict
Roe v. Wade

Introduction

The Supreme Court's decision in *Roe v. Wade* placed the Court and Congress, as well as all state legislatures and courts, in the center of the abortion controversy. The focus of debate shifted temporarily from courts to legislatures as opponents of abortion attempted to override the Supreme Court's decision to legalize abortions—or at least restrict access by some groups of women to abortions—through amendments to legislation, or "riders," and amendments to the Constitution.

A major legislative method of restricting the availability of abortions is to prohibit use of government funds, e.g. Medicaid, for elective abortions, which effectively prevented low-income women from electing to have an abortion. Other legislative vehicles of restriction include requiring consent of parents or husbands, allowing abortions to be performed only in hospitals, and mandating a waiting period before surgery. These restrictions were promptly challenged in the courts by pro-abortion groups.

In *Harris v. McRae,* the most prominent

of these cases, the Supreme Court ruled that government funds need not be used for elective abortions. State supreme courts, however, remain free to interpret their own state constitutions as requiring state funding of abortions or not, as they see fit.

Amendments to pending legislation are to be distinguished from proposed amendments to the Constitution. Legislatures can modify the effects of Supreme Court decisions by legislation, but they cannot change the Court's interpretation of the Constitution. If the Court does not overrule its prior decision, an amendment to the Constitution is necessary to override the Court's constitutional interpretation. Unlike ordinary legislation, constitutional amendments must be passed by two-thirds of both houses of Congress and be ratified by the legislatures of two-thirds of the states.

Other Supreme Court Abortion Ruling. The court June 4, 1973 upheld, 9–0, a lower court ruling rejecting an argument that abortions should not be covered by Medicaid, as the practice would interfere with the rights of a living, but unborn child.

Bans on federal-paid abortions lose—The Senate Sept. 17, 1974 approved an amendment to the fiscal 1975 Health, Education and Welfare (HEW)-Labor Department appropriations bill prohibiting use of federal funds to pay for abortions or abortion referrals, except to save the lives of mothers.

A similar, but more restrictive antiabortion amendment to the House version of the HEW-Labor appropriations bill had been defeated in the House June 27, and the Senate proposal was eliminated in joint conference committee before the two houses of Congress passed the appropriations bill Nov. 26.

The Senate amendment's sponsor, Dewey F. Bartlett (R, Okla.), indicated that the funding cutoff was aimed at the HEW Medicaid program, which he said had helped to pay for abortions in at least 14 states. Opponents of the Bartlett measure contended that it would discriminate against poor women, who, unlike higher income women, could not afford abortions except with the assistance of Medicaid.

The following year the Senate April 10, 1975 rejected, by 54–36 vote, an amendment to a health measure that would have prohibited federal funding of abortions under the Medicaid program for the poor.

Sen. Bartlett said HEW spent more than $40 million for 270,000 abortions in 1973, contended that the federal government had adopted a policy of encouraging abortions despite the national controversy surrounding the issue. "If this amendment is passed into law," Bartlett said, "we can eliminate those programs whose purpose is the taking of human life."

Opponents of the amendment on the other hand, avoided the emotional side of the issue and maintained that the amendment was illegal, vaguely written and unfair to women too poor to afford abortions without Medicaid.

In 1976, Congress Sept. 30 passed a controversial Labor-HEW bill containing a provision, approved by President Ford, that barred the use of federal funds disbursed through Medicaid for most abortions.

Both chambers had approved the bill's spending levels in August. The bill had not cleared Congress then because the House and Senate had disagreed on abortion. The House wanted a provision barring outright the use of the bill's fund to pay for or promote abortions; the Senate would not agree to such a provision. The final version incorporated a provision, worked out in a House-Senate conference committee, that barred use of the funds to pay for abortions "except where the life of the mother would be endangered if the fetus were carried to term."

Opponents of the abortion curb charged that it was discriminatory and unconstitutional because it would effectively deprive poor women of the right to an abortion. Supporters of the curb contended that the government should not fund operations that were considered immoral by a substantial percentage of citizens. (The New York Times Sept. 16 cited official HEW figures which showed that in 1975 between 250,000 and 300,000 women had received abortions that were paid for by Medicaid.)

Further Court Action

Stay on Medical abortion funds refused. The Supreme Court Nov. 8, 1976 refused to stay a lower-court order barring the federal government from withholding Medicaid funds for elective abortions. The lower-court order issued Oct. 22 by Judge John F. Dooling Jr. in U.S. District Court in Brooklyn, N.Y. had been sought by Planned Parenthood, the New York City Health and Hospitals Corp. and other parties. They had brought suit after Congress incorporated a ban on Medicaid funding for abortions in the fiscal-1977 appropriations bill for the Department of Health, Education and Welfare.

The stay, which would have barred the use of Medicaid funds for abortions while the case was under appeal, had been requested by Sen. James I. Buckley (R-Cons., N.Y.), Rep. Henry J. Hyde (R. Ill.) and others. Hyde was the sponsor of the aid cutoff amendment to the HEW funding bill.

The Planned Parenthood suit had contended that the cutoff on abortion funds discriminated against poor women by effectively denying them their constitutional right to an abortion.

HEW and the Justice Department had defended the law but did not endorse the request for a stay. In a communication to the Supreme Court concerning the request for the stay, the departments said they believed Dooling's ruling was "erroneous and [would] be reversed on appeal."

The Supreme Court ruling did not touch on the basic question of whether the Hyde amendment was constitutional. However, the ruling insured that federal Medicaid funding for abortions would continue until, or unless, the district court ruling was overturned on appeal.

The high court rejected the stay request in a one-sentence statement that did not record the views of individual justices.

(The following year the Supreme Court June 29, 1977 vacated, without comment, Dooling's 1976 decision that barred Congress from cutting off Medicaid funds for elective abortions.)

1972 ruling on Medicaid reaffirmed—A three-judge U.S. District Court in Brooklyn March 10, 1976 had reaffirmed a decision it had handed down in 1972 barring the state from denying Medicaid reimbursements for voluntary abortions.

The state Social Services Department had appealed the district court's 1972 ruling to the U.S. Supreme Court, which had sent the case back to the lower court for reconsideration.

The lower court's 1972 ruling had been limited to the question of indigent women. The 1976 ruling broadened the issue to include all women, regardless of economic status. Also, for the first time, the state was prevented from withholding Medicaid reimbursements from women having abortions for other than health reasons.

Government funding of abortions is issue in confirmation.

Joseph Califano was confirmed as Secretary of Health, Education and Welfare by a 95–1 vote of the Senate Jan. 24, 1977. Sen. Robert W. Packwood (R, Ore.) dissented as a protest against the nominee's views on the abortion issue, namely that he was against it personally but would follow the courts' decisions on use of federal funds for voluntary termination of pregnancy.

Califano Jan. 13 had told the committee he would work actively to prevent the use of federal funds to pay for abortions under any federal health programs. He added that if the courts ruled that pregnant women had a constitutional right to receive federal funds for abortions, he would "enforce the law." (Califano the same day had made a courtesy appearance before the Labor and Public Welfare Committee.)

Senate differs from House on abortion. The Senate June 29, 1977, approved, as the House of Representatives had previously, a

curb on the use of Medicaid funds for abortions. Unlike the House, the Senate voted to allow relatively broad exceptions. The vote on abortion, and votes on such other controversial topics as busing and affirmative action requirements, came during the Senate's consideration of the fiscal 1978 appropriations bill for the departments of Labor and Health, Education and Welfare (HEW). [See p. 478B1].

The funding bill was approved by the Senate June 29 by a 71–18 vote. The bill appropriated $5.9 billion for the Department of Labor, $53.4 billion for HEW and $1.3 billion for related agencies.

The total was more than the Carter Administration had requested. In May, Carter had warned he might veto spending legislation he considered excessive, but most of the debate in the Senate was not directed to the spending levels set in the bill. The Senate June 28 rejected, 62–32, an amendment by Sen. William Proxmire (D, Wis.) that would have limited appropriations in each program category to the amount asked by Carter. Proxmire said the amendment would have shaved $1.8 billion from the bill.

Federal funding for abortions was the subject of a series of votes on the Senate floor June 29. An amendment offered by Sen. Jesse Helms (R, N.C.) that would have barred the use of Medicaid funds except when a mother's life was endangered was rejected, 65–33. The Senate then voted down, 56–42, an amendment by Sen. Bob Packwood (R, Ore.) removing from the bill any curbs on funding of abortions. Pro-abortion forces then won adoption, 56–39, of an amendment providing federal funding when a doctor deemed an abortion "medically necessary."

As finally approved by the Senate, the curb on funding for abortions made exceptions for cases when a mother's life would be endangered by carrying the pregnancy to term, when a doctor said an abortion was medically necessary and when a pregnancy resulted from rape or incest. The House curb

19

had barred Medicaid funding for abortions under any circumstances.

Packwood said that inclusion of the exception for medically necessary abortions meant that most poor women would be able to obtain federal funding, since a doctor could take into account "physical, emotional, psychological, familial" and other factors in determining the necessity of abortion. However, the Senate language would face probable opposition from House conferees when the bill was sent to conference committee.

State funding not mandatory. The Supreme Court June 20, 1977 held, 6–3, that states and localities were not constitutionally required to fund elective abortions for indigent women. The decision, which came on separate cases in Pennsylvania, Connecticut and Missouri, was regarded as a major victory for the right-to-life movement.

The Missouri case, *Poelker v. Doe,* involved a campaign by St. Louis Mayor John H. Poelker to prevent abortions at his city's public hospitals. In an unsigned opinion, the Supreme Court, reversing a lower court ruling, held that the Constitution did not "forbid a state or city, pursuant to democratic processes, from expressing a preference for normal childbirth as St. Louis has done."

Justice Lewis F. Powell Jr. wrote for the majority in both the Pennsylvania and Connecticut cases. The issue in the Pennsylvania case, *Beal v. Doe,* was whether the state could deny public funds for elective abortions without violating the federal Social Security Act. Powell, rejecting a lower court ruling, wrote that "encouraging normal childbirth" was an "unquestionably strong and legitimate interest" of any state and that there was nothing in the wording of the Social Security Act that would make the pursuit of that interest "unreasonable."

In the Connecticut case, *Maher v. Roe.* the high court reversed a lower court ruling that had found the state's bar on Medicaid-funded elective abortions beyond the first three months of pregnancy in violation of a poor woman's right to equal protection of the laws. (Connecticut continued to supply Medicaid funds for childbirths.) Powell wrote, "The state may have made childbirth a more attractive alternative, thereby influencing the woman's decision, but it has imposed no restriction on access to abortions that wasn't already there."

Powell said, "The indigency that may make it difficult and in some cases, perhaps, impossible for some women to have abortions is neither created nor in any way affected" by state regulations. The issue of whether the federal government itself legally could limit Medicaid funds for abortions was not addressed.

Powell rejected the argument that the withholding of Medicaid funds for abortions was an act of unlawful discrimination against the poor. "An indigent woman desiring an abortion," he contended, did not belong in "the limited category of disadvantaged classes" entitled to constitutional protection. Powell claimed the majority was not "unsympathetic to the plight" of such women and that its decisions in these cases signaled "no retreat" from the court's landmark 1973 rulings.

Justices William J. Brennan Jr., Harry A. Blackmun and Thurgood Marshall each issued sharp dissenting opinions. Brennan said the present rulings "seriously eroded the principles" of the 1973 decisions. Blackmun, the author of the 1973 majority opinions, called the present action "punitive and tragic" and said it would be an "invitation" for public officials under pressure from the right-to-life movement "to approve more such restrictions."

Marshall characterized the majority decisions as "vicious" and said they would "have the effect of preventing nearly all poor women from obtaining safe and legal abortions." He contended that the rulings would have a disproportionate effect on nonwhite women, those most dependent on Medicaid for health care.

The Supreme Court June 27 also vacated decisions of lower federal courts that had invalidated New York State and South Dakota restrictions on the use of Medicaid funds for elective abortions. The court also refused to review a New Jersey Supreme Court decision voiding bans placed on elective abortions by some nonprofit hospitals in that state.

Abortion—Carter endorsed recent Supreme Court decisions on abortion as "adequate" and "reasonably fair." "The federal government should not be required or encouraged to finance abortions" except when the woman's life was threatened or the pregnancy was a result of rape or incest, he said. He thought the court's decision against federal funding of elective abortions "ought to be interpreted very strictly."

Carter was asked if it was fair that a woman who could afford an abortion could have one and a woman who could not afford it was "precluded from this."

"Well, as you know, there are many things in life that are not fair, that wealthy people can afford and poor people can't," he replied. "But I don't believe that the federal government should take action to try to make these opportunities exactly equal, particularly when there is a moral factor involved."

States rule on abortion funding. Since the Supreme Court's ruling June 20, 1977, that states were not required to provide free abortions to poor women, 13 states had decided to continue to use public funds for that purpose, a private research organization reported Oct. 12. The Alan Guttmacher Institute, formerly a division of the Planned Parenthood Federation of America, conducted the survey to assess the status of abortion financing following the cutoff of federal Medicaid funds.

(In all states, legal abortions continued to be available to women who could afford to pay for them.)

In Alaska, California, Colorado, Hawaii, Illinois, Maryland, Massachusetts, Michigan, New York, Oregon, Washington, West Virginia and Wisconsin, low-income women could still receive free abortions on demand.

Thirty-one states had terminated free

abortions except in cases where a woman's life was in danger. Idaho and Pennsylvania would pay for medically necessary abortions. Oklahoma, Virginia and Wyoming had not yet taken a stand on the issue. Arizona was unaffected by the recent rulings since it had never used Medicaid funds to finance abortions.

In 1976, about 300,000 indigent women obtained abortions subsidized by some combination of federal and state funds at a cost of about $61 million. Dr. Louis Hellman, former deputy assistant secretary of health, education and welfare, June 1 said a total of 1,115,000 legal abortions were performed in 1976.

Planned Parenthood Funds Ban Upset. Judge Donald Alsop of the U.S. District Court in St. Paul,Minn. ruled Feb. 23 that Planned Parenthood, a nonprofit organization that operated an abortion clinic in St. Paul, could not be denied state money for pre-pregnancy family planning services.

A section of a 1978 Minnesota state law that set aside $1.3 million to be distributed by the Minnesota Health Department specifically excluded Planned Parenthood. Judge Alsop declared the ban unconstitutional, holding that the statute denied the agency equal protection under the law as guaranteed by the 14th Amendment to the Constitution.

Planned Parenthood was the state's largest family planning agency.

Abortion-funding issue continues. Health, Education and Welfare Secretary Joseph A. Califano Aug. 4 banned all federal subsidies for abortions except when the mother's life was in danger. The ban was announced immediately after U.S. District Court Judge John F. Dooling in New York City vacated a temporary restraining order he had issued that had required continued federal reimbursement for elective abortions. The Supreme Court June 29 had vacated an earlier injunction Dooling had issued against the abortion ban.

The Hyde Amendment (after Rep. Henry Hyde, Republican of Illinois), which prohibited the use of Medicaid funds for elective abortions, had been temporarily nullified by Dooling's injunction. The amendment was part of the fiscal 1977 appropriations bill for the departments of Labor and HEW and applied only to the 1977 fiscal year, which ended Sept. 30.

The two chambers of Congress differed on extending the Hyde Amendment, which, according to an opinion issued July 27 by Attorney General Griffin Bell, prohibited federally funded abortions even in cases of rape and incest. (Califano noted in his Aug. 4 announcement that the government would reimburse other medical procedures, such as the morning-after pill (DES) or dilation and curettage (D&C), which were often used after rape or incest.)

For the 1978 fiscal year, which began Oct. 1, the House favored retaining the Hyde Amendment, which allowed Medicaid abortions only for women whose lives were endangered by carrying the pregnancy to full term. The Senate favored an amendment that would pay for abortions in cases of rape, incest and nonspecific medical necessity.

The abortion question was the sole remaining obstacle to final passage of the 60.2-billion Labor and HEW appropriations bill for fiscal 1978. In a letter to Democratic congressional leaders Oct. 11, Califano urged that either a bill be enacted "this week" or a continuing resolution be passed that would temporarily fund HEW salaries and operations.

Califano described the poor and federal and state employees as "hostages" of the abortion deadlock, inasmuch as the lack of government funding would force the curtailment of various programs and services.

HEW-Labor funds OK'd with abortion curb. Legislation providing $60.2 billion in fiscal 1978 appropriations for the departments of Labor and Health, Education and Welfare cleared Congress Dec. 7, 1977 when the House and the Senate finally reached an agreement over language curbing federal funding of abortions.

The bill had been stymied for months be-cause of the abortion dispute. The House, when it first passed the bill, had barred any use of federal funds for abortions. The Senate had also included a ban on abortion funding but had allowed exceptions in various cases, including when a doctor deemed an abortion "medically necessary."

(HEW and the Labor Department had been able to meet their payrolls and other cash obligations by means of congressional resolutions that provided funding in October and November at fiscal 1977 levels.)

With intensive lobbying by pro- and anti-abortion groups, the two chambers remained deadlocked for months. Finally, agreement was reached over the following provisions:

Federal funds for abortion were barred unless a continued pregnancy would endanger the woman's life or, in the judgment of two doctors, carrying the pregnancy to term would result in "severe and long-lasting physical health damage" to the woman.

Federal funds were permitted for "medical procedures" to treat rape and incest victims, provided the rape or incest had been reported promptly to the police or to public health authorities.

Federal funds were approved for birth control drugs and devices and for operations to end tubal pregnancies.

There was some disagreement among members of Congress over how the final language should be interpreted. Supporters of federally funded abortions argued that abortions were among the "medical procedures" that rape and incest victims could obtain. Anti-abortion legislators contended that abortions did not fall within the scope of that phrase. There were also differences as to what would count as "prompt" notification of rape or incest.

The legislation required HEW to promptly issue regulations enforcing the abortion provisions. Since there was no clear consensus on what the bill's language meant, observers agreed, the impact of the abortion provisions would be determined in considerable part by the HEW interpretation.

Supporters of federally funded abortions were not happy with the final version. The National Abortion Rights Action League termed the abortion provision "inhumane and quite possibly unconstitutional."

Anti-abortion groups were more pleased with the bill. William Cox, executive director of the National Committee for a Human Life Amendment, called the final provision "maybe a two-thirds victory for us." Cox added: "The most important aspect of this entire thing is that the pro-life movement established itself as a major political force in this Congress. We'll come back much wiser and better prepared to get a narrower provision next year."

Besides the abortion provisions, the bill included language barring HEW from using federal funds as a means to require, directly or indirectly, the busing of students to schools other than the one to which they were nearest.

The bill also barred the Occupational Safety and Health Administration from fining businesses for non-serious health or safety violations on a first inspection, unless 20 or more violations were cited.

In its funding sections, the bill made the following fiscal 1978 appropriations:

—Labor Department: $5.68 billion (the Administration had asked $6.38 billion).

—HEW: $53.186 billion (the Administration had requested $53.09 billion). The HEW appropriation broke down as follows: health, $6.24 billion; education, $10.13 billion, and welfare, $36.64 billion.

—Related agencies: $1.30 billion (the Administration request was $1.12 billion). Included in the related agencies appropriation was $596 million for the Community Services Administration, $117 million for ACTION and $88.5 million for the National Labor Relations Board.

The bill cleared Congress Dec. 7 when the House approved the abortion provision by a 181–167 vote and the Senate concurred by voice vote.

For parliamentary reasons, the bill was attached to a joint resolution that also extended funding for the District of Columbia at fiscal 1977 levels.

HEW Issues Final Abortion Rules. Regulations authorizing federally funded abortions in limited cases were announced Jan. 26, 1978, by Health, Education and Welfare Secretary Joseph Califano Jr. The regulations applied to abortions for low-income women whose lives would be endangered by continuing pregnancy, for those for whom giving birth (in the opinions of two doctors) would cause "severe and long-lasting damage to physical health" and for victims of rape or incest (providing the incident was reported within 60 days).

Legislation passed by Congress in December 1977 had provided that Califano, in issuing rules for implementation, would interpret the meaning of certain compromise terms included in the law.

Anti-abortion figures who had written the amendment forbidding Medicaid-financed abortions considered the "prompt" reporting period in cases of rape or incest as too long. But legislators who supported subsidized abortions for indigent women were pleased by the decision that the phrase "medical procedures necessary for the victims of rape or incest" would include abortion.

HEW's 62-page report accompanying the new rules specified that "anyone may report [rape or incest] on behalf of the victim." Since the law used the general term rape, not the term forcible rape, any pregnant girl under the age of consent would qualify for a federally financed abortion since she would be considered to have been raped.

Bangor, Me. Town Meeting (Feb. 17, 1978)—About 2,400 people attended the 90-minute meeting, which was held in the municipal auditorium.

Among the subjects that came up was abortion.

Carter did not favor use of federal funds for abortions. He was willing "to use federal funds if the pregnancy is the result of rape or incest," he said.

But he stressed that the federal regulations

"should be administered in such a way that women are not encouraged to lie about it, and use that legal congressional mandate as an excuse for abortions when no rape or incest has taken place."

"If it appears to me that the ruling is being abused," he said, "then I would favor tightening up the HEW regulations."

House votes to further restrict funds for abortions.

On a separate issue, the House June 13, 1978 rejected, 212–198, an attempt to include in the bill the same compromise curb on funds for abortions that had been approved in 1977. The compromise language would have allowed Medicaid funding for abortions in cases when the mother's life would be in danger, when the mother was the victim of rape or incest or when, in the judgment of two doctors, birth would cause the mother severe and long-lasting physical problems.

Instead, the House approved a sharper restriction. The House bill allowed federal funding of abortions only when the mother's life would be endangered by carrying the pregnancy to term.

The House leadership urged that the 1977 compromise language be adopted. The 1977 compromise had been achieved after a months-long deadlock between the House and the Senate, which had a more liberal attitude towards abortion funding. House Majority Leader James Wright (D, Tex.) said that by adopting the compromise at the start "the members might save themselves time and the agony of prolonged debate and bitter dissension. . . ."

But Rep. Henry Hyde (R, Ill.), a leader of the anti-abortion forces, said the lengthy 1977 contest had prevented many abortions. He also charged that the regulations drawn up by HEW to implement the funding curb had interpreted the language so loosely that what resulted was "abortion on demand."

Hyde continued, "The House position was torpedoed by the people who really run this country—the regulators."

An amendment offered by Rep. Louis Stokes (D, Ohio) that would have eliminated any curb on funding for abortions was rejected, 287–122.

Abortion Funding Curb Voted—The House Aug. 9, 1978 adopted, by a 226 to 163 vote, an amendment to the bill that barred the use of any defense money for abortions except when the mother's life would be endangered by giving birth.

Rep. Robert K. Dornan (R, Calif.) sponsored the amendment. He said that "26,000 abortions are performed by the military using defense dollars, and I'm sure the irony of the word "defense' comes home to all of us."

Rep. Elizabeth Holtzman (D, N.Y.), who opposed the funding curb, said that "all it will do is discourage men and women from entering our armed services" and therefore hurt the national defense.

Karen Mulhauser, executive director of the National Abortion Rights Action League, commented, "Today's regressive action marks yet another step towards abridging rights for all women."

'79 Appropriations Bill Enacted. Racing to meet defense payrolls, the 95th Congress sent a record-breaking $117.3-billion defense appropriations bill to President Carter Oct. 12. Final action came in the House on a voice vote and in the Senate on a 77–3 roll call vote.

President Carter signed the spending measure Oct. 13, 1978 allowing the Pentagon to meet its first payroll of fiscal 1979. The House-Senate conferees substituted more liberal language for the original stringent abortion restrictions of the House version. The final bill banned abortions for military personnel funded with federal money unless the pregnancy was the result of a crime or endangered the mother's health.

Medicaid Abortions Decline 99%. Health, Education and Welfare Secretary Joseph Califano Jr. issued a report March 8, 1979, that said congressional limits on federal funding of Medicaid abortions, had reduced the annual rate to 2,421 for the period February to December 1978 from an estimated

250,000 Medicaid-financed abortions in 1977. See 1978, p. 743A3]

Medicaid abortions were reported in 37 states. Sixteen states and territories reported no abortions under terms of the new funding. Ohio was reported to have accounted for roughly one-third of the 2,421 abortions.

The government report said that 80% of the abortions were approved because of danger to the woman's life, 17% were for possibly severe and long-lasting health damage and 3% for rape or incest.

Continuing Funding Resolutions Passed. Congress passed two resolutions to provide funds for government agencies whose regular, annual appropriations bills had not been cleared when fiscal 1980 began at midnight Oct. 1.

On Oct. 12, 1979 the Senate and the House finally compromised on a continuing appropriations resolution as only three of 13 regular appropriations bills had been cleared. President Carter signed the resolution Oct. 12. It was to expire Nov. 20.

Conferees worked out an agreement that preserved most of the restrictions on federally funded abortions that existed in 1978. A compromise also gave members of Congress and top-level executive bureaucrats a 5.5% pay increase. The compromise language stated that abortions could be funded only to save the life of the mother and in case of reported rape or incest.

The deadlock over the resolution, which had continued for weeks, centered on the Senate's reluctance to vote for a congressional pay increase and on the House's demand for tough, restrictive language on federally funded abortions.

On Nov. 16, Congress cleared another continuing appropriations resolution and on Nov. 20, the day the first resolution expired, President Carter signed it.

The resolution, which retained the earlier compromise language on federally-funded abortions, provided continuing funds at current levels through Sept. 30, 1980 for five major departments: Interior, Defense, Transportation, Labor and Health, Educa-

tion and Welfare; and for foreign assistance and military construction programs.

It also provided funding for the Federal Trade Commission through March 15, 1980, and prohibited the FTC from implementing any new regulations made final after Aug. 30, 1979, or issuing any new final rules, or initiating any new investigations.

When Congress did pass fiscal 1980 appropriations bills for the departments involved, the resolution stated, their funding would be set at that level.

Teen-Age Abortion Notice Law Upheld. The Supreme Court ruled, 6–3, March 23, 1981 that a state could make it a criminal offense for a physician to perform an abortion on a teen-age girl without first notifying her parents. However, the court suggested that such notice was not required if the girl in question was mature and independent.

The case, *H.L. v. Matheson,* involved a class action challenge by a pregnant 15-year-old girl to Utah's parental notification law. Three other states had similar laws.

The plaintiff, identified only as H.L., contended that the Utah statute violated her right to privacy and was unconstitutional because it failed to differentiate between mature and immature teen-age girls. The law had been upheld in Utah courts.

The Supreme Court also upheld the statute, but not in its entirety. Writing for the majority, Chief Justice Warren E. Burger held that "the Utah statute is reasonably calculated to protect minors in [the] appellant's class by enhancing the potential for parental consultation concerning a decision that has potentially traumatic and permanent consequences. . . . As applied to immature and dependent minors, the statute plainly serves the important considerations of family integrity and protecting adolescents."

Burger carefully noted that the law did not require parental consent for abortions on teen-agers. The statute, he explained, "gives neither parents nor judges a veto power over the minor's decision." (The Supreme Court

25

had struck down parental-consent abortion laws in the 1970s.)

The Utah law applied only to those pregnant girls seeking abortions who were unmarried, under 18 years old and were dependent on their parents. H.L. was living at home and was being supported by her parents at the time she filed suit.

The high court majority indicated that Utah, and other states with similar laws, had to make a legal exemption for those girls who had demonstrated maturity and were leading independent lives. (From a legal standpoint, a mature person was one who was capable of making informed decisions about his or her health or welfare. H.L. apparently had failed to convince the Utah courts that she was such a person.)

Justices Lewis F. Powell Jr. and Potter Stewart, while endorsing Burger's opinion, wrote separately that a minor who could demonstrate that parental notification "would not be in her best interests" should also be exempted.

Justice John Paul Stevens did not endorse Burger's opinion. Instead, he wrote a separate opinion stating that the Utah statute should have been ruled valid for all minors, regardless of their maturity or independence.

Justice Thurgood Marshall wrote the dissent, joined by Justices William J. Brennan Jr. and Harry A. Blackmun.

Marshall maintained that the Utah law hampered privacy and burdened "the minor's fundamental right to choose with her physician whether to terminate her pregnancy."

Abortion Limits Cases Argued. The Supreme Court Nov. 30, 1982, heard oral arguments on five cases dealing with the power of states and localities to regulate legal abortions.

The five cases, all accepted for review in May, were: *Akron v. Akron Center* and *Akron Center v Akron, Planned Parenthood v. Ashcroft* and *Ashcroft v. Planned Parenthood,* and *Simopoulos v. Virginia.* The first two cases came from Akron, Ohio, the second two from Missouri and the third from Virginia.

The cases involved a variety of laws that made it more difficult for women in those areas to obtain legal abortions. The statutes ranged from required hospitalization for second-trimester abortions (all three areas) to parental consent for abortions on minors (Akron and Missouri). Akron also mandated a 24-hour waiting period before each abortion and required physicians to counsel pre-abortion on the negative aspects of the operation.

Seven lawyers faced the justices. The high point of the arguments was a confrontation between Solicitor General Rex E. Lee and Justice Harry A Blackmun. Lee was presenting the Reagan administration's position in support of the Akron restrictions. Blackmun had authored the majority opinion in *Roe v. Wade,* the 1973 high court ruling that legalized abortion.

Blackmun asked Lee if he was asking the Supreme Court to overrule *Roe v. Wade.*

"No I am not," Lee replied.

"It seems to me," Blackmun said, "that your brief asks either that or the overruling of *Marbury v. Madison.*" The reference was to an 1803 landmark decision that set the precedent for the Supreme Court review of legislation on constitutional grounds.

Lee responded that he had no such intent, because "at the end of the day, the ultimate decision is still for the courts." But, he added, "the courts must be mindful of the choices already made" by elected officials.

"Did you personally write this brief?" Blackmun angrily demanded as he held a set of papers aloft.

"Substantial portions," the solicitor general answered curtly.

Alan G. Segedy, a lawyer representing the city of Akron, explained to the justices that "the right is not a right to have an abortion, but the right to make a decision: abortion or childbirth. . . . The state has an interest in protecting the woman's freedom of choice whether or not to have an abortion." He said that states or localities should not have to show a "compelling" reason for limiting abortions.

On the other side, Stephen Landsman, an attorney for a group of Akron abortion clinics, contended that the city ordinance treated "women as if they are not to be trusted to know their own minds and to make rational decisions."

William G. Broaddus, Virginia's chief deputy attorney general, defended his state's hospitalization requirement against suggestions that new medical procedures had made second-trimester abortions safer.

Justice John Paul Stevens asked him if Virginia restricted any other types of surgery to hospitals.

"I am not aware of any [other such laws]," he replied.

"So under Virginia law a surgeon could perform brain surgery at home, I suppose," Justice Stevens said.

Stevens pursued the same reasoning with questions to John Ashcroft, Missouri's attorney general.

Ashcroft said that he was unaware of any other types of operations that had to be performed in hospitals under Missouri law. However, he argued that the state legislature could constitutionally require "all childbirth except for emergencies to take place in a hospital."

"That would be a little hard to enforce, wouldn't it?" Stevens noted.

Frank Susman, a lawyer for Planned Parenthood Federation of America, which was opposing the Missouri law, argued that the "very foundations of liberty" were attacked by the notion that abortion regulation should be in the hands of state and local officials.

Abortion Funding Cases Accepted. The Supreme Court Nov. 26, 1979 agreed to review three Illinois cases dealing with the issue of congressional restrictions on federal funds for abortion. The cases, consolidated for argument, were: *Williams v. Zbaraz, Quern v. Zbaraz,* and *U.S. v. Zbaraz.*

The cases involved the so-called Hyde Amendment, named after its sponsor, Rep. Henry J. Hyde (R, Ill.). The amendment, which had been attached as a rider to appropriations bills since 1976, limited Medicaid funds for abortions to instances of pregnancy through rape or incest or instances in which the woman's life was jeopardized by the pregnancy.

An earlier version of the amendment had included a provision that would permit Medicaid funding for abortion if two doctors concluded that a woman would suffer "severe and long-lasting health damage" without an abortion. This provision, which was the subject of the Zbaraz cases, was dropped from the amendment for the fiscal years 1978 and 1979.

A U.S. District Court judge in Chicago, John F. Grady, had ruled in 1978 that the Hyde Amendment, as well as a state abortion-funding law, were unconstitutional.

One issue before the high court was whether the question of a constitutional violation had been properly raised in the lower court. If the Supreme Court decided that the issue was not raised, it could decline to review the merits of the cases.

Federal Aid Ban Struck Down. A federal judge ruled Jan. 15, 1980, that legislation restricting federal financing of abortions under Medicaid was unconstitutional.

The ruling by Judge John F. Dooling Jr., of the federal district court in Brooklyn, N.Y., ordered government officials to authorize expenditures of federal Medicaid funds to help pay for "medically necessary abortions provided by duly certified providers."

The decision by Judge Dooling defined medically necessary abortions as those "that are necessary in the professional judgment of the pregnant woman's attending physician, exercised in the light of all factors, physical, emotional, psychological, familial and the woman's age, relevant to the health-related well-being of the pregnant woman."

The ruling in the three-year case, the longest in the turbulent legal history of the abortion issue, struck down legislation known as the Hyde Amendment.

That Amendment permitted federal Medicaid payments for abortions only in cases in which a woman's life was endangered or pregnancy had resulted from rape or incest that had been promptly reported.

The plaintiffs in the New York case had contended that the fedral government's restrictions on abortion aid constituted discrimination on the basis of economic status, race and sex and also infringed on the rights of privacy, due process and equal protection of the laws.

The plaintiffs further argued that the federal statute abridged the constitutional separation of church and state by enacting into law the religious beliefs of those who regarded the fetus as a human being from the time of conception.

Government attorneys on the other side argued that the belief that the fetus was a human being was based on biological, not religious evidence. They also maintained that religious support for a belief did not by itself make a law supporting that belief unconstitutional.

Government attorneys also contended that a lack of financial means to exercise a right did not constitute a denial of that right.

Publicly financed payments for abortions for low-income women eligible for Medicaid began nationally in 1973 with the legalization of abortion by the U.S. Supreme Court.

Stay on Abortion Aid Order Lifted. The Supreme Court voted, 6–3, Feb. 19, 1980, to lift a stay on a lower court order requiring the federal government to resume financing abortions for poor women.

The order had been issued Jan. 15, effective Feb. 15, by Judge John F. Dooling Jr. of the U.S. District Court in New York City. Dooling struck down the use of the so-called Hyde Amendment by Congress to prohibit the use of federal funds for abortions under the Medicaid program.

Dooling's order had been stayed Feb. 14 by Justice Thurgood Marshall, who referred the issue to the full court.

The high court lifted Marshall's stay and announced that it would review the case, *Harris v. McRae,* during the current term. The court had already agreed to review three Illinois cases on the same issue. All of the cases were to be argued together and ruled upon before the end of the term.

Chief Justice Warren E. Burger and Justices Lewis F. Powell Jr. and William H. Rehnquist voted to continue Marshall's stay.

(The Department of Health, Education and Welfare Feb. 19 began notifying states of the resumption of Medicaid financing of "medically necessary" abortions. The states were henceforth barred from refusing to pay their share of Medicaid abortion costs.)

Abortion Funding Cases Argued. The Supreme Court April 21 heard arguments on an issue that might lead to the most important ruling of the 1979–80 term: whether Congress or the states could refuse to fund abortions for poor women.

The arguments involved three Illinois cases—*Williams v. Zbaraz, Miller v. Zbaraz* and *U.S. v. Zbaraz*—and one New York case, *Harris v. McRae.*

Five lawyers spoke before the justices while about 50 persons demonstrated outside the Supreme Court building, some in favor of abortion restrictions, others against.

The arguments revolved around the validity of the so-called Hyde Amendment, a rider attached by Congress since 1976 to the funding bills for the Department of Health, Education and Welfare. The amendment prohibited the use of Medicaid funds to finance abortions for indigent women, unless their pregnancies were life-threatening, or were the result of incest or rape.

Several states, including Illinois, had passed laws based on the Hyde Amendment barring the use of state funds for abortions.

U.S. Solicitor General Wade H. McCree defended the Hyde Amendment, saying that it was a legitimate tool to help "preserve human life and encourage childbirth." McCree noted that in 1977, the high court had ruled that state government had a rational interest in promoting childbirth and that this interest did not violate the equal protection rights of poor women when states refused to fund elective abortions.

Justice Byron R. White told McCree that there was "another interest" to be considered in the 1980 cases: "the life and health interest of the women."

McCree stated that the two interests were not so separate that they would "require a different [constitutional] analysis."

Justice John Paul Stevens asked the solicitor general if he would make the same argument if the Hyde Amendment did not "contain an exception for the life of the mother?"

McCree said that he would. "A pregnant woman is the only person seeking medical services in a case where a potential human life is at stake."

William W. Wensel, an assistant attorney general of Illinois, defended the right of the states to determine what types of medical treatment for indigents they would fund. He said Illinois had decided not to pay for abortions, just as it would not pay for infertility treatments or transsexual surgery.

Rhonda Copeland, an attorney with the Center for Constitutional Rights in New York City, spoke against restrictions on government-funded abortions. "The Hyde Amendment," she contended, "precludes the exercise of sound medical judgment about the health of a pregnant woman. The preference for fetal life at the expense of maternal health and life is irrational."

Justice William H. Rehnquist asked Copeland if she meant by "irrational" that "those who voted to adopt the Hyde Amendment belong in a loony bin? Were they just off the wall?"

Copeland replied that, as a legal matter, she "would not make that judgment."

Observers noted that Rehnquist appeared to be the most vocal proponent of the Hyde Amendment, while Stevens seemed to be its most evident opponent among the justices.

At one point in the 2½-hour proceedings, Rehnquist compared the congressional limitations on Medicaid abortions to the Supreme Court's limitations on access to pornography.

Stevens, who was regarded as an important "swing vote" on the issue, continually returned to the question of how the denial of Medicaid abortions affected the health of poor women.

Chief Justice Warren E. Burger and Justice Potter Stewart repeatedly asked the opponents of the Hyde Amendment if they believed that the Supreme Court should tell Congress how to exercise its spending power.

In another, related argument, Robert W. Bennett, a law professor at Northwestern University, contended that any limit on Medicaid abortions discriminated against poor women.

A Chicago lawyer, Victor G. Rosenblum, rejected this view, saying that curbs on public funding did not prevent women from having legal abortions.

Medicaid Abortion Funding Limits Upheld by Supreme Court

'Hyde Amendment' Backed in 5–4 Vote. The Supreme Court ruled, 5–4, June 30, 1980, that neither the federal government nor the states were constitutionally required to fund abortions for poor women. The decision upheld the so-called "Hyde Amendment," used by Congress to limit Medicaid abortions, as well as similar state restrictions.

The cases, consolidated for judgment, were *Harris v. McRae, Williams v. Zbaraz, Miller v. Zbaraz* and *U.S. v. Zbaraz.*

The Hyde Amendment named after Rep. Henry J. Hyde (R, Ill.), prohibited the Department of Health, Education and Welfare (now the Department of Health and Human Services) from using Medicaid funds for abortions except in instances of pregnancies that were the result of incest or rape or if the life of the mother would be endangered by carrying the fetus to term.

At least 40 states had also restricted or banned the use of Medicaid funds for abortion. (Medicaid was funded jointly by the federal government and the states.)

Decisions by two federal district judges, John F. Dooling Jr. in New York City and John F. Grady in Chicago, had found the funding limits unconstitutional.

The Supreme Court overturned those judgments, holding, among other things, that it was not the province of the courts to "decide whether the balance of competing interests reflected in the Hyde Amendment is wise social policy."

Chief Justice Warren E. Burger and Justices Potter Stewart, Byron R. White, Lewis F. Powell Jr. and William H. Rehnquist made up the five-member majority.

The majority, led by Stewart, rejected all of the arguments advanced by those opposed to the Hyde Amendment: that it discriminated against poor women and indigent pregnant teen-agers; that it was the imposition of the religious beliefs of Catholics and other faiths opposed to abortion, and that the amendment impinged on the freedom of choice established in the Supreme Court's landmark 1973 decision making legal abortions available to women.

Poor people in general, and pregnant teen-agers in particular, were not a "class" specifically protected by the Constitution, Stewart reasoned. He further held that the policy of paying for Medicaid childbirths while limiting Medicaid abortions, rather than being an act of discrimination, was an expresssion of "the legitimate congressional interest in protecting potential life."

As to the religious issue, Stewart maintained that the Hyde Amendment was "as much a reflection of traditionalist values toward abortion as it is an embodiment of the views of any particular religion."

Nor did the amendment interfere with a woman's freedom of choice in relation to abortion, Stewart said. "It simply does not follow," he explained, "that a woman's freedom of choice carries with it a constitutional entitlement to the financial resources to avail herself of the full range of protected choices. . . . Although government may not

place obstacles in the path of a woman's exercise of her freedom of choice, it need not remove those [obstacles] not of its own creation."

On the question of state funding, Stewart wrote that the laws governing Medicaid did not require any state "to assume a unilateral funding obligation for any health service. If Congress chooses to withdraw federal funding for a particular service, a state is not obligated to continue to pay for that service as a condition of continued federal financial support for other services."

The majority's stand brought angry dissents from Justices Thurgood Marshall, William J. Brennan Jr., John Paul Stevens and Harry A. Blackmun.

Marshall said that the ruling would have "a devastating impact on the lives and health of poor women," and predicted a sharp rise in the fatalities of such women through illegal or self-induced abortions.

Brennan contended that the decision would serve to "coerce indigent pregnant women to bear children that they would otherwise elect not to have."

Blackmun, who wrote for the majority in the 1973 ruling, assailed the government for "punitively" impressing "upon a needy minority its own concepts of the socially desirable, the publicly acceptable and the morally sound."

Stevens opined that the Hyde Amendment was "tantamount to [the] severe punishment" of poor women.

Reaction to the Decision—The reaction to the ruling June 30 fell along predictable lines, with antiabortion groups and individuals praising the decision, and abortion rights advocates damning it.

Rep. Henry Hyde described his own feelings as "exultant, delighted, pleased and happy."

Terence Cardinal Cooke of New York City said that the decision strengthened the efforts of those "working for human life amendment to the Constitution."

A spokesman for Planned Parenthood called the ruling "a national disgrace."

The American Civil Liberties Union charged the high court with abandoning "the constitutional guarantee of equal justice."

Court Denies Abortion Funding Review. The Supreme Court Sept. 17, 1980, rejected a petition to rehear the cases on Medicaid abortion funding limits it had decided June 30. In that ruling, the high court had upheld the authority of Congress to impose such restrictions.

The denial of petitions for rehearing was usually a routine Supreme Court action. However, this rejection was significant because it would halt almost all federally funded abortions.

The Department of Health and Human Services had continued to pay for about 1,000 Medicaid abortions a week despite the decision June 30. Secretary Patricia Roberts Harris had maintained that the ruling would not become final until the Supreme Court denied a rehearing.

A spokesman for the department said that states would be notified immediately of a cutoff of Medicaid abortion funds.

Abortion Aid Restrictions Passed—The Senate, in a 52–43 vote, May 21, 1980, approved an amendment sponsored by Sen. Helms that placed stringent restrictions on federal funding of abortions. Already approved by the House, the amendment permitted federal aid only when the life of the mother was endangered. It eliminated previous exceptions made for rape or incest.

The new restrictions were passed as a rider on a supplemental appropriations bill for the remainder of the current fiscal year, and would thus remain in effect through Sept. 30, 1981. Many Republican fiscal leaders objected to the treatment of the abortion issue as a postscript to the budget-writing process. During the lively and acrimonious debate that the amendment aroused, Sen. Packwood accused its proponents of "imposing on the country a Cotton Mather morality." Helms referred to a "set of instructions that came down from Mount Sinai" about the "deliberate taking of an innocent human life."

In other developments:

Six former U.S. attorneys general May 1 sent a letter to Sen. Max Baucus (D, Mont.) denouncing the proposed antiabortion bill as unconstitutional. In the letter, the three Republicans and three Democrats said Congress was not empowered to overturn the 1973 Supreme Court ruling merely through passage of a bill. Their objections echoed those contained in a previous letter sent by 12 constitutional scholars.

Six women were arrested April 23 when they interrupted a crowded Senate hearing with shouts of "Stop the hearing! Not the church, not the state, women must decide their fate!" The demonstrators were applauded by pro-abortionists in the room, who objected to the alleged 'stacking' of the witness list in favor of anti-abortionists.

New Jersey court permits Medicaid funding of all medically necessary abortions. The New Jersey Supreme Court ruled in 1982 that a state law prohibiting Medicaid funding of abortions except when the mother's life would be endangered by carrying the pregnancy to term violates the state constitution's equal protection clause. In *Right to Choose v. Byrne,* the court held that the state's legitimate interest in protecting the unborn child may not outweigh the mother's interest in her health. The statute's unconstitutional discrimination against women for whom abortion is medically necessary, but for whom giving birth would not be fatal, is an impermissible state influence on the decision of whether to abort the pregnancy. The court did hold, however, that the state may protect its interest in potential life by prohibiting medicaid funding of abortions where neither the life nor the health of the mother would be threatened by giving birth.

Massachusetts Sets Strict Law. Massachusetts Governor Edward J. King June 12, 1979, signed what was described as the strictest anti-abortion law in the U.S.

The bill prohibited the use of state funds for nearly all abortions sought by Medicaid clients and state employees covered by the state's group health insurance program.

Under the new law, government funded abortions would be permitted only to save a woman's life. The bill made no provisions for victims of rape or incest.

Mass. Court Overrules Abortion Curbs. The Massachusetts Supreme Court ruled Feb. 18, 1981, that the state constitution required the state to pay for all "medically necessary" abortions for women on welfare, even if their lives were not in danger.

The 6–1 decision, written by Justice Francis J. Quirico, overturned a 1979 state law that limited state-financed abortions to women confronted with life-threatening health complications. The court held that the due process provision in the state constitution was violated by such restrictions.

The court case involved claims of three unidentified Medicaid-eligible women who had each decided, after consultation with a physician, to have an abortion. The physician in each instance had determined that an abortion was "medically indicated" but not needed to prevent death, the decision said.

The court held that since the state chose to subsidize child-bearing and health costs, it must do so with "genuine indifference." Each of the affected women, the court said, was "entitled to non-discriminatory funding of lawful, medically necessary abortion services."

'80 D.C. Appropriations Bill Signed. President Carter Oct. 30, 1979, signed into law a fiscal 1980 District of Columbia appropriations bill after Congress had agreed to a compromise on anti-abortion language.

The Senate had adopted the final version Oct. 22 on a 64-to-19 vote. The House passed the bill Oct. 16, by voice vote.

As cleared by Congress, the measure appropriated $374 million in federal funds and approved a fiscal 1980 budget for the city of $1.5 billion.

The abortion question was resolved by a compromise proposed by Rep. Charles Wilson (D, Texas) limiting the use of federal, but not city-generated, funds to pay for Medicaid abortions. The compromise also adopted language that stated federal money

could not be spent to end a pregnancy unless the mother's life were endangered or in case of rape or incest.

'Right-to-Life' Proposals to Amend the Constitution

Anti-abortion amendment introduced. Sen. James L. Buckley (R, N.Y.) and five co-sponsoring senators May 31, 1973, introduced in the Senate a constitutional amendment prohibiting abortions except to save the life of the mother.

The amendment, designed to circumvent the Supreme Court decision striking down abortion laws, defined life as beginning when the fertilized ovum implanted itself on the wall of the uterus, a period usually four–seven days after fertilization. Under this definition, "morning after" pills would be considered contraceptive, and therapeutic treatment given to women immediately after rape would be legal.

Co-sponsors of the amendment were: Mark Hatfield (R, Ore.), Wallace F. Bennett (R, Utah), Carl T. Curtis (R, Neb.), Milton R. Young (R, N.D.), Harold Hughes (D, Iowa) and Dewey F. Bartlett (R, Okla.). All sponsors except Buckley and Bartlett were Protestants.

Hearings on amendments. The Senate Judiciary Constitutional Amendments Subcommittee held hearings March 6–7, 1974 on two proposed constitutional amendments aimed at rescinding the 1973 Supreme Court decision upholding a woman's right to decide whether or not to have an abortion. An amendment offered by Sen. Jesse Helms (R, N.C.) would guarantee, without exception, the right to life at the instant of conception. The other amendment, offered by Sen. James Buckley (R-Conservative, N.Y.), would allow abortion only when a reasonable medical certainty existed that the mother's life would be endangered by the continuation of the pregnancy.

Testifying before the subcommittee March 6, Buckley expressed a desire to restore the "traditional understanding" of the 14th Amendment, which he construed as the right to life. "It matters not, under my amendment," he said, "whether one is come to full term in a mother's womb." Buckley opposed abortions after rape but favored establishment of professionally-staffed treatment centers for rape victims.

Rep. John M. Zwach (R, Minn.), sponsor of an abortion amendment in the House, told the panel March 6 that framers of the Declaration of Independence said all men were "created equal," not that they were born equal.

John Cardinal Krol, archbishop of Philadelphia and president of the U.S. Catholic Conference, told the subcommittee March 7, "The right to life is not an invention of the [Roman] Catholic church or any other church. It is a basic human right which must undergird any civilized society." Humberto Cardinal Medeiros, archbishop of Boston, testified that the Catholic church opposed abortion, even to save the mother's life.

Rabbi J. David Bleich, who spoke for the Rabbinical Council of America and orthodox Judaism, said March 7 that fetal life was entitled to all the safeguards afforded all members of society.

Appearing in opposition to the amendments was Rep. Bella Abzug (D, N.Y.), who warned March 6 that the amendments "would impose a particular religious or moral ethic upon a nation that at its inception . . . rejected any dogma or creed as mandatory for all."

Colgate University professor Barbara McNeal testified March 7: "Should a male dominated [Catholic] religious hierarchy determine the moral posture and legal status of the opposite sex when the woman in question is caught up in a dilemma no man can fully understand? . . . A church that proclaims celibacy to reflect the highest levels of excellence and that takes the dimmest

possible view of scientific methods of birth control is not in a logical position to impose its view on abortion on the remainder of the citizenry."

Rabbi Balfour Brickner, who as a representative of the Union of American Hebrew Congregations appeared as a spokesman for reform Judaism, testified March 7 that he interpreted Judaic law to mean that the fetus was not a person until it was born. Brickner said abortion was not wrong.

Women's groups vs. amendments. Rep. Ronald V. Dellums (D, Calif.) inserted in the Congressional Record March 12, 1974 letters in which women's groups opposed the proposed antiabortion amendments.

Alice Travis, as chairperson of the Women's Caucus of the California Democratic Council (CDC), said in a Feb. 25 letter to Dellums that the CDC remained "diametrically opposed to any governmental infringement" on the "right of a woman to have an abortion on demand."

Sue Wimmershoff-Caplan, president of the Professional Women's Caucus, told Dellums in a Jan. 22 letter:

> We are convinced that the right of every woman to control her reproductive processes is an elementary Constitutional Right upon which all of her other efforts and aspirations toward equality are based. We would like you to know that at our annual convention held in New York City at the end of September, 1973, the following resolution was adopted:
>
> Since control over our bodies is the very cornerstone of any equality for women, passage of the so-called "Right to Life Amendment" to the Constitution, which is now in the Judiciary Committee of the United States House of Representatives, would be an unmitigated disaster to the cause of women in the United States. It is an anomaly indeed, that while we still lack a Constitutional Amendment giving equal protection to women, we are now faced with the very real prospect of passage of a Constitutional Amendment granting greater rights to the fetus. Accordingly, defeat of the proposed "Right to Life Amendment" now in the Judiciary Com-

33

mittee in the House of Representatives in the United States Congress is imperative.

Dellums July 18 inserted in the Congressional Record a July 11 letter in which Black Women Organized for Action (BWOA) expressed concern at a proposed antiabortion amendment that read:

"Neither the U.S. nor any state shall deprive any human being (from the moment of) conception of life without due process of law; nor deny any human being from the moment of conception, within its jurisdiction the equal protection of the law. Neither the U.S. nor any state shall deprive any human being of life on account of illness, age or incapacity."

Dellums, often a spokesman for black views in Congress, said in a statement in the July 18 issue of the Record that he considered it "the basic human right of each woman to decide when to acquire a legal abortion."

'Operation Avalanche.' Rep. Donald M. Fraser (D, Minn.) told Congress July 16, 1974 that a recent "sharp increase in antiabortion form letters" to Congress members had been organized by the Committee of Ten Million, "a national pro-life organization" headquartered in Glendale, Calif. Fraser inserted in the Congressional Record of July 17 a copy of "a cover letter to 18,000 bishops and pastors" that was written by Gilbert Durand, national chairman of the committee. The letter said in part:

1. Operation Avalanche will force enactment of the Human Life Amendment in 1975.

2. Operation Avalanche will deliver 10 million anti-abortion letters to Congress during the week of July 4, 1974.

3. Operation Avalanche will automatically organize 20,000 local pro-life political action groups. There are more groups than the Democratic and Republican Parties have, combined.

4. Operation Avalanche will elect a pro-life Congress.

5. Operation Avalanche will force state ratification of the Human Life Amendment by July 4, 1976.

"We consider the passage of a pro-life constitutional amendment a priority of the highest order."

"In all of this, well-planned and coordinated political organization by citizens at the nation, state and local levels is of highest importance."

"Our system of government requires citizen participation, and in this case, there is a moral imperative for political activity."

Now that it is clear what needs to be done, the question remains: how best to do it? For months the Committee of Ten Million has worked on this problem. Its carefully considered solution is entitled *Operation Avalanche*.

Operation Avalanche is a serious, realistic and uniquely effective response to the Bishop's recitation of what needs to be done. It is our best means of discharging our moral responsibilities in this election year—this crucial year.

Operation Avalanche will *quickly* organize 20,000 local pro-life political action groups—a splendid follow-up to the Bishop's suggestion. It will unleash 10 million letters on the Congress in one week. Its power will force enactment of the Human Life Amendment.

Ford for amendment. A White House spokesman indicated Sept. 5, 1974 that Gerald R. Ford, who had succeeded Richard Nixon as Prsident, favored a constitutional amendment permitting states to decide whether or not to allow abortions. Characterizing this stance as consistent with past Ford positions on abortion, the spokesman also pointed to Ford's opposition to a 1972 Michigan referendum to permit abortion on demand.

Betty Ford, the President's wife, said at a Sept. 5 news conference that her views on abortion were "definitely closer" to those of Vice President-designate Nelson A. Rockefeller than Sen. James Buckley (R-Conservative, N.Y.). (As governor of New York, Rockefeller had favored abortions; Buckley was the sponsor of a constitutional amendment to prohibit abortions.)

The White House subsequently issued a statement that the views of the President and Mrs. Ford were not far apart. Their essential concern, the spokesman said, was that there must be a remedy in cases of serious illness or criminal attack.

Antiabortion proposals rejected. The Senate Judiciary Subcommittee on Constitutional Amendments Sept. 17, 1975 rejected eight proposed amendments to the Constitution that would have prohibited or restricted the right to abortions. The amendments ranged from one completely outlawing abortion to another that would have allowed each state to determine its own stand on abortion. The votes followed 18 months of subcommittee hearings on the controversial issue.

Sen. Birch Bayh (D, Ind.), chairman of the subcommittee, said after the votes, ''I think the committee has spoken, at least for the duration of this Congress.''

In 1976, the Senate voted April 28, by 47–40, to table another in a series of proposed constitutional amendments that would have outlawed abortions. While the vote was technically on a procedural question—whether the proposed amendment should be debated on the Senate floor—Jesse A. Helms (R, N.C.), the amendment's sponsor, said that a vote to table would be regarded as a vote for abortions.

The amendment sponsored by Helms would have barred all abortions, including those for women who had been raped or whose lives were endangered by pregnancy. Thirty-two Democrats and 15 Republicans voted in favor of the tabling motion; 20 members of each party voted against it.

Senate Panel Backs Antiabortion Amendment. The Senate Judiciary Committee's Constitution subcommittee Dec. 16, 1981, unanimously approved a proposed constitutional amendment that would give ''concurrent power'' to Congress and the states to ban or regulate abortion. The so-called ''human life federalism'' amendment was approved 4 to 0 only an hour after hearings on it ended.

Stating that ''a right to abortion is not secured by this Constitution,'' the amendment gave precedence to the more restrictive law

in the event that state and federal legislation conflicted.

The amendment, sponsored by Sen. Orrin G. Hatch (R, Utah), was an attempt by ''gradualists'' to facilitate passage of an antiabortion measure. ''Absolutists,'' who favored the so-called ''human life statute'' sponsored by Sen. Jesse Helms (R, N.C.) or a total ban on abortions, labeled the amendment a ''sellout.''

Sen. Patrick Leahy (D, Vt.) abstained, saying: ''I think the precedent the subcommittee sets today does material harm to the tradition of public participation in the lawmaking process,'' adding that the rapid vote would indicate to the public that senators felt free to ignore testimony.

The amendment had the backing of the National Right to Life Committee and the National Conference of Catholic Bishops.

ACLU announces abortion drive. The American Civil Liberties Union announced Oct. 6, 1977, that the right of women to obtain elective abortions would be its priority issue for 1978. The chairman of the ACLU's 80-member board, Norman Dorsen, said that recent restrictive actions by the Congress, the Supreme Court and the Carter Administration suggested that ''freedom of choice is gravely in danger.''

Dorsen noted that to date nine states—Indiana, Louisiana, Massachusetts, Missouri, Nebraska, New Jersey, Rhode Island, South Dakota and Utah—had adopted legislation calling for a national constitutional convention to amend the Constitution to prohibit all abortions. An additional 25 states would have to pass similar resolutions in order for Congress to call such a convention, which would be the first since 1787.

Senate Panel Passes Amendment. The Senate Judiciary Committee March 10, 1982, approved, by a vote of 10 to seven, a proposed constitutional amendment that would enable Congress and each state to restrict or ban abortions.

The amendment, if passed, would have the effect of nullifying the 1973 Supreme Court ruling that upheld the right of women to seek abortions.

It now joined a rival bill already on the Senate calendar, sponsored by Sen. Jesse Helms (R, N.C.), which sought to legally redefine life as beginning at conception, thereby entitling a fetus to the same protections as any other individual.

The amendment passed March 10, sponsored by Sen. Orrin G. Hatch (R, Utah), would require approval by two-thirds of both the House and the Senate to become part of the Constitution, as opposed to the simple majority necessary to pass the Helms bill.

The proposed amendment gave Congress and the states "concurrent power to restrict and prohibit abortion," but prohibited the states from passing less restrictive laws than the national one. Hatch, in urging the passage of the amendment, stated that it "puts us in the middle" between "the two extremes dominating the debate." The measure was deplored by groups who supported legalized abortions and those who felt stronger antiabortion legislation was needed.

Endorses Antiabortion Proposal—In a letter to nine senators Sept. 8, Reagan announced his support for Sen. Helms' antiabortion legislation and called for an end to the liberal filibuster of that proposal.

Despite Reagan's endorsement, the motion for cloture to end the filibuster was easily defeated the next day.

Reagan did not disclose the names of the nine senators, but said their votes would be important in winning approval of the cloture measure.

He called the Helms proposal "moderate," and said it would provide an opportunity "for the Supreme Court to reconsider its usurpation of the role of the legislatures and state courts."

"It is vitally important for the Congress to affirm, as this amendment does, the fundamental principle that all human life has intrinsic value," he wrote.

Reagan sent a separate letter to Senate Majority Leader Howard H. Baker Jr. (R, Tenn.), commending him for his effort to end the filibuster. "You are providing the Senate with an opportunity to stand up and be counted on what I think is one of the most important issues of our times," he wrote.

The President's endorsement of Helms' proposal stirred criticism in Congress. Sen. Robert Packwood (R, Ore.) a leader of the filibuster, said Reagan's endorsement represented "one more nail in the coffin" of the Republican Party. He criticized the President for following the advice of those who "are convinced that America doesn't want equal rights for women and minorities."

Sen. Max Baucus (D, Mont.) called Reagan's support of the proposal "a token appeasement of the right wing." "My personal view is that he doesn't have his heart in it," Baucus said.

In his letter to the nine senators, Reagan asserted that his endorsement of the Helms legislation was not intended as a rejection of a proposed constitutional amendment introduced by Sen. Orrin G. Hatch (R, Utah). The Hatch amendment would give states the authority to regulate or prohibit abortions. Reagan maintained that he was writing in favor of the Helms proposal because "it is crucial that a filibuster not prevent the representatives of our citizens from expressing their judgment on so vital a matter."

Abortion Debated. The Senate Aug. 16–20, 1982, debated abortion. But a filibuster led by liberal senators was successful in delaying votes on amendments offered by Sen. Jesse Helms (R, N.C.) until after Congress reconvened from its Labor Day recess Sept. 8.

The debate centered on Helms' amendments to a bill authorizing an increase in the ceiling on the federal debt. That bill would have to be approved before Oct. 1 for the government to continue its operations.

The Helms amendments proposed to:

Declare that the Supreme Court had "erred" in its 1973 decision guaranteeing abortion rights by "excluding unborn children from the safeguards afforded by the equal protection and due-process provisions of the constitution'';

Require a direct appeal to the Supreme Court of any lower court decision affecting state antiabortion laws;

Declare, in a preamble that would have no legal bearing, that it was a "finding of Congress" that "scientific evidence demonstrates that the life of each human begins at conception";

Make permanent the restrictions voted by Congress for each of the last five years prohibiting the use of federal funds to obtain an abortion, and

Declare that the Supreme Court "shall not have jurisdiction to review" state laws allowing voluntary prayer in public schools.

Packwood Begins Filibuster—The debate on the abortion amendment began Aug. 16, when Helms introduced a two-word amendment and Sen. Robert Packwood (R, Ore.) immediately seized the Senate floor and began a filibuster.

Helms introduced only the heading for his amendment, "Title II." But Packwood took the floor and read from a book on the history of abortion in America for more than two hours in order to stall debate.

Packwood began the filibuster after it had become known that Helms intended to delete from the legal text of his amendment a provision stating that life began at conception. Without that provision in the amendment, Packwood said, he feared that he did not have the votes to defeat it.

The filibuster continued Aug. 17.

Helms Loses Preliminary Vote—Helms suffered a setback Aug. 18 when his proposal to limit the authority of the Supreme Court drew outraged responses in the Senate, and led to his defeat in a preliminary vote.

Helms introduced the text of his amendments, surprising the Senate with his linking of the abortion and school prayer issues and with the provision to curtail the Supreme Court's jurisdiction.

"We have before us the greatest constitutional crisis since the Civil War," shouted Sen. Daniel Patrick Moynihan (D, N.Y.). He said Congress would be guilty of an "abomination" if it passed the Helms amendments and directed its "rage and irresponsible fury" against the Supreme Court.

"If the court is to be a subordinate branch . . . of the U.S. Congress, then we are no longer the republic founded at Philadelphia in 1787," he said.

The first test vote on the issue came when Sen. Lowell P. Weicker Jr. (R, Conn.) introduced an amendment intended to counter Helms' amendment. It reaffirmed the authority of the federal courts to enforce the Constitution, regardless of the language of the Helms amendment.

The Senate then easily defeated an effort by Helms to table Weicker's amendment, by a vote of 59 to 38.

Opponents of Helms' amendments declared victory following the vote. They said the vote indicated that Helms had gone too far and had lost his support in the Senate, and that his amendments on school prayer and abortion were effectively dead for the year.

Helms denied defeat, saying it was "outrageous" to suggest that the fight was over.

Helms Calls for Vote—As the Senate prepared to adjourn for its Labor Day recess, Sen. Helms Aug. 19 proposed to end the debate and bring all amendments up for an immediate vote.

Opponents of the Helms amendments refused the proposal, however. That meant that the Senate would continue to consider the abortion and school prayer amendments following the recess.

Helms Proposal Tabled. The Senate Sept. 15, 1982, voted to table the antiabortion amendment sponsored by Sen. Jesse Helms (R, N.C.), thus ending weeks of filibusters and legislative maneuvers aimed at delaying a vote on the controversial proposal.

Earlier that day, another antiabortion proposal had been removed from consideration, when Sen. Orrin G. Hatch (R, Utah) withdrew a proposed constitutional amendment that would give Congress and the states the right to prohibit abortions. Hatch said he would reintroduce the amendment in 1983, when campaign pressures and time limits would not interfere with Congress' consideration of it.

The vote to table the Helms amendment came after a vote on a third cloture motion had failed to break the liberal filibuster. (A second cloture motion had been defeated Sept. 13.) In the third cloture vote, Helms supporters could muster only 50 votes, 10 short of the number needed to limit debate on the amendment.

A motion by Sen. S. I. Hayakawa (R, Calif.) to table the Helms amendment then passed by a vote of 47 to 46, after Senate Majority Leader Howard H. Baker Jr. (R, Tenn.) withheld his vote.

Helms' school prayer amendment, attached to the same debt-ceiling bill as the abortion proposal, was unaffected by the vote and would have to be considered separately.

Leaders of the filibuster were jubilant following the vote. Sen. Robert Packwood (R, Ore.) attributed the legislative victory to public support. "By any measure of public opinion, people are two-to-one in favor of a pro-choice position on abortion," he said.

Sen. Lowell P. Weicker Jr. (R, Conn.) said "We just weren't going to get rolled over . . . We just weren't going to get snowed under by a moralistic crusade."

Reagan Says 3-Month Fetus Survives. President Reagan, speaking to a group of religion editors Sept. 14, mistakenly maintained that infants had been born after a three-month gestation period and lived to "grow up and be normal."

"I think the fact that children have been prematurely born even down to the three-month stage and have lived to, the record shows, to grow up and be normal human beings, that ought to be enough for all of us," the President said.

White House spokesmen later conceded that Reagan had been mistaken, and that he had meant to say four and a half months, not three. They pointed to the birth, after

an 18-week gestation, of a boy weighing one pound, 10 ounces, on Jan. 1, 1972 in Cincinnati. The boy, named Marcus Richardson, was now healthy and "above average" at the age of 10, they said.

White House spokesman Larry Speakes said the President's misstatement did not detract from his central point. Speakes paraphrased the point this way: "As long as there is no scientific proof as to when life begins, it is better to err on the side of saying that it begins at conception."

At the same meeting, Reagan criticized antiabortion groups for their failure to unite in support of a single piece of antiabortion legislation.

"They've been divided behind . . . several amendments, and that's what kept us from bringing this to the floor and getting a determination," he said.

The President reiterated his strong support for antiabortion legislation. But he expressed pessimism on the future of the antiabortion proposal of Sen. Jesse Helms (R, N.C.), saying it was "cluttered up with a lot of extra and extraneous resolutions which have weakened support for it and probably is one of the reasons we are not able to get cloture to shut off the filibuster."

Other State Court Decisions and Legislation

Court orders elective abortions. The New Jersey Supreme Court ruled, 6–1, Nov. 17, 1976, that private, nonsectarian hospitals receiving government funds could not refuse to perform elective abortions. "Moral concepts cannot be the basis of a nonsectarian, nonprofit eleemosynary [charitable] hospital's regulations where that hospital is holding out the use of its facilities to the general public," Associate Justice Sidney M. Schreiber wrote in the majority opinion.

The decision overturned a ruling by Justice Herbert Horn of state Superior Court, who in October 1974 had upheld the regulations of three hospitals barring elective but not therapeutic abortions at their facilities.

The current ruling was in a suit originally filed on behalf of two South Jersey women, both on welfare, who had been denied elective abortions at the three hospitals named as defendants in the suit. The hospitals were Bridgeton Hospital, Salem County Memorial Hospital in Mannington and Newcomb Hospital in Vineland.

Since the three hospitals were tax-exempt and received financial support from the federal and state governments, Justice Schreiber reasoned, they were effectively "quasi-public institutions" that "must serve the public without discrimination." He added that there was "no valid distinction which justifies permission to utilize hospital facilities and equipment for therapeutic but not elective abortions."

The new decision altered the operational meaning of New Jersey's "conscience law" providing that no hospital would be subject to legal liability for refusing to perform elective or therapeutic abortions. To continue to follow this interpretation would be contrary to federal court decisions establishing the "constitutional right to an abortion during the first trimester. . .," Schreiber said.

The decision affected at least 80 hospitals. It did not address itself to the right of hospitals run by religious organizations to refuse to perform abortions, nor did it clarify a staff doctor's individual right to withhold abortion services. The case was *Doe v. Bridgeton Hospital Association, Inc.* (1976).

Boston doctor convicted in abortion case. A Boston jury Feb. 16 found Dr. Kenneth C. Edelin guilty of manslaughter in the death of a male fetus after a legal abortion. Judge James P. McGuire sentenced him to one year's probation and immediately stayed the sentence pending the outcome of an appeal.

(The Massachusetts Supreme Judicial Court unanimously reversed Edelin's conviction Dec. 17, 1976.)

The prosecution contended the fetus was alive at the time of the abortion, some 23 weeks after the onset of the pregnancy. Its star witness, Enrique Giminez-Jimeno, a fellow hospital resident, testified Edelin held the fetus in the uterus for three minutes, suffocating it to make sure it would not live.

Dr. Edelin, who was black, said Feb. 16 that racial and religious prejudice had made a fair trial in Boston impossible. Ten of the 12 members of the jury were members of the Roman Catholic Church, which opposed abortions. Edelin said two alternate jurors had told him of instances of racial slurs made against him while the jury was sequestered, but the jury foreman denied the charge.

Members of several medical groups and women's rights advocates said the decision would make doctors fearful of performing second trimester abortions and could lead to having some aborted fetuses being kept alive by expensive medical technology. Anti-abortion advocates read the verdict as a victory in their drive to limit the effects of the 1973 Supreme Court decision that gave women and their doctors the right to terminate most pregnancies without government interference.

(In reversing the conviction Dec. 17, 1976, the state's highest court ruled that Edelin could have been guilty of manslaughter only if he had deliberately ended the life of a fetus that had been definitely alive outside the mother's body. The prosecution had accused Edelin of suffocating the fetus before it emerged from the uterus.)

Mistrial in Abortion Death. The 16-week trial of a Los Angeles obstetrician accused of murdering an infant that survived a legal saline abortion ended in a mistrial May 5, 1978. The jurors advised the California Superior Court trial judge that they were hopelessly deadlocked, 7–5, in favor of acquittal.

The defendant, Dr. William Waddill Jr., performed the unsuccessful abortion March 2, 1977 on an unwed, 18-year-old woman who had told him she was 22 weeks pregnant. Instead, a 28 to 31 week-old three-pound infant girl was delivered. The infant was breathing and had a heartbeat.

The doctor was accused of strangling the infant, which he denied. He further contended that if the infant had survived it would have suffered severe brain damage from the salt solution.

At issue was the legal definition of death and whether the child was alive when Waddill saw her or whether she had suffered "brain death."

The jury was initially instructed that death was "the permanent disappearance of all vital signs" and ordered to return a verdict of guilty if the doctor had omitted any effort to save the baby. After eight days of deliberation, the judge withdrew that definition and told the jury death was the "total and irreversible cessation of all brain function."

The prosecutor said a retrial would be justified if only to gain a verdict that would set a precedent on the question of "brain death."

Waddill also faced a $17-million damage suit for malpractice filed by the mother, who contended he had been negligent in determining the length of her pregnancy.

During the trial, the prosecution had charged that fear of a law suit was the motive for murder.

Woman Not Guilty in Self-Abortion. A 22-year-old woman, Maria Elaine Pitchford, accused of having performed an abortion on herself, was found not guilty by reason of insanity Aug. 30, 1978, in Bowling Green, Ky. She was believed to be the first woman in the U.S. charged with criminally aborting her own fetus.

At the time of the incident, in which she thrust a knitting needle into her body "during a moment of panic," Pitchford was 20 to 24 weeks pregnant. She had sought a legal abortion at a Louisville, Ky. clinic. The clinic refused to perform the abortion because her pregnancy was too advanced.

The 1974 state statute under which she was prosecuted allowed abortions to be performed only by licensed physicians in the second trimester of pregnancy. (During the first three months, a woman could perform the operation herself under a doctor's supervision.) If convicted, Pitchford could have been sentenced to between 10 and 20 years in prison.

The Kentucky law had been enacted in response to the 1973 Supreme Court decision that states could not prevent abortions during the first six months of pregnancy, but could restrict abortions beyond the first three months to protect a woman's health.

One witness who testified for the defense at the trial was an obstetrics specialist who had been a Kentucky lawmaker at the time the abortion statute was passed. He contended that the law was intended to prevent quacks from performing abortions and there was no law preventing Pitchford from aborting her own child. "She can take out her own appendix if she's foolish enough," he said.

Pitchford's fiancee testified under immunity at the trial that he had insisted she get a legal abortion and had driven her to the clinic. He had broken their engagement after the loss of the child.

An additional charge of manslaughter had been quashed by the judge prior to the trial on the ground that a fetus had no legal standing as a person.

Pitchford, who had spent most of her life in a rural community and was a college sophomore, became a cause celebre for feminists, who contributed money and counseling for her defense.

Ky. County Abortion Ordinance—Jefferson County (Ky.) commissioners passed an ordinance Aug. 22, 1978, for all of the county except the city of Louisville, that cut off county funds for abortions and required that a woman be shown a photograph of a fetus before an abortion would be permitted. In addition, if a woman were under 18 years of age her parents (or husband, if married) would be notified of the abortion plans.

In other state actions:

A stringent new abortion law that was to have gone into effect in Louisiana Sept. 8,

1978 was delayed by a federal district court restraining order Sept. 7 in connection with a law suit filed to have the law declared unconstitutional.

The law required parental notice for an unmarried pregnant woman under 18 seeking an abortion, and it mandated a 24-hour waiting period and counseling by a doctor. The woman would have to acknowledge her "informed consent" in writing that the physician had told her that "the unborn child is a human life from the moment of conception" and that an "unborn child may be viable" (able to survive outside the womb) if the woman was more than 22 weeks pregnant.

The law required the doctor to describe "in detail" the characteristics and appearance of the fetus, including "mobility, tactile sensitivity including pain, perception or response, brain and heart function, the presence of internal organs and the presence of external members." He was also to advise that abortion was "a major surgical procedure which can result in serious complications," and give information about availability of agencies as an alternative to abortion.

All abortions after the first trimester would have to be performed in hospitals. Clinics and doctors' offices where abortions were performed would be required to pay annual license fees of $1,000, plus $500 for each doctor doing abortions.

The Louisiana legislation, with the exception of the licensing provision, had been patterned after an Akron, Ohio ordinance passed Feb. 28.

An Illinois abortion law prohibiting abortion without the consent of a woman's parents or spouse if she was under the age of 18 was overturned by a federal appellate court April 13.

A part of Missouri's abortion law requiring physicians to advise women that they would lose custody of any child born alive during an attempted abortion was declared unconstitutional Sept. 13 by the Eighth U.S. Circuit Court of Appeals. The court also noted that the Missouri law required the doctor to certify that a fetus was unable to survive an abortion in order for it to be performed, making the live-born warning "meaningless."

The Nebraska legislature gave approval March 19, 1979, to a new abortion statute requiring women to wait 48 hours after asking for an abortion and girls under the age of 18 to consult with their parents or guardians before having an abortion. The bill had been introduced to bypass constitutional problems in a previous abortion law.

A federal judge suspended portions of the new law April 20, including the 48-hour waiting provision, and ordered the state not to enforce the provisions until constitutional challenges were resolved in the courts.

The Utah House approved Feb. 16 a bill requiring doctors to give a woman seeking an abortion printed material on the medical procedure along with details on what was done with aborted fetuses, physical characteristics of developing babies and alternatives to abortion.

Women's abortion rights extended. The Supreme Court, ruling on several cases in which abortion laws of Missouri and Massachusetts were contested, held, 6–3, July 1, 1976 that states could not require a woman to obtain her husband's consent before having an abortion. The court also ruled, 5–4, that states could not adopt a hard-and-fast requirement that women under the age of 18 get parental consent for an abortion. The court did say, however, that some form of state regulation for minors seeking abortions might not be unconstitutional.

In its landmark 1973 ruling, the court had affirmed the right of women to abortions during the first six months of pregnancy. (States were allowed to place certain restrictions designed to protect the health of the pregnant women on abortions during the second trimester.) The 1973 ruling, however, had not resolved a number of issues related to abortions, of which consent by parents or husband was one.

A Missouri law, enacted in 1974, placed

a number of curbs or legal requirements in those areas that the 1973 decision had left open. The court ruled on each as follows:

Upheld unanimously a requirement that a woman give written "informed consent" in advance of an abortion.

Upheld unanimously the state's right to require doctors to keep detailed records of abortions, so long as the requirement was not "abused or overdone" by state officials.

Struck down, 6–3, a prohibition against employing "saline amniocentesis" after the first 12 weeks of pregnancy. The procedure was the most commonly used method of effecting abortions after the first trimester.

Upheld unanimously the definition of fetal "viability" as the stage of development "when the life of the unborn child may be continued indefinitely outside the womb by natural or artificial life-supportive systems." The 1973 ruling allowed states to ban abortions of viable fetuses.

Struck down, 6–3, a requirement that doctors performing an abortion endeavor to save the life of the fetus just as if the intention were that it be born alive.

Ruled that doctors had standing to challenge in court laws barring use of Medicaid funds for elective abortions, because of their own interest in the matter (by a 9–0 vote) and because they could press the interests of their patients (by a 5–4 vote).

In the ruling on spousal consent for abortions, Justice Harry A. Blackmun, writing for the majority, said, "The obvious fact is that when the wife and the husband disagree . . . only one of the two marriage partners can prevail. Since it is the woman who physically bears the child and who is the more directly and immediately affected by the pregnancy . . ., the balance weighs in her favor."

Dissenting from the ruling were Justices Byron R. White and William H. Rehnquist and Chief Justice Warren E. Burger. The same bloc formed the minorities in the other rulings, except for the one regarding the legal standing of doctors contesting Med-icaid laws. In the ruling on parental consent, they were joined by Justice John Paul Stevens.

The parental consent issue appeared in cases both from Missouri and Massachusetts. The Missouri statute was voided on this requirement, with the court reasoning (in Blackmun's words) that "the state does not have the constitutional authority to give a third party an absolute, and possibly arbitrary, veto over the decision of the physician and his patient . . . . Any independent interest the parent may have in the termination of the minor daughter's pregnancy is no more weighty than the right of privacy of the competent minor mature enough to have become pregnant."

The court, however, unanimously refused to uphold a federal court in Massachusetts that had struck down a section of a Massachusetts law that required parental consent for abortions by unmarried minors. The court noted that the law made an exception for minors who went to court and convinced the judge that there was good reason for an abortion. Therefore, the court held, the law might be interpreted in such a way as to "avoid or substantially modify" a constitutional challenge. The federal court should have waited to see whether the state courts interpreted the law in that light before ruling on it, the high court held.

The cases from which the rulings emerged were: *Planned Parenthood of Missouri v. Danforth* (74–1151), *Danforth v. Planned Parenthood* (74–1419), *Singleton v. Wulff* (74–1393), *Bellotti v. Baird* (75–73) and *Hunerwadel v. Baird* (75–109).

(The Supreme Court Jan. 15, 1975 had rejected an appeal by the state of Pennsylvania to reinstate the state's new abortion law, which restricted the right to an abortion by requiring a woman to obtain her husband's consent or her parents' approval if she were under 18. The law, which had been enjoined by a lower court pending further review, also banned use of public funds for abortions.)

Other Supreme Court Decisions.

Ruling Jan. 13, 1975, the Supreme Court unanimously affirmed a decision of a lower court that had overturned a Louisiana law that allowed the revocation of a doctor's license because he had performed an abortion before the Supreme Court legalized most abortions in January 1973.

The court June 16 held as an unconstitutional infringement on the freedom of the press a Virginia law—since amended—making it a misdemeanor to publish an advertisement for an abortion service operated in a state where abortions were legal.

The court Nov. 11, in a 9–0 opinion, warned state courts that they had "misinterpreted" the 1973 Supreme Court ruling legalizing abortion if they permitted persons who were not physicians to perform abortions. The high court said it had set aside anti-abortion laws as they applied to doctors but that it "did not go so far" as to immunize non-doctors.

State courts in Connecticut and Minnesota had applied the 1973 decision to protect non-physicians from prosecution, while New Jersey and Michigan courts had held that anti-abortion laws still applied to non-doctors.

The court Dec. 1, 1975 upheld a ruling permitting a private hospital that was government-funded to bar a doctor from performing abortions.

The Supreme Court March 1, 1976 declined to review a lower court decision allowing private hospitals that received federal funds to refuse to perform abortions and sterilization operations.

The Supreme Court Nov. 29, 1976 also upheld a decision of a lower court striking down an Indiana law that required abortions during the first trimester to be performed in a hospital or licensed health facility. The lower court found the bar to abortions in doctors' offices "clearly unconstitutional"

in light of the Supreme Court's 1973 abortion decision. In upholding the ruling, the high court did not hear arguments or issue an opinion. Justice Byron R. White, in a dissent joined by Chief Justice Warren E. Burger and Justice William H. Rehnquist, objected to the summary treatment of the case by the court. White also contended that the 1973 high court bar to state interference in abortions during the first trimester should not be so interpreted as to prohibit regulations for health or safety.

Gary–Northwest Indiana Women's Services v. Bowen. The high court Jan. 25, 1977 affirmed without comment the decision of a lower court that barred Indiana officials from enforcing a state law that required minors seeking abortions in the first 12 weeks of pregnancy to get parental permission.

The court May 23 also affirmed a lower federal court decision voiding a Connecticut law requiring minors committed to the state's care to obtain the written consent of a state official before getting an abortion. *Lady Jane v. Maher.*

Affirmed without comment a lower-court order barring Indiana officials from enforcing a state law that required minors seeking abortions in the first 12 weeks of pregnancy to get parental permission.

Affirmed, without comment, a lower federal court decision voiding a Connecticut law requiring minors committed to the state's care to obtain the written consent of a state official before getting an abortion.

Vacated lower court rulings that had invalidated New York State and South Dakota restrictions on the use of Medicaid funds for elective abortions. The court also refused to review a New Jersey Supreme Court decision voiding bans placed on elective abortions by some nonprofit hospitals in that state.

In other actions June 29, the court:

Vacated, without comment, a 1976 decision by U.S. District Court Judge John F. Dooling Jr. of Brooklyn barring Congress from cutting off Medicaid funds for elective abortions. Dooling was given 25 days to lift the injunction he had placed on implementation of the so-called "Hyde Amendment."

Refused to accept for judgment a case involving the Illinois Abortion Control Act of 1975. A U.S. district court had found several provisions of the law unconstitutional. The state attempted to take its appeal directly to the Supreme Court, bypassing the U.S. 7th Circuit Court of Appeals.

Declined to review a decision upholding the legality of a Cleveland zoning ordinance barring abortion service in certain parts of the city. The ordinance was challenged by a private abortion clinic as a violation of the 1973 Supreme Court ruling that allowed women unrestricted access to abortions in the first three months of pregnancy. The U.S. 6th Circuit Court of Appeals backed the ordinance. The case was *Westside Women's Services Inc. v. Cleveland*.

Pa. Abortion Control Law Voided. The Supreme Court ruled, 6–3, Jan. 9, 1979 that a state law requiring physicians to try to preserve fetal life during abortions was illegal. The case was *Colautti v. Franklin*.

The case concerned the Pennsylvania Abortion Control Act of 1974. Under the statute, a doctor performing an abortion had to determine if the fetus "is viable," or determine if there was "sufficient reason to believe that the fetus may be viable." If such a determination was made, the physician was required to use the technique "which would provide the best opportunity for the fetus to be aborted alive." Doctors who violated the law were subject to civil suits and/or criminal charges.

The law had been enacted a year after a landmark Supreme Court decision enabled women to obtain abortions in their first trimester of pregnancy without state interference. The same ruling allowed states to intervene in abortions in the second three months of pregnancy, but only if the woman's life was believed endangered by the proceeding. States could also halt abortions in the final 10 weeks of pregnancy because fetuses were thought to be viable during that period. (A fetus was viable, according to the high court's 1973 definition, when it "presumably has the capability of meaningful life outside the mother's womb.")

The Pennsylvania law was struck down by a three-judge federal panel in 1977. The Supreme Court upheld the lower court. Writing for the majority, Justice Harry A. Blackmun found the language of the law unconstitutionally vague, particularly singling out the phrase "may be viable" as wording that illustrated "double ambiguity."

Blackmun, who also wrote the 1973 majority opinion, said that the Pennsylvania statute could have a "profound chilling effect on the willingness of physicians to perform abortions near the point of viability in the manner indicated by their best medical judgment."

The majority also held that the law could permit the state to prosecute a physician for murder if he used saline solution to abort a fetus. (A saline-induced abortion was almost always fatal to the fetus. It was the most widely used method of abortion in the latter stages of pregnancy.)

The dissenters, led by Justice Byron R. White, argued that the ruling withdrew "from the states a substantial measure of the power to protect fetal life that was reserved to them" in the 1973 decision. White held that the phrase "may be viable" meant "potentially able to live" outside the womb, and was therefore in agreement with the 1973 guideline.

The minority disagreed with the majority on whether a physician in violation of the law could be prosecuted for murder under the statute.

White was joined in dissent by Chief Justice Warren E. Burger and Justice William H. Rehnquist.

Several states and cities had laws similar to, although not identical with, the Pennsylvania law.

Affirmed was a decision that struck down a Missouri law requiring any physician consulted by a woman seeking an abortion to inform the woman that if the infant was delivered alive, it would become a ward of the state. The case was *Ashcroft v. Freiman.*

Nullified, by an 8–1 vote, a lower court ruling that had voided a South Carolina abortion law and barred the prosecution of a doctor who had allegedly violated the law. The statute made any physician who performed an abortion in the third trimester of pregnancy subject to prosecution for murder. The lower court was ordered to reconsider its decision in light of past Supreme Court abortion rulings and the high court's policy against the interference of federal courts in state court prosecutions. Justice Brennan dissented in the case, *Anders v. Floyd.*

In other actions May 14, the court:

Refused to review a lower court decision in support of a Massachusetts law that barred the use of state funds to finance Medicaid abortions, except in cases where the mother's life was in danger or in instances of rape or incest. The lower court had held that the Hyde Amendment—which prohibited the use of federal funds for most abortions—relieved the state of any obligation to provide its own money for the procedure. The case was *Baird v. Sharp.*

Mass. Abortion-Consent Law Voided. The Supreme Court voted, 8–1, July 2, 1979 to strike down a Massachusetts law that required an unmarried minor to obtain the permission of both parents or a judge before having an abortion. The cases, consolidated for judgment, were *Bellotti v. Baird* and *Hunerwadel v. Baird.*

Affirming a lower court ruling, eight of the Supreme Court justices found the law unconstitutional, but they were divided in their reasonings.

Justice Lewis F. Powell Jr., writing for one faction, indicated that the law was illegal because it might deny an abortion to a "mature minor."

Powell wrote that "every minor must have the opportunity—if she so desires—to go directly to a court without first consulting or notifying her parents. If she satisfies the court that she is mature and well-informed enough to make intelligently the abortion decision on her own, the court must authorize her to act."

Powell's group, which included Chief Justice Warren E. Burger and Justices Potter Stewart and William H. Rehnquist, suggested that if a judge found that a pregnant girl was not "mature," he should still consider authorizing an abortion, if he believed it would be in the girl's best interest.

Justice John Paul Stevens issued a separate opinion criticizing the Powell faction for endorsing an "advisory opinion" on how Massachusetts could modify the statute to satisfy the Supreme Court.

Stevens held that the law was invalid because it was "potentially even more restrictive" than a Missouri law struck down by the high court in 1976.

Justices William J. Brennan Jr., Harry A. Blackmun and Thurgood Marshall joined the Stevens opinion.

Justice Byron R. White was the lone dissenter. "Until now," he wrote, "I would have thought inconceivable a holding that the United States Constitution forbids even notice to parents when their minor child who seeks surgery objects to such notice and is able to convince a judge that the parents should be denied participation in the decision."

The Court refused to stay a lower court order requiring the state of Arizona to honor its contract with the state branch of Planned Parenthood. Under that contract, Arizona subsidized the organization with federal family planning funds. The state legislature had passed a budget amendment barring the transfer of such funds to organizations that performed abortions or abortion counseling. The case was *Arizona v. Planned Parenthood.*

Indiana Abortion Limit Case Refused. The Supreme Court April 27, 1981 refused to review, thus letting stand, an Indiana law that made it a felony for second-trimester abortions to be performed anywhere but in a hospital. The case was *Gary-Northwest Indiana Women's Services v. Orr.*

45

The Indiana law had been challenged by the staff of a Gary abortion clinic as an illegal infringement on the right of women to have abortions during their fourth through sixth months of pregnancy. They contended that many hospitals in the state refused to perform second-trimester abortions.

The Supreme Court had ruled in 1973 that states could not prevent women from having abortions in the first six months of pregnancy.

Justices William J. Brennan Jr., Thurgood Marshall and Harry A. Blackmun voted to hear the Gary case.

More than 16 states had laws similar to the Indiana statute, but Indiana was believed to be the only state where non-hospital second-trimester abortions were a felony offense.

Supreme Court Curbs State, Local Limits on Abortion

No Retreat from Landmark '73 Ruling. The Supreme Court June 15 curbed the power of state and local governments to limit access to legal abortions. In doing so, the court strongly reaffirmed its landmark 1973 ruling in *Roe v. Wade,* which gave women an unrestricted right to abortions in their first three months of pregnancy.

The 1983 action came in three decisions in five cases: *Akron v. Akron Center* and *Akron Center v. Akron* (from Ohio); *Planned Parenthood v. Ashcroft* and *Ashcroft v. Planned Parenthood* (from Missouri), and *Simopoulos v. Virginia.* The cases had been argued before the high court in November 1982.

Justice Lewis F. Powell Jr. wrote the majority opinion in all three decisions. Justice Sandra Day O'Connor authored the key dissent, in the Akron decision.

Taken together, the decisions bolstered the 1973 ruling. Many pro-choice advocates

had feared that the court would retreat from *Roe v. Wade* by allowing states and localities wide latitude in regulating abortions.

Powell wrote that since the 1973 ruling, "the court repeatedly and consistently has accepted and applied the basic principle that a woman has a fundamental right to make the highly personal choice whether or not to terminate her pregnancy.

"Arguments continued to be made that we erred in interpreting the Constitution," he noted. "Nonetheless, the doctrine of stare decisis, while perhaps never entirely persuasive on a constitutional question, is a doctrine that demands respect in a society governed by the rule of law. We respect it today, and reaffirm *Roe v. Wade.*"

(Stare decisis is a doctrine under which, once a court has established a legal principle based on a set of facts, its future decisions adhere to that principle given similar facts.)

The Akron Decision—The Supreme Court voted, 6–3, to overturn an Akron, Ohio city ordinance that had placed several restrictions on access to legal abortions. The decision was a victory for the Akron Center for Reproductive Health, which had challenged the ordinance. The ruling upheld in part and reversed in part a decision by the U.S. 6th Circuit Court of Appeals.

The Akron statute had mandated a 24-hour waiting period for all abortions; hospitalization for all abortions after the first trimester of pregnancy; parental consent for abortions performed on girls under 16 years of age, and a procedure under which doctors were required to inform pre-abortion patients of the dangers of abortion and that the fetus was a human being from the moment of conception.

On the waiting-period issue, Powell wrote that once a woman had given her written permission to a medical facility to perform an abortion, "a state may not delay the effectuation of that decision."

By requiring hospitalization for second trimester abortions, he said, "Akron has imposed a heavy, and unnecessary, burden on women's access to a relatively inexpensive, otherwise accessible, and safe abortion procedure.'' (Powell cited studies by the American College of Obstetricians and Gynecologists indicating that advances in abortion procedures, particularly in dilation and evacuation, had made abortions safer.)

On the doctors' "informed consent" provision, Powell asserted: "It is fair to say that much of the information required is designed not to inform the woman's consent, but rather to persuade her to withhold it altogether.'' Physicians, not governments, were the only ones "to decide what information a woman must be given before she chooses to have an abortion,'' he opined.

Justice O'Connor's dissent in the Akron decision was the first public airing of her views on abortion since her confirmation hearings in 1981. At that time, antiabortion forces had opposed her appointment to the high court on the ground that she supported legal abortion.

Quoting from previous Supreme Court opinions, O'Connor reminded her fellow justices that "we must always be mindful that 'the Constitution does not compel a state to fine-tune its statutes so as to encourage or facilitate abortions. To the contrary, state action encouraging childbirth except in the most urgent circumstances, is rationally related to the legitimate government objective of protecting potential life.' ''

O'Connor criticized as "completely unworkable" the three trimester approach adopted in *Roe v. Wade*. Such an approach, she said, could not possibly accommodate "the conflicting personal rights and compelling state interests that are involved in the abortion context.''

O'Connor also quarreled with Powell's notion that medical advances justified a relaxation of controls on second trimester abortions. "The Roe framework," she maintained, "is clearly on a collision course with itself. As the medical risks of various abortion procedures decrease, the point at which the state may regulate for reasons of maternal health is moved further forward to actual childbirth.'' (Under the 1973 ruling,

authorities could intervene in second-trimester abortions only to preserve the health of the pregnant woman.)

She continued: "As medical science becomes better able to provide for the separate existence of the fetus, the point of viability is moved further back toward conception . . . The state interest in potential human life is extant throughout pregnancy. In Roe, the court held that although the state had an important and legitimate interest in protecting potential life, that interest could not become compelling until the point at which the fetus was viable. The difficulty with this analysis is clear: potential life is no less potential in the first weeks of pregnancy than it is at viability or afterward.''

O'Connor concluded: "Accordingly, I believe that the state's interest in protecting potential human life exists throughout the pregnancy.''

Justices William H. Rehnquist and Byron R. White endorsed her dissent.

The Missouri Decision—The Supreme Court voted, 6–3, to strike down a section of a Missouri law requiring hospitalization for second-trimester abortions. However, the justices voted, 5–4, to uphold other provisions of the law, including one that required parental consent for abortions on "unemancipated" girls under 18 years old. The ruling upheld a decision by the U.S. 8th Circuit Court of Appeals on a challenge brought by Planned Parenthood Federation of America.

The hospitalization provision was overturned on the same rationale as was used to void the similar provision in the Akron ordinance. The alignment of justices was also similar, with O'Connor, Rehnquist and White dissenting.

Unlike the Akron decision, the justices upheld parental notification in Missouri because that law took into account previous high court decisions requiring states to differentiate between teen-age girls who were mature enough to make their own abortion decisions and those who were not.

The other provisions upheld by the court

required a pathologist's analysis of the aborted fetal tissue, and required at least two physicians to be present during third-trimester abortions.

Justices Harry A. Blackmun, Thurgood Marshall, William J. Brennan Jr. and John Paul Stevens dissented.

The Virginia Decision—The Supreme Court voted, 8–1, to uphold the conviction of Dr. Chris Simopoulos for violating a Virginia law that required second-trimester abortions to be performed either in a hospital or an outpatient clinic licensed by the state. Simopoulos, a Woodbridge, Va. gynecologist, had performed an abortion on a teen-aged girl in his office.

The doctor had been sentenced by a state court to two years in prison. All but 20 days of the sentence had been suspended.

The high court, with only Justice Stevens dissenting, refused to overturn the state law. Powell noted that the statute, unlike the required hospitalization provisions in Akron and Missouri, permitted mid-trimester abortions at clinics.

Decisions Praised, Damned—The Supreme Court's decisions June 15 drew predictably strong reactions from individuals and organizations on both sides of the abortion issue.

Janet Benshoof, director of the American Civil Liberties Union's reproductive rights project, hailed the Akron ruling as a "total victory for a woman's right to choose abortion." The ACLU had represented the Akron Center for Reproductive Health in its fight against the city's abortion ordinance.

Benshoof criticized as "unprincipled" the dissent issued by Sandra Day O'Connor, the Supreme Court's only woman justice.

Sen. Robert W. Packwood (R, Ore.) said he was "delighted" by the decisions because they affirmed "a constitutional right that state legislatures cannot nibble away at."

Dr. Chris Simopoulos, who lost his case before the high court, nevertheless said he was "delighted" that he court had "decided for women's rights."

Solicitor General Rex E. Lee, who had argued before the high court in favor of abortion limits, contended that the rulings represented neither a "major victory" nor a "major defeat . . . We won some and we lost some."

Douglas Johnson, legislative director of the National Right to Life Committee, maintained that the decisions demonstrated "the extremism of the court on abortion" and underscored the need for a constitutional amendment banning the procedure. "The court has defended the interests not of women, but of the assembly-line abortion industry."

Richard A. Viguerie, a prominent New Right activist, said that the decisions would "delight only those abortionists who are interested in running as many women as possible through their clinics so as to maximize profits."

Gary Curran, a spokesman for the American Life Lobby, contended that it was clear that a majority of the justices cared "little or nothing for the humanity of the unborn."

Sen. Orrin G. Hatch (R, Utah) called the decisions an "abomination." Hatch was the sponsor of an antiabortion constitutional amendment that was scheduled to come before the Senate in late June or early July. However, he conceded that there was little chance that the Senate, "with its present makeup," would pass the measure.

Sen. Roger W. Jepsen (R, Iowa), the co-sponsor of a bill that would extend legal rights to the unborn, was more optimistic about the passage of antiabortion legislation. "The furor and emotion that this has generated will help us," he said.

Terence Cardinal Cooke, the leader of New York City's Roman Catholics, June 16 joined the call for federal legislation to protect the unborn. Cooke criticized the Supreme Court for dealing a "lethal blow" to human values.

Reagan: Antiabortion Law Needed—President Reagan, reacting to the Supreme Court's abortion decisions, June 16 urged Congress to pass legislation to "restore legal protections for the unborn."

In a statement issued at the White House, the president said that society was "confronted with a great moral issue, the taking of the life of an unborn child. Accordingly, I join millions of Americans expressing profound disappointment at the decisions announced by the Supreme Court in striking down several efforts by states and localities to control the circumstances under which abortion may be performed."

Echoing the dissent by Justice Sandra Day O'Connor, whom he had appointed to the high court, Reagan contended that "the legislature is the appropriate forum for resolving these issues. The issue of abortion must be resolved by our democratic process."

The statement concluded: "Once again, I call on Congress to make its voice heard against abortion on demand and to restore legal protections for the unborn, whether by statute or constitutional amendment."

Other Congressional Action

The Question of Abortion—The President said a constitutional amendment prohibiting abortion might be unneeded if Congress determined when human life began.

If Congress determined that a fetus was a human being, "then there isn't really any need for an amendment," he said. "Because once you have determined this, the Constitution already protects the right of human life."

The President reasserted his belief that, "in an abortion we are taking a human life."

The question was in reference to legislation introduced in Congress for a declaration that human life began at the moment of conception. The legislation was sponsored by Sen. Jesse Helms (R, N.C.) and Rep. Henry Hyde (R, Ill.).

Doctors Testify Against Senate Bill. Eight eminent physicians May 20, 1981, criticized efforts in Congress to pinpoint the moment a human life began. Their criticism came at the resumption of Senate hearings on proposed antiabortion legislation. The bill, if passed, would place the legal commencement of human life at the moment of conception.

The eight physicians assailed the bill as scientifically unjustifiable. Dr. George M. Ryan, president of American College of Obstetricians and Gynecologists, stated that "when Congress equates cellular life to personhood it is taking a substantial leap beyond the current views of the medical and scientific community." His testimony and that of seven other doctors reinforced a resolution passed in April by the National Academy of Sciences, which stated that the proposed bill's definition of life "cannot stand up to the scrutiny of science."

The single opposing medical witness May 20 was Dr. Mildred F. Jefferson of Boston University Medical School, a prominent figure in the right-to-life movement. Her remarks in turn echoed those of five antiabortion physicians whose testimony had opened the first round of hearings April 23. She and they insisted that it was an established fact that life began with the meeting of sperm and egg, in accordance with textbook definitions.

The legislation under debate, designed to outlaw abortions by granting constitutional rights to a zygote, or newly fertilized egg, was sponsored by Rep. Henry J. Hyde (R-Ill.) and Senator Jesse Helms (D, N.C.).

The hearings were convened by Sen. John P. East (R, N.C.), a Helms protege and one of the most outspoken new conservatives in Congress. Senator Orrin Hatch (R, Utah) had withdrawn as co-chairman of the hearings, citing questions about the bill's constitutionality and about the potentially one-sided nature of the proceedings. Sen. East subsequently pledged to expand later hearings and make them "fair, extensive and exhaustive."

Passage of the bill would overturn a 1973 Supreme Court ruling, *Roe v. Wade,* which gave women the constitutional right to abortion.

The bill was introduced because a constitutional amendment to bar abortion would be much more difficult to pass. Both feminists and doctors voiced concern, however, that the implications of the bill would extend beyond abortion to contraceptive practices. Under the definition of life in the bill, the use of either an intrauterine device or birth control pills would in effect become illegal, as both methods were believed to act after conception. Amniocentesis, the procedure used to detect birth defects in unborn babies, would also come under question.

Senate Ends Hearings. The third round of Senate hearings on a bill designed to ban abortions ended June 18, 1981. No conclusion was reached on the eighth and final day of impassioned arguments between the bill's supporters and opponents before the Judiciary Committee's subcommittee on the separation of powers.

The issues that provoked the strongest disagreement were those of the constitutionality of the bill, its potential to create complicated legal tangles in cases where the interests of a mother would conflict with those of her unborn child, and its possible application to matters beyond abortion, including some birth control methods.

Sen. East (R, N.C.), who had chaired the hearings, said the panel would write the final draft of the bill by the end of July; if approved by the full Judiciary Committee, it was expected to reach the Senate floor in late autumn.

Pro-Abortionists' Testimony—Sarah Weddington, a lawyer who had served as adviser on women's affairs under President Carter and successfully argued the 1973 Supreme Court case that legalized abortion, was a key witness against the passage of the proposed bill.

Testifying on behalf of 75 national organizations with 34 million members, Weddington charged that the proposed legislation "blatantly disregards the integrity of the constitutional process, the separation of powers, the religious liberty of our citizens, the will of the people, the sound practice of medicine and the desperate needs of women facing problem pregnancies." In any case, she said, the bill would not reduce the number of abortions "because you will not have eliminated the reasons that women feel compelled to seek abortions."

Some of those reasons were outlined in letters from parents of children who suffered from severe genetic diseases and defects. The letters were read to the panel by singer Judy Collins.

Dr. Joseph F. Boyle, of the American Medical Association, objected to the bill on legal grounds: "Under the bill, the physician would be responsible for the welfare of every fetus, whose legal and health interest would, in the eyes of the law, be equal to, but may be in conflict with, those of the woman." The AMA had previously stated its opposition to the bill's assumption that a human life began at conception.

Opposition was also voiced by a representative of the American Psychiatric Association, Dr. Naomi Goldstein of the New York University Medical School. She stressed the difficulties encountered by children of unwanted pregnancies, including "abuse, neglect, mental illness and deprivation." She also cited the high rate of suicide among women who did not want the babies they were carrying, and the "medical complications of self-induced and medically incompetently performed abortions."

Supporters Voice Their Views—In response to charges of unconstitutionality, Rep. Hyde (R, Ill.) asserted there was "nothing wrong with a little congressional activism" to reverse the 1973 Supreme Court ruling. He went on to call abortion "a sort of humane holocaust of the unborn," and praised Sen. East for withstanding "an incredible display of journalistic abuse." Hyde, who together with East had sponsored the bill, called its opponents "wildly confused" and accused them of using "scare tactics" to prevent its passage.

East, permanently paralyzed by polio, said that denying life to the handicapped "smacks of a Nazi-like mentality."

Testimony in support of the bill was also given by Dr. Carolyn F. Gerster, a physician and former president of the National Right to Life Committee, who told of her own miscarriage experience in the 13th week of pregnancy.

Theological Dispute—Several theologians of different faiths testified on both sides of the abortion issue before the committee June 12. A Roman Catholic seminary professor, Dr. Rosemary Radford Ruether, defended a woman's right to decide to have an abortion: "The issue is not pro-life versus pro-abortion. The issue is legal, safe abortions versus illegal, unsafe abortions."

A similar view was expressed by Rabbi Henry Siegman, executive director of American Jewish Congress: "The proper role of government in a free society is to allow the different religious traditions to inculcate their own beliefs about the appropriateness of abortion and to leave the final decision to the woman, answering to God and conscience."

Rabbi Seymour Siegel, of the Jewish Theological Seminary of America, however, stated that under Jewish law abortion was permitted only when the life of the mother was endangered.

2 Ex-Solicitors General Oppose Bill—The issue of the bill's constitutionality was addressed June 1 by two former solicitors general, Archibald Cox and Robert H. Bork. Both maintained in appearances before the committee that passage of the bill would violate the authority of the Supreme Court as outlined in the Constitution.

Bork, a law professor at Yale University, said: "Only if we are prepared to say that the [Supreme] Court has become intolerable in a fundamentally democratic society and that there is no prospect whatever for getting it to behave properly, should we adopt a principle which contains within it the seeds of the destruction of the court's entire constitutional role."

Cox argued against passage of the bill, saying that "the very function of the Constitution and court is to put individual liberties beyond the reach of both congressional majorities and popular clamor."

Professor Uddo of Loyola University Law School disagreed with Cox and Bork, saying it was within Congress's power to "decide a question not answered by an applicable Supreme Court decision."

12 Law Professors Support Bill. A letter signed by 12 law professors and mailed June 18 to Sen. East advanced arguments in support of the constitutionality of the proposed antiabortion legislation.

The letter read in part: "Congress does have constitutional authority to declare by statute that unborn children are human beings, and that all human beings are 'persons' within the meaning of the 14th Amendment to the Constitution." (The 14th Amendment says that no person can be deprived of "life, liberty, or property, without due process of law.")

The letter took a view opposing two sent earlier by constitutional scholars and six former attorneys general.

4 Congressmen Quit Pro-Life Group. Three U.S. representatives and one senator resigned June 3 from the advisory board of the National Pro-Life Political Action Committee after the antiabortion group issued a list of nine congressmen targeted for defeat in 1982.

All four complained that they had not been consulted about the so-called hit list, although their names were listed on the committee's letterhead. Said Sen. Jake Garn (R, Utah), "Members of a group's advisory board should be asked to advise, and since I was not, I intend to resign." He and Reps. Henry J. Hyde (R, Ill.), Marty Russo (D, Ill) and Robert A. Young (D, Mo.) also expressed distaste for the tactic of issuing such lists. "I'm not in any way going to participate in anything that is set up to defeat sitting members," said Russo.

Peter B. Gemma Jr., executive director of the committee, explained the rationale behind the issuing of the list: "We're out to influence those congressmen, senators and candidates from both parties who are ambivalent or undecided on this matter of life versus death. If we can knock off some highly visible officeholders, it sends a signal to the mushy middle, as I call them."

Although some of the congressmen the committee hoped to defeat had frequently cast antiabortion votes, all nine had refused to endorse a constitutional amendment to make all abortions illegal.

Gemma said the committee would spend $250,000 in 1981 preparing for the 1982 elections, and as much as $400,000 altogether to defeat the designated candidates. The group had spent $210,000 in the 1980 elections.

Panel Delays Dr. Koop's Nomination. House-Senate conferees June 17 effectively blocked the nomination of Dr. C. Everett Koop, 64, to be surgeon general.

The conference committee approved a credit card bill that carried a rider permitting the president to appoint as surgeon general someone over 64. The rider did not, however, lift the age barrier for members of Commissioned Corps of the U.S. Public Health Service, to which Koop would have to be appointed in order to qualify as a surgeon general nominee.

Koop's nomination had been opposed by several public health groups because of his outspoken opposition to abortion. An eminent pediatrician, he had attacked what he called "antifamily trends," including many forms of contraception. He had termed amniocentesis, the detection test for birth defects, a "search and destroy mission." He had also been widely criticized as a nominee because of his lack of experience in the public-health field.

Senate Panel Passes 'Human Life' Bill. The first congressional step toward overturning the 1973 Supreme Court ruling that had legalized abortion was taken June 9, 1981, when the U.S. Senate Judiciary Committee's subcommittee on the separation of powers approved legislation known as the human life bill.

The vote came after months of acrimonious debate in hearings conducted before the subcommittee, chaired by Sen. John P. East (R, N.C.). In its final version, amended slightly by East, the bill stated that, "The Congress finds that the life of each human being begins at conception," and went on to add "Congress further finds that the 14th Amendment to the Constitution of the United States protects all human beings." The bill would extend the 14th Amendment's right to due process of law to an unborn fetus.

The bill had previously been worded as follows: ". . . present scientific evidence indicates a significant likelihood that the life of each human being starts at conception."

Vote Is Close, Party Divided—The approval of the bill, by a vote of three to two, divided the subcommittee along party lines. Voting for the bill were the subcommittee's three Republican members: Sen. East, Sen. Orrin Hatch (Utah) and Sen. Jeremiah Denton (Ala.). Opposing the bill were its two Democrats, Max Baucus (Mont.) and Howell Heflin (Ala.)

Although approving the bill, the subcommittee members agreed to delay a decision by the full Judiciary Committee of 18 members until hearings were held on a proposed constitutional amendment that would specifically deny a woman the right to terminate her pregnancy. Passage of an amendment would require a two-thirds majority, rather than the simple majority necessary for a bill.

East declared that he was "extremely delighted" by the favorable vote. Hatch, who had expressed a preference for passage of a constitutional amendment, was plainly not delighted despite his pro vote, expressing "serious constitutional reservations" about the bill.

Hatch, who chaired the Senate Judiciary Committee constitution subcommittee, said that this group would hold hearings on the amendment to ban abortion in the fall, thereby delaying final action on either measure until sometime in 1982. He voted for the bill, he said, because "on an issue of this magnitude, I would prefer that the collective wisdom of the entire Judiciary Committee, rather than only this subcommittee, be called into play."

Baucus expressed dismay about the practical effect of the bill on contraceptive measures, maintaining as well that it "undermines the role of the judiciary as it has existed in this nation and will lead to an undercutting of the role of the states in our federal system." Heflin, who believed the Supreme Court would without doubt refuse to overrule the *Roe v. Wade* decision, called the bill "an exercise in futility," although reaffirming his antiabortion views: "As a former fetus, I'm opposed to abortion."

Both Sides Claim Victory—The vote was a step forward for antiabortionists. Said a spokesman for the Ad Hoc Committee in Defense of Life; "It's definitely a win for us . . . it's the first substantive piece of legislation on abortion ever to be reported out of subcommittee."

Pro-abortionists, however, were far from despondent because of the vote, and expressed optimism about defending legal abortion. "We have managed to push this bill onto the back burner," said a spokeswoman for National Abortion Rights Action League, "and it shows we have some real political strength."

Political Platforms

No 1972 abortion planks. Neither of the major political parties mentioned abortion in the platforms adopted for the 1972 Presidential election campaign. The Democratic National Convention's Platform Committee June 27 rejected proposals to include a call for legalized abortions.

1976
Party Platforms. In its 1976 platform, the Democratic Party said:

We fully recognize the religious and ethical nature of the concerns which many Americans have on the subject of abortion. We feel, however, that it is undesirable to attempt to amend the U.S. Constitution to overturn the Supreme Court decision in this area.

The Republican platform said:

The question of abortion is one of the most difficult and controversial of our time. It is undoubtedly a moral and personal issue but it also involves complex questions relating to medical science and criminal justice. There are those in our party who favor complete support for the Supreme Court decision which permits abortion on demand. There are others who share sincere convictions that the Supreme Court's decision must be changed by a constitutional amendment prohibiting all abortions. Others have yet to take a position, or they have assumed a stance somewhere in between polar positions.

We protest the Supreme Court's intrusion into the family structure through its denial of the parents' obligation and right to guide their minor children. The Republican Party favors a continuance of the public dialogue on abortion and supports the efforts of those who seek enactment of a constitutional amendment to restore protection of the right to life for unborn children.

Ford explains on TV.—In a television interivew with Walter Cronkite of CBS Feb. 3, President Ford stated his "moderate" position on the abortion issue, that he did not believe "in abortion on demand," did not agree with the Supreme Court decision of 1973 nor think that a constitutional amendment was "the proper remedy."

He favored "some flexibility." There were instances, such as rape or illness of the mother, he said, when abortion should be permitted.

The court decision, which struck down laws against abortion, "went too far," in his opinion, as did a constitutional amendment as a solution.

If there had to be action on the issue, Ford said, "it ought to be on a basis of what each individual state wishes to do under the circumstances."

He gave assurance that even though he disagreed with the Supreme Court decision, he would uphold the law as defined by the court.

If the constitutional amendment approach were taken, he preferred that it provide the states with more authority to restrict abortion than they had under the 1973 court ruling.

Campaign statements.—During the campaign, neither candidate seemed particularly anxious to turn the abortion situation into a major campaign issue.

Carter, speaking in Manchester, N.H. Aug. 3, touched on the issue of abortion. "We need to do something about teen-age pregnancies," he said. "We need a strong family planning program, better adoption procedures, better education, strong moral leadership to reduce or eliminate the need for abortions."

At a Sept. 8 news conference on the White House lawn, Ford supported the Republican Party platform plank urging constitutional protection of unborn children. It "coincides with my long-held view," he said, but he also said that "there should be a constitutional amendment that would permit the individual states to make the decision based on a vote of the people in each of the states."

Carter Sept. 9 said that abortion was a "very serious problem" for him. It was a "legitimate" issue, he said, and he understood the "deep feelings" of the anti-abortion demonstrators who were dogging his campaign trail and considered it proper for them to dramatize their view. But, he said, it would be "inappropriate" for him to "change my position to try to get their votes." Carter said he thought there would be an "adverse reaction" against any presidential candidate "who tried to take political advantage of an emotional issue like this."

1980 Democratic Platform Drafted. A draft of the Democratic Party's 1980 platform was adopted by the Democratic Party Platform Committee June 24.

The 40,000-word document conformed in most respects to the political wants of President Carter, whose supporters held a majority of nearly 2–1 on the committee, a proportion approximating the number of delegates won in the primaries and caucuses.

The President's supporters successfully withstood repeated attempts by backers of Sen. Edward Kennedy (D, Mass.) to gain planks he preferred, such as endorsements of wage and price controls, gasoline rationing and decontrol of domestic oil prices.

The President's forces did give ground on two key issues—nuclear power and abortion—and narrowly averted a setback on a plank opposing the MX mobile missile system, which Carter favored.

A call for phasing out nuclear power plants came from a Carter delegate from Minnesota—Carrie Wasley. When it appeared likely that the Wasley proposal might pass, the Carter strategists decided to compromise.

The compromise plank called for retirement of nuclear power plants as soon as alternative sources of energy became available. It also called for a moratorium on licensing new plants until tighter safety standards were issued.

(The plank contrasted with the policy statement signed by President Carter and other Western leaders in Venice June 23 supporting an expanded role for nuclear power.)

The abortion plank, strongly supported by almost all of the women delegates from both the Carter and Kennedy camps, declared the party's opposition to "any constitutional amendment" that would restrict the 1973 Supreme Court ruling on abortion rights.

The Carter camp would have preferred a provision describing a constitutional amendment on the subject as "not appropriate."

GOP National Convention

Skirmishes on Platform. Skirmishing on the abortion issue broke out in the Republican Party's drafting of a platform July 7–10.

The abortion plank adopted by the platform committee on July 9 called for a constitutional ban on abortion. The current statutory ban on use of public funds to finance abortions for the poor was endorsed.

An attempt to kill the antiabortion plank was rejected by a vote of 75 to 17.

On this issue conservatives pushed through tougher versions of more moderate provisions prepared at the staff level.

The abandonment of the party's traditional stand on the Equal Rights Amendment was protested July 9 by Mary D. Crisp, outgoing vice chairman of the Republican National Committee. "We are about to bury the rights of over 100 million American women under a heap of platitudes," she told the panel.

"Even worse is the fact that our party is asking for a constitutional amendment to ban abortions," she said. "I personally believe that these two actions could prevent our party from electing the next president of the United States."

Party Platform. The Republican National Convention July 15 adopted the longest party platform in American history. The document was entitled "Family, Neighborhood, Work, Peace, Freedom."

Its abortion plank stated:

There can be no doubt that the question of abortion, despite the complex nature of its various issues, is ultimately concerned with equality of rights under the law. While we recognize differing views on this question among Americans in general—and in our own Party—we affirm our support of a constitutional amendment to restore protection of the right to life for unborn children. We also support the Congressional efforts to restrict the use of taxpayers' dollars for abortion.

We will work for the appointment of judges at all levels of the judiciary who respect traditional family values and the sanctity of innocent human life.

Excerpts from Republican Party Platform

Women's Rights

We acknowledge the legitimate efforts of those who support or oppose ratification of the Equal Rights Amendment.

We support equal rights and equal opportunities for women, without taking away traditional rights of women such as exemption from the military draft. We support the enforcement of all equal opportunity laws and urge the elimination of discrimination against women. We oppose any move which would give the federal government more power over families.

Ratification of the Equal Rights Amendment is now in the hands of state legislatures, and the issues of the time extension and rescission are in the courts. The states have a constitutional right to accept or reject a constitutional amendment without federal interference or pressure. At the direction of the White House, federal departments launched pressure against states which refused to ratify ERA. Regardless to one's position on ERA, we demand that this cease.

Total integration of the work force (not separate but equal) is necessary to bring women equality in pay;

Girls and young women must be given improved early career counseling and job training to widen the opportunities for them in the world of work;

Women's worth in the society and in the jobs they hold, at home or in the workplace, must be reevaluated to improve the conditions of women workers concentrated in low-status low-paying jobs;

Equal opportunity for credit and other assistance must be assured to women in small businesses; and

One of the most critical problems in our nation today is that of inadequate child care for the working mother. As champions of the free enterprise system, of the individual, and of the idea that the best solutions to most problems rest at the community level, Republicans must find ways to meet this, the working woman's need. The scope of this problem is fully realized only when it is understood that many female heads of households are at the poverty level and that they have a very large percentage of the nation's children.

We reaffirm our belief in the traditional role and values of the family in our society. The damage being done today to the family takes its greatest toll on the woman. Whether it be through divorce, widowhood, economic problems, or the suffering of children, the impact is greatest on women. The importance of support for the mother and homemaker in maintaining the values of this country cannot be overemphasized.

Antiabortion Candidates Lose. Two congressional candidates won nomination in the Massachusetts primary Sept. 16, 1980, despite a bid by the Catholic Church to have voters reject candidates with proabortion views.

Shortly before the election, Cardinal Humberto Medeiros, Catholic archbishop of Boston, issued a message stressing the church's opposition to abortion. The message stopped just short of saying that a vote for a pro-abortion candidate was a sin.

Fifth District incumbent Rep. James M. Shannon (D) and state Rep. Barney Frank (D), seeking nomination in the 4th District, won despite their suport for federal funding of abortions for the poor. Both were up against conservative, antiabortion challengers.

Shannon took 54% of the vote. Frank, who was strongly backed by retiring Rep. Robert F. Drinan, won 52%. Drinan, a Roman Catholic priest, had stepped down from the seat after an order from Pope John Paul II barring priests from seeking political office.

Women Add Seats in Congress. The Nov. 4 election gave women 19 seats in the House and two in the Senate, which meant that women would have more of their number in Congress than ever before.

Still, the nation-wide swing to the right caused many feminists to view the election with dismay. With the victory of Ronald Reagan and many right-wing Republican senators abortion rights looked like they might come under siege.

Sarah Weddington, an aide to President Carter who had worked for abortion rights, commented, "It's going to take a major effort not to go backward in the next four years, let alone trying to move ahead."

Maryland. Charles McC. Mathias Jr. retained his Senate seat, easily defeating Democratic state Sen. Edward T. Conroy, 811, 925–423,879. Although a Republican, Mathias took traditionally liberal stands on abortion, the Equal Rights Amendment and defense.

Oklahoma. The GOP candidate, state Sen. Don Nickles, defeated Andy Coats (D), a former district attorney of Oklahoma County, to take the U.S. Senate seat of retiring Sen. Henry Bellmon (R).

Although a Catholic, Nickles won the support of many fundamentalist Protestant churches in Oklahoma. Nickles favored drastically reducing the role of the federal government and had worked in support of a constitutional amendment to outlaw abortion.

Religious Views

Bishops vs. abortions. A pastoral letter issued Feb. 13, 1973 by the National Council of Catholic Bishops warned Catholic laymen that anyone undergoing or performing an abortion "would place themselves in a state of excommunication." The message also contained unprecedented advice regarding disobediance of "any civil law that may require abortion."

According to the bishops, the Jan. 22, 1973

upreme Court decision permitting abortions
n demand was "wrong and entirely con-
ary to the fundanemtal principles of mo-
ality . . . The Supreme Court has certainly
verstepped itself in making law rather than
interpreting it." The bishops said they were
exploring all the possibilities" of overriding
the court's decision.

Jesuit dismissed on abortion issue. The
Rev. Eamon Taylor, provincial supervisor
f New York Sept. 6, 1974 announced the
ismissal of the Rev. Joseph O'Rourke, a
member of the West Side Community of the
Society of Jesus, who Aug. 20 had baptized
the 3-month-old son of a Massachusetts
woman who publicly favored a woman's
ight to have an abortion.

A local newspaper had reported Mrs.
Carol Morreale, a member of the Immaculate
Conception parish in Marlborough, favored
pening a Parents Aid Society abortion clinic
perated by William Baird. After the Rev.
ohn J. Roussin, a parish priest, postponed
the baby's baptism pending a review of the
mother's beliefs, Mrs. Morreale's friends
ontacted O'Rourke, a board member of
Catholics for a Free Choice, to conduct the
aptism. Taylor said O'Rourke had been
orbidden to perform the baptism.

In a related development, three Connect-
cut Roman Catholic bishops Aug. 13 warned
Catholic doctors, nurses and other medical
personnel that they would face excommun-
cation if the bulk of their work involved
bortions.

Catholic Conference sued. The Women's
Lobby, an organization with a registered
obbyist concerned with legislation affecting
women, sued the United States Catholic
Conference to force it to register with Congress as a lobbying organization, or to refrain
rom influencing legislation, it was reported
May 20, 1974.

At issue was the conference's antiabortion
activities in Congress aimed at overturning
he 1973 Supreme Court decision on abor-
ion.

The plaintiffs asserted that the "principal"

activity of Msgr. James T. McHugh, director
of the Conference's Family Life Division,
was to secure antiabortion legislation.

The conference said only a small portion
of its $17 million budget was applied to leg-
islation, $100,000 to the Family Life Division
and $128,000 to its Office of Government
Liaison.

According to Internal Revenue Service
statutes, a non-profit organization could not
maintain its tax exemption if registered as a
lobby.

Conference takes action—The U.S. Catholic Conference announced Jan. 7, 1976 that
it had formally asked the Supreme Court to
reverse itself on liberalizing access to abortion. The conference also requested that the
unborn's "legal personhood" be protected
under the Fifth Amendment to the Constitution. In their campaign to amend the 1973
decision, the bishops contested the Court's
creation of the category of "potential life."

Strong Vatican stand. A 5,000-word
document issued Nov. 25, 1974 by the congregation for the Propagation of the Faith
and approved by Pope Paul VI, according
to Vatican sources, said that "never, under
any pretext may abortion be resorted to . . .
as a legitimate means of regulating births."
Instead, the paper said, social reforms including improved adoption laws and aid for
unwed mothers were appropriate.

Quakers accept abortion. A statement
opposing efforts to ban abortion was adopted
by the Quakers' General Committee at its
annual meeting in Washington Jan. 26, 1975.
The statement said:

Members of the Religious Society of
Friends (Quakers) have a long tradition and
witness of opposition to killing of human
beings, whether in war or capital punishment or personal violence. On the basis of
this tradition, some Friends believe that
abortion is always wrong.

Friends also have a tradition of respect
for the individual and a belief that all persons should be free to follow their own
consciences and the leading of the Spirit.
On this basis some Friends believe that the

problem of whether or not to have an abortion at least in the early months of pregnancy is one primarily of the pregnant woman herself, and that it is an unwarranted denial of her moral freedom to forbid her to do so.

We do not advocate abortion. We recognize there are those who regard abortion as immoral while others do not. Since these disagreements exist in the country in general as well as within the Society of Friends, neither view should be imposed by law on those who held the other.

Recognizing that differences among Friends exist, nevertheless we find general unity, in opposing the effort to amend the United States Constitution to say that abortion shall be illegal.

Baptists accept some abortions. Messengers to the 12.3 million-member Southern Baptist Convention were reported June 16, 1974 to have voted for the approval of abortion in cases of rape, incest, fetal deformity or possible damage to the health of the mother.

Methodists oppose abortion foes. The council of bishops of the United Methodist Church adopted a resolution April 4, 1975, after a meeting in Minneapolis, which upheld the "sanctity of human life" but opposed any amendment to the U.S. Constitution that would "outlaw abortion." Deleted from the resolution was a section which scored "one segment of the American religious community," a reference to Roman Catholicism, for trying to impose its values on the rest of the country. The deletion was made in order to preserve ecumenical relations between Methodists and Catholics.

1978 Gallup Poll of Roman Catholics. It was found in the survey that 69% of all those polled (74% of the college educated) thought divorced Catholics should be permitted to remarry in the church and that 73% (83% college educated) thought the church should permit contraception.

On the abortion issue, 44% of all those who answered felt the church should "relax its standards forbidding all abortions under any circumstances."

U.S. Catholics Polled on issues. American Roman Catholics, according to a New York Times/CBS News Poll, endorsed the right to an abortion by almost as great a percentage as Protestants, it was reported Nov. 11, 1979. But a plurality in both religious groups disapproved of an acquaintance having an abortion.

The same poll also showed that 50% of the Protestants and 40% of the Catholics favored women in the clergy. But the percentage of Catholics opposed to the idea had jumped to 55% from 45% in two years.

New York Times/CBS pollsters interviewed 1,385 voting-age Americans from Oct. 29 to Nov. 3.

On the issue of abortion, the poll asked for a response to the statement, "The right of a woman to have an abortion should be left entirely to the woman and her doctor."

Sixty-nine percent of the Protestants and 64% of the Catholics agreed, while 27% of the Protestants and 32% of the Catholics disagreed. The same question, when asked in an October 1977 poll, found that 69% of the Catholics agreed with the pro-abortion statement.

A second question pertaining to abortion was asked in the current poll, "Would you approve or disapprove of someone you know having an abortion?"

Thirty-two percent of the Protestants and 27% of the Catholics approved, while 37% of the Protestants and 44% of the Catholics did not. For both religious groups, 25% answered, "It all depends."

The figures compiled by the poll on the abortion question suggested according to some observers, that abortion was no strictly a "Catholic" issue but rather a broad-based moral question that divided people along religious and nonreligious lines.

A study by Dr. Judith Blake, a sociologist at the University of California at Los Angeles, was cited. It maintained that regular church attendance was a far more common characteristic of abortion opponents than age, race, sex, income or religious denomination.

N.Y. Clerics Protest Catholic Stand—Nearly three dozen Jewish and Protestant clergy Jan. 22, 1979, led about 500 men and women to the steps of St. Patrick's Cathedral in New York to present a petition protesting anti-abortion statements and actions of Roman Catholic church leaders.

The leader of the group attached a scroll, signed by 43 church leaders, to the center door of the church. The scroll bore a "declaration of religious conscience on the spirit of intolerance."

It said, among other things, that Roman Catholic leaders, by comparing hospitals and abortion clinics to Auschwitz and Buchenwald and calling advocates of abortion murderers and Nazis, "have opted for a kind of demagoguery that destroys the spirit of dialogue and sows the seeds of bitter religious discord."

It added that the tactics and theology of the Catholic leaders "are a threat to the civil peace if pursued with the same clear disregard for others' convictions."

The ministers and rabbis denied that their action was an anti-Catholic protest, saying it was a plea for "tolerance and sensitivity" to the views of others. One clergyman added, "If we were in Salt Lake City, we would probably march into the Mormon temple."

Pope Signs New Code of Canon Law. Pope John Paul II Jan. 25, 1983, approved a new set of laws to govern the Roman Catholic Church, marking the first revision in the church's canon law since it was first codified in 1917.

The revised code, which would govern the religious lives of more than 735 million Roman Catholics worldwide, was to take effect Nov. 27. It incorporated many of the changes in church practice that had come about since the Second Vatican Council of 1962–1965. The Pope signed the new canon law on the 24th anniversary of the decision by Pope John XXIII to convoke that council and to modernize church laws.

It decreased, to six from 37, the number of offenses for which the automatic penalty was excommunication from the church. The six such offenses remaining were: aiding in or having an abortion; assaulting a pope; profaning the consecrated Communion host; violating the confidentiality of confession; absolution by a priest of his accomplice in an illegal act, and ordination of a bishop without approval of the Pope.

Nun Quits Order Over Abortion Stand. A Roman Catholic nun May 11, 1983 announced that she had given up her religious vows to avoid expulsion from her order, the Sisters of Mercy. Sister Agnes Mary Mansour had been ordered by the Vatican to resign as director of Michigan's Department of Social Services because the agency administered state funds for abortions.

When Mansour had been appointed to head the welfare agency in December 1972, Archbishop Edmund Szoka of Detroit had said he would oppose her acceptance of the post unless she publicly denounced state-funded abortions.

Mansour expressed a personal opposition to abortion but refused to take the position that the operation should be denied only to women who could not afford to pay for it. Szoka then had taken the issue to the Vatican for consideration.

Mansour subsequently had requested a leave of absence from her religious order to direct the state welfare department. Bishop Anthony Bevilacqua of Brooklyn, N.Y., a representative of Pope John Paul II, May 9 denied her request. He told her that if she did not resign, she would be subject to a church trial and possible dismissal from the order.

Mansour said at a news conference May 11 that her "vow of service to the poor, sick, uneducated and oppressed" was more meaningful than her "vow of obedience" to the church.

The Vatican May 13 confirmed that it had released Mansour from her vows and was allowing her to remain a Roman Catholic.

200,000 March and Pray In Washington Rally of Conservative Christians. Some 200,000 evangelical Christians assembled for a "Washington for Jesus" rally marched and prayed April 29, 1980, in Washington D.C.

Carrying Bibles, American flags and placards reading "America for Jesus" and "America Must Repent or Perish," the crowd gathered on the Washington Mall, prayed for God's intercession in what one of their leaders called "a world aflame in sin."

The rally, sponsored by One Nation Under God, a coalition of mostly conservative church groups, featured 60 speakers, including well-known evangelists and broadcast preachers. Many of the speakers at the demonstration warned of the moral and military deterioration of the United States and denounced, among other things, abortion, divorce, pornography and homosexuality.

The Christian rally climaxed a two-day gathering in Washington that included a series of religious meetings and a youth rally. The gathering also included mass lobbying on Capitol Hill, although the organizers of the rally said that they were trying to avoid any political involvement.

A group of Christian, Jewish and secular leaders charged April 29 that the organizers of the evangelical rally were "right-wing" with "a hidden political agenda" for the United States. The group charged that that agenda included defeating the proposed equal rights amendment, limiting abortion, opposing homosexual rights, discontinuing welfare programs and blocking affirmative action.

Said the Rev. David Eaton, minister of the All Souls Unitarian Church in Washington, D.C.: "Many of the organizers have political track records that are not only conservative but almost reactionary. Some of these persons have hoarded millions and millions of dollars and seek to completely ignore the social gospel. They seem to have no understanding of what it means to be poor in this country."

Nominee Assailed at Pro-Life Rally. Conservative and fundamentalist Christian groups held a "Rally for Life" in Dallas Sept. 3, 1981, at which the Supreme Court

nomination of Judge Sandra Day O'Connor was criticized. The rally attracted about 6,000 participants.

Edward E. McAteer, president of the Religious Roundtable, maintained that O'Connor's "public record" was one of "consistent and unequivocal support of abortion." He further contended that she had attempted to conceal her abortion stance from the Reagan administration.

While McAteer and several other rally leaders forthrightly attacked O'Connor's nomination, others adopted a more cautious attitude and said they would take a public stand when her Senate confirmation hearings were completed.

The second group included the Rev. Jerry Falwell, head of the Moral Majority, and the Rev. James Robison, a prominent evangelist.

Other Public Views

Report links decrease in abortion deaths to legalization. A report made by a panel of the National Academy of Sciences showed a sharp decline in maternal deaths and injuries related to abortion since the liberalization of abortion laws. The report, released May 27, 1975, said that women who had had abortions since legalization had displayed no measurable increase in mental problems.

The project was led by 11 specialists in the health and behavioral sciences who were named by the science academy's Institute of Medicine in early 1974. They were commissioned to make what members called "as objective an analysis as possible" of available abortion facts.

The impetus for the report was the 1973 Supreme Court decision that greatly liberalized states' abortion laws and the subsequent number of protests.

The report, titled "Legalized Abortion and the Public Health," noted that in 1961, when illegal abortions were common, there were 320 known abortion-related deaths. This contrasted with 47 deaths in 1973, with 16 attributed to illegal abortions.

The report noted that a healthy woman undergoing a competently performed abortion during the initial three months of pregnancy had only about six chances in a thousand of a major medical complication. During the second six months, however, the risk increased to 21 chances in a thousand.

Figures as to the number of medical complications when abortions were illegal were difficult to calculate, the committee said. But it cited a sharp drop in admissions to New York City municipal hospitals for two serious complications of abortion between 1969 and 1973. Incoming patients from septic and incomplete abortions, the report said, went from 6,524 to 3,253 in those years. Most restrictions on legal abortion in New York City were dropped in 1970.

At a news conference the day the report was released, a member of the committee said that a return to restrictive laws would probably lead to a rise in illegal abortions and the dangerous health consequences they entailed.

The committee also found that estimates of post-abortion psychoses (serious mental breakdowns) ranged from .2 to .4 per 1,000 legal abortions. This compared with the one or two associated with normal deliveries. Depression or guilt feelings reported by some women after abortions were usually described as mild and temporary.

The study panel cited figures indicating that 745,400 legal abortions were performed in the United States in 1973 and 900,000 in 1974. Of these, a third of the women were under 20, a third were between 20 and 25 and the remainder over 25. One in four was married and two-thirds were white.

The Associated Press reported May 26 that a Harris Poll survey had found that 54% of the American people supported legalized abortion, 38% opposed it and 8% were unsure.

In a related research development, Dr. William Peterson, a Washington gynecologist, reported May 20 he had developed a process that extended by a month the time in which a woman could have a suction abortion safely. He said he had performed the surgery on over 2,000 women who were beyond the third month of pregnancy.

Most doctors set three months as the outer limit for doing a suction abortion which surveys had found to have been the safest and least costly method presently in use.

Pentagon liberalizes rule. In a memorandum issued Sept. 17, 1975, the Pentagon reversed its policy restricting abortions performed in military hospitals. In 1971, President Nixon had ordered military hospitals to follow the abortion policies of the states in which they were located.

The Pentagon memo ordered base commanders in all services to heed the Supreme Court ruling.

Administration women challenge Carter. Some 40 high-ranking women in the Carter Administration met July 15, 1977, in the office of Margaret (Midge) Costanza, a presidential aide for public liaison, to protest President Carter's opposition to the use of Medicaid funds to pay for abortions. Carter July 12 had expressed his support for the withdrawal of funds.

The women had originally planned to send Carter a memorandum they had jointly drawn up, but after the President expressed displeasure about their meeting, they instead agreed to address him individually.

White House and government agency appointees who challenged Carter's abortion stand were praised for their action Aug. 15 by a coalition of 27 women's and public interest groups. In a letter to the President, the coalition said his top-level employees were "sensitive to and cognizant of the feelings of women throughout the nation."

End to unwanted pregnancies urged. Six major family planning and health groups, describing the Carter Administration's anti-abortion stance as "harsh" and "abhorrent," urged the federal government July 19 to increase financial support for birth control programs and other social services that would help prevent unwanted pregnancies.

The group called the Administration's proposed abortion alternative—a plan to increase adoptions—"ineffective" and a means of "bribing an unfortunate class of women to be breeders for the more fortunate."

A three-year, $1.7-billion education and research plan was submitted by the six organizations—Planned Parenthood Federation of America, American Public Health Association, National Family Planning Forum, Population Council, Zero Population Growth Inc. and Great Lakes Family Planning Coalition. (The Department of Health, Education and Welfare had budgeted $225 million for similar projects in fiscal 1978.)

Frederick S. Jaffe, the main spokesman for the groups, said their pregnancy prevention effort would be aimed at teenagers and the poor. Planned Parenthood had reported that one million teenaged women became pregnant each year, resulting in 608,000 births—one fifth of the annual total in the U.S. Planned Parenthood said those figures, and others that showed that one-fourth of the nation's illegitimate children were born to women 17 or under, indicated an "epidemic of pregnancies" among adolescents.

The public's attitude toward abortion had changed very little in recent years, according to a Gallup Poll reported Apr. 22, 1979. A survey in February of 1,534 adults indicated that 22% of those responding thought abortion should be legal under all circumstances; 54% believed it should be legal in certain circumstances, and 19% felt it should be illegal under any circumstances.

Only 25% of the Catholics interviewed felt that abortion should be illegal under all circumstances, indicating that most did not agree with the church's view.

Legalized Abortion 6th Year Marked. The sixth anniversary Jan. 22 of the Supreme Court ruling that legalized abortion was marked by protests and counterprotests in Washington and New York.

An almost all-white crowd estimated at 60,000, including large numbers of school-age children bused from Catholic schools, according to march participants, walked from the White House to the Capitol in a "March for Life." They carried posters with captions such as "Thank God, Jesus Wasn't Aborted" and "I Was Adopted, Not Aborted, Thank God."

Speakers on the steps of the Capitol called for a moratorium on the number of abortions that they said was close to three million and took credit for several election defeats of politicians with pro-abortion voting records. They said they were seeking the passage of a constitutional amendment outlawing abortions and noted they had been instrumental in getting federal Medicaid funds for abortions cut off.

Earlier in the day, the National Organization for Women held a press conference announcing it had invited some 40 anti-abortion and "pro-choice" organizations to meet and seek areas of common interest, such as birth control and family planning, and to try to end the "polarization and violence that surrounds this issue."

The invitation was rejected by the March for Life organization, whose president Nellie J. Gray, said, "Pro-life people will not negotiate with baby killers."

National Abortion Rights Action League president Karen Mulhauser accepted NOW's invitation. NARAL had held a press conference Jan. 21 to announce establishment of a "Rosie Jiminez Fund" to aid low-income women who would have qualified for Medicaid-fund abortion before Congress restricted the use of federal funds. (The effect of the cutoff was a 98% drop in federally funded abortions, NARAL said.)

Jiminez, who died in 1978, was the first reported victim of an illegal abortion following the restrictions put on Medicaid funds.

Gloria Steinem, speaking at the NARAL press conference, called the differences between the anti-abortion groups and the "pro-choice" groups "a kind of intimate Vietnam for women."

She said it was a War of the Roses. March for Lifers said they carried red roses "as a beautiful living reminder of the pre-born child." Steinem said the "pro-choice" groups would be sending legislators "one dead Rose—the story of Rosie, a real woman who was once alive, and who died at the age of 27."

Arizona Judge Sandra O'Connor Picked. President Reagan made history July 7, 1981, when he nominated Judge Sandra Day O'Connor as the first woman Supreme Court justice.

The nomination was received with elation by women's right advocates and with consternation by antiabortion organizations.

Reagan, following his announcement, said he was "completely satisfied" with O'Connor's position on abortion and declined to comment further on the issue.

O'Connor met with reporters in Phoenix July 7. She said that she was "extremely honored and happy" to be named to the high court. If confirmed, she promised to do her best "to serve the court and [the] nation in a manner that will bring credit to the President," her family and the American people.

Pro-Life Groups Oppose Nomination— Judge O'Connor's nomination to the Supreme Court was greeted by antiabortion groups with dismay and anger. Their anger was focused on O'Connor's voting record as an Arizona state senator. The groups said her voting record reflected a "pro-abortion" and "antifamily" slant.

In 1970, in a Republican Party caucus, O'Connor had voted for a bill to legalize abortion in Arizona. In 1974, she had voted against a rider that would have prevented abortions at the tax-supported University of Arizona hospital. Also in 1974, O'Connor had voted against state senate resolution calling on Congress to pass a Human Life Amendment to the Constitution.

The only notably "antiabortion" vote on her record came in 1973, when she backed a bill to allow physicians and nurses to refuse to participate in abortions against their will.

Also of concern to those opposed to her nomination was O'Connor's vocal support for the passage of a federal Equal Rights Amendment and women's rights in general.

Dr. J.C. Willke, chairman of the National Right to Life Committee, called O'Connor's appointment "a grave disappointment to the pro-life public nationwide." Willke accused Reagan of repudiating the Republican 1980 national platform.

(One plank of the platform supported the appointment of federal judges "who respect traditional family values and the sanctity of innocent human life.")

The Moral Majority issued a statement decrying O'Connor's nomination as a "disaster for men and women" and one that would "further undermine the traditional family."

Peter Gemma, chairman of the Pro-Life Political Action Committee, vowed to lobby the Senate against her confirmation. "I'm not sure we'll defeat her," he said. "But we want to send the President a clear signal at how much of an insult this is, and how his next court appointment had better be pro-life."

Kidnapped Abortion Doctor Released. The owner of an abortion clinic and his wife Aug. 20, 1982, were released unharmed after being abducted and held captive for a week. An antiabortion group that called itself the Army of God claimed responsibility for the kidnapping.

Dr. Hector Zevallos and his wife, Rosalie, Aug. 13 had disappeared from their home in Edwardsville, Ill., 12 miles (about 20 kilometers) east of St. Louis. Zevallos was the owner of the Hope Clinic for Women in Granite City, Ill., where hundreds of abortions were performed annually.

An anonymous phone call to authorities Aug. 15 led to the discovery, in a St. Louis park, of a tape recording and 43 pages of letters signed by a group called the Army of God.

In the letters, called "epistles" by the group, the Army of God took credit for the abduction and condemned the legalization of abortion. As a condition for the release of the couple, the group demanded that President Reagan appear on television by Aug. 18 to denounce abortion.

Reagan, who had frequently spoken out against abortion, declined comment on the kidnapping.

Authorities said the content of the epistles was "in effect, that man is evil, man's institutions have become instruments of evil and are working to deprive man of life, liberty and prosperity in defiance of God's will."

The Army of God was unknown to the Federal Bureau of Investigation and to both pro-choice and antiabortion groups. But the St. Petersburg, Fla. police department Aug. 19 confirmed that a group by that name had claimed responsibility for the firebombings of two abortion clinics in the St. Petersburg area May 29.

Zevallos' clinic had been damaged Jan. 23 by a fire, which police ruled had been caused by arson. However, no arrests had been made either in that case or in the two bombing cases in Florida.

The FBI Aug. 18 appealed to the Army of God to make contact with it so that "your demands can be discussed." The FBI appeal said that "any adverse action taken by you against the Zevalloses will be detrimental to the cause to which you are committed."

The Zevalloses were released on a dirt road a mile and half from their home at four a.m. Aug. 20. The FBI said that no ransom had been paid for their release.

Women Voters Backs Abortion Rights. The League of Women Voters Jan. 19, 1983, endorsed for the first time the right of women to obtain a legal abortion.

"The League of Women Voters believes that public policy in a pluralistic society must affirm the constitutional right of privacy for the individual to make reproductive choices," the League's statement said.

Dorothy S. Ridings, president of the 110,000-member organization, said, "This is not a statement that implies moral approval or disapproval of the procedure of abortion." Rather, she said, the league believed women should be allowed to make their own decisions about abortion and other issues involving reproduction.

Ridings said the league's board had decided to issue the statement after years of neutrality on the abortion issue when a poll showed that 92% of the league's chapters supported legalized abortion.

Heckler Sworn in to Cabinet. Margaret Heckler was sworn in March 9, 1983 as secretary of health and human services. The oath was administered by Supreme Court Associate Justice Sandra Day O'Connor in a ceremony in the Oval Office of the White House.

Heckler had been confirmed by the Senate by an 82–3 vote March 3. The negative votes were cast by Republicans—Sens. Jesse Helms (N.C.) and John East (N.C.) and Bob Packwood (Ore.).

At her confirmation hearing before the Senate finance Committee Feb. 25, Heckler, a former member of Congress, was questioned about some positions she had taken in the past that were contrary to Reagan administration policy.

In fact, according to a study by Congressional Quarterly, a weekly publication, Heckler had voted against the President's position more frequently than any other Republican member of the House in 1982.

Heckler told the panel that she had been representing one congressional district in casting those votes, but that she would be serving the whole country in the cabinet post.

She assured the committee she would pursue an appeal of a court decision blocking the administration's rule to have federally aided clinics notify parents when minors requested contraceptives. In the past, she had urged the administration to withdraw the rule. "My own prior views are personal views," she said.

Heckler expressed firm opposition to abortion. She refused the committee's repeated attempts to express opposition to proposals to curtail the Supreme Court's jurisdiction over the issue. "My own strong convictions on the right to life will dominate my own thinking," she told the committee.

The committee approved her nomination March 2.

Abortions, Illegitimate Births Rise. There were 854,853 legal abortions in the U.S. in 1975, or 272 abortions for every 1,000 live births, the bureau of the Census reported Aug. 10. In 1976, there were 312 legal abortions for every 1,000 live births, the federal Center for Disease Control reported May 24.

The Census Bureau's statistics showed that unmarried women had three out of four of the abortions. There was wide state-by-state variation in the total number of abortions. New York reported the highest ratio, 624 abortions for every 1,000 live births, and West Virginia reported the lowest, three abortions for every 1,000 live births.

There were 448,000 illegitimate births in 1975, with teen-agers accounting for more than half the number, the Census Bureau said. Illegitimate births were 14.3% of all births in 1975, up from 3.6% in 1940. Blacks accounted for 39% of the births out of wedlock; whites accounted for 7.3%.

The Center for Disease Control study showed that 65% of the women obtaining legal abortions were under 25 years of age, 67% were white, 75% were unmarried, and 48% had no other living children.

The number of deaths attributed to legal abortions declined in 1976 for the first time since 1972, although the number of abortions increased. There were 10 deaths attributed to legal abortions in 1976, compared with 29 in 1975, 27 in 1974, 26 in 1973 and 24 in 1972.

Also, the number of deaths associated with all abortions, including spontaneous abortions, continued to decline. There were 25 such deaths in 1976, compared with 45 in 1975, 52 in 1974, 56 in 1973 and 89 in 1972.

Other abortion related news:

In 19 opinion polls taken between 1972 and 1977, most of those surveyed generally believed women should be able to obtain a legal abortion, the Washington Post reported Aug. 9.

A five-year survey by the National Opinion Research Center in Chicago found that 88% of the adults questioned agreed that a legal abortion should be available to a woman whose health was endangered, while only 45% approved abortion for a married woman who did not want more children. The approval ratings were said to have increased each year of the survey.

A December 1977 Gallup poll found 22% of those surveyed thought abortion should be legal in all circumstances; 55% said it should be legal in certain circumstances, and 19% felt it should be illegal under all circumstances.

Violence against abortion and birth control clinics was on the rise throughout the U.S., according to the National Abortion Rights Action League March 7. At least 15 such clinics had been bombed, burned or vandalized during the past year, it said. Another firebombing of a clinic was reported May 17.

The March of Dimes announced March 8 that it was phasing out its support of programs diagnosing prenatal birth defects. Spokesmen denied pressure from anti-abortionists was responsible. Opponents of the program had called the foundation's screening and testing programs, which were able to detect birth defects such as mongolism, sickle cell anemia and Tay-Sachs disease, a "search and destroy" operation. The March of Dimes said the decision followed a policy of limiting foundation support to five years. There were 83 projects on genetic disease in the U.S. that would lose about $2 million in March of Dimes grants.

Abortions in 30% of Pregnancies. Nearly 30% of all pregnancies in the U.S. in 1978 were terminated by legal abortions, it was reported Jan. 9, 1980.

According to a new study, published in the latest issue of Family Planning Perspectives, there were an estimated 1,374,000 legal abortions in 1978, terminating 28.9% of all pregnancies in the U.S., excluding those ending in natural miscarriages. The 1978 figure was an increase of 54,000 over 1977.

The study said that about one-third of the abortions were for teen-agers and about three-quarters were obtained by unmarried women.

In 1977, the latest year for which figures were available by localities, the District of Columbia had by far the highest proportion of abortions to total pregnancies (excluding those that ended in natural miscarriages). About 59 of every 100 such pregnancies ended in legal abortions. New York State was second with 44 per 100. Mississippi had the lowest rate of legal abortion—5.5 per 100 pregnancies.

The study, conducted by the Alan Guttmacher Institute, also showed that more than nine-tenths of all abortions were obtained in urban areas where abortion facilities were more available and that more than nine-tenths took place in the first three months of pregnancy.

In 1973, according to the U.S. Center for Disease Control in Atlanta, Ga., the total number of legal abortions was 745,000. But in the wake of the U.S. Supreme Court decision striking down state antiabortion laws, the number of legal abortions had gone up sharply.

The number of illegal abortions, estimated in 1973 at several hundred thousand a year, had shown a decrease to about 10,000 or fewer a year.

Contraception

Introduction

Birth control practices (with the exception of abortion) had gained wide acceptance in the U.S. by the 1960s despite the opposition of the Roman Catholic Church and other religious authorities to specific contraceptive methods.

Recent issues considered by courts, executive agencies and legislatures include whether legislative prohibitions of sales of contraceptives, many dating from the nineteenth century, continue to be valid, and whether mandatory notification and consent of parents of teenagers receiving contraceptive services constitutes an invasion of privacy.

Public Policy & Controversy

"Family planning" defined. By the end of the 1960s, the term "family planning" had come into wide use in the public discussion and controversy over birth control. A "discursive" definition of the term "family planning" was prepared by the staff of the U.S. House Commerce Committee's Subcommittee on Health & the Environment. The definition:

family planning: the use of a range of methods of fertility regulation to help individuals or couples to avoid unwanted births; bring about wanted births; produce a change in the number of children born; regulate the intervals between pregnancies; and control the time at which births occur in relation to the age of parents. It may include an array of activities ranging from birth planning, the use of contraception and the management of infertility to sex education, marital counselling and even genetic counselling. Family planning has succeeded the older term, birth control, which is now felt to be too negative and restrictive in meaning. Birth control can be separately defined as the prevention of pregnancy by contraception, abortion, sterilization or abstinence from coitus.

Family planning bill passed. A bill authorizing $382 million for fiscal 1971–73 for family planning services and population research activities was approved by the House Dec. 8, 1970 and Senate Dec. 10 by voice votes. The measure sent to the President called for establishment of an Office of Population Affairs within the Health, Education and Welfare Department.

It also required development of a five year plan for extension of family-planning services to all persons desiring them, for research programs and for training of personnel. Grants to state agencies were authorized to help provide family planning services. Low-income families were to have priority in receiving cost-free family planning services.

The original Senate version of the bill had

67

been adopted by voice vote July 14. The bill, passed by the Senate Labor Committee July 7, was approved on the Senate floor without debate or dissent. It had been introduced by Sen. Joseph D. Tydings (D, Md.) with 30 co-sponsors.

The Nixon Administration had backed a more limited measure with open-ended authorizations. However the committee, reporting the bill later passed by the Senate, had said that the funds authorized in the measure would make it possible to meet President Nixon's stated goal of serving the five million women in the nation estimated to be in need of family planning services.

The report of the Senate committee emphasized that the legislation included safeguards to insure that acceptance of family planning services would be on a voluntary basis and would not be a prerequisite for receiving other financial or medical aid.

A more limited House version was passed by 298–32 vote Nov. 16 before the final compromise bill was worked out.

Expanded research sought. Roy Hertz, an associate director of the Population Council, asserted April 9, 1970 that advanced breakthroughs in contraceptive technology would require expanded research into the reproductive process. Hertz said "growing disillusionment" with present methods of contraception necessitated development of other techniques.

Hertz, addressing the annual seminar of the American Association of Planned Parenthood Physicians in Boston, said the reasons for the disillusionment were the known and unknown medical hazards and the difficulty in gaining widespread acceptance of the oral contraceptives and other currently available contraceptive methods among poorly motivated persons.

He said he was attempting to draw up blueprints for new birth control techniques that would circumvent the problems that had negated the overall success of the methods now in use. One approach, Hertz said, involved the vitamin folic acid, originally

found in leafy vegetables. Folic acid was essential to the growth of the womb during pregnancy and to survival of the fetus. Hertz said he was seeking a substance that would interfere with the body's ability to use the folic acid. He said a substance known as prostagladin F2 Alpha was under study in England, Sweden, and parts of Africa, as an abortion-causing agent. Hertz suggested that should Alpha 2 prove to be safe to the woman, it could conceivably be used as a morning-after type of contraceptive.

Massachusetts law voided. The Supreme Court March 22, 1972 voided as unconstitutional a 93-year-old Massachusetts law that prohibited distribution of contraceptive devices to single persons although the same devices were legally available to those who were married.

Under Massachusetts law, persons who sold or gave birth control devices to unmarried persons were subject to prison terms.

Only Wisconsin, which had a similar restrictive law, appeared to be affected by the court's decision. The court's vote in voiding the law was 4–3.

The issue came to the court in a case involving William R. Baird, a crusader for birth control. Baird was convicted in April 1967 of distributing birth control devices to a coed at Boston University and sentenced to three months in jail. State courts sustained his conviction but the 1st U.S. Circuit Court of Appeals voided the law under which he was convicted.

The opinion of the majority in the 4–3 vote was written by Justice William J. Brennan Jr., the only Roman Catholic on the bench. In his report, Brennan rejected the state's argument that the law was a proper exercise of the state's power to discourage fornication and protect people from harmful products. Brennan said this could not have been the state's real purpose because the statute applied only to unmarried persons.

Justices William Douglas, Potter Stewart and Thurgood Marshall agreed with Brennan. Chief Justice Warren Burger and Justices Harry Blackmun and Byron White dissented.

In a separate vote in the same case, the court voted 6–1 to overturn Baird's conviction. Only Burger dissented. The case was *Bellotti v. Baird*.

N.Y. curbs on contraceptives voided. A New York State law that prohibited the distribution and sale of contraceptives to persons under 16 was ruled unconstitutional July 2, 1975. The suit was seen as a test case whose results might spur other states into similar action. Among other provisions, the law had made it a crime to display or advertise contraceptives. The law also prohibited the sale of nonprescription birth-control devices—such as condoms—to minors by anyone other than physicians and limited the sale of nonprescription contraceptives to adults from licensed pharmacists. The case was *Carey v. Population Services International*.

U.S. drops condom-stamp plan. A plan for sending low-income teenagers sex information and condom stamps, first introduced in 1971, was dropped, it was reported April 28, 1975. The stamps were worth $1 for purchasing condoms. More than 43,000 boys, mostly in Philadelphia and Cleveland which were target areas for the first year's mailing, were sent the stamps, but only 254 were redeemed. The plan cost $100,000. The project director said the government's main concern was that the mailings might be construed as an invasion of privacy.

Condoms advertised on TV—Television station KNTV, an ABC affiliate in San Jose, Calif. broadcast the first condom commercial in the U.S. July 23. It was for the Trojan brand. Following a deluge of criticism from viewers the station tentatively decided not to run it again.

But July 25 the station ran a Trojan commercial as part of its news broadcast and when it asked for viewer attitudes toward the spot it received calls that it said were 8–1 in favor of running the commercial. As a result of the response, KNTV decided to reinstate the ads.

The station was able to act independently because it did not adhere to the National Association of Broadcasters' code of ethics, which banned such commercials. Four hundred sixteen U.S. stations, about 60%, subscribed to the code and over 40% (about 3,000) of radio stations.

Family-planning service lack cited. Fewer than half of the 510,000 Pennsylvania women with low or marginal incomes who were in need of family-planning services were receiving them, according to a study released Feb. 12, 1976 by the Alan Guttmacher Institute, the research and development division of the Planned Parenthood Federation of America. The report estimated that meeting the needs of the 263,900 women in need of the services would require the expenditure of $30.6 million on family planning—$22 million more than the estimated $8.6 million spent in the state in 1974. It noted that the federal government provided 75% of the funds for the 175 clinics in the state operated by 100 agencies, with 20% coming from private sources and 5% from state and local governments.

The study, based on 1974 figures but said by an institute spokesman to be still valid, was prepared under a grant from the M.K. Kellogg Foundation as part of a nationwide series for the Guttmacher Institute.

Other items mentioned in the report included:

Of an estimated 220,000 teenagers of all income levels in need of family counseling, approximately 150,000 remained unserved.

Ony 58 of Pennsylvania's 241 general hospitals reported the availability of family-planning services.

Of all women between the ages of 15 and 19 served by organized programs, 56% lived in Allegheny and Philadelphia counties.

More than 29,810 abortions were performed in the state during 1973, virtually all of them in metropolitan counties. Of the 39 hospitals reporting abortion services, 15 did not have identified family-planning programs.

Restraints on contraceptives voiced. The Supreme Court June 9, 1977, voided several provisions of a New York State law that had limited the advertising and sale of contraceptives within the state. Among other things, the provisions had made it a crime to display or advertise contraceptives. The law also prohibited the sale of nonprescription birth-control devices—such as condoms—to minors by anyone other than physicians and limited the sale of nonprescription contraceptives to adults from licensed pharmacists. The case was *Carey v. Population Services International.*

Justice William J. Brennan Jr. wrote for the majority in the 7—2 decision, which affirmed a lower court ruling. On the issue of advertising, members of the majority concurred with Brennan in reiterating the court's position that certain forms of commercial expression were protected by the First Amendment.

On the other issues, the majority agreed, in various combinations, that the state had failed to prove its contention that access to contraceptives would increase sexual activities among the young; that minors, like adults, had a right to privacy in their sexual relations; that the Constitution did not support blanket prohibitions on the right of minors to obtain contraception (since it could not prevent them from obtaining abortions), and that the statutes discriminated against married New York State females aged 14–16, who were subject to the same restrictions as unmarried females in the same age group.

Chief Justice Warren E. Burger dissented without comment. Justice William H. Rehnquist also dissented, saying the decision "enshrined in the Constitution the right of commercial vendors of contraceptives to peddle them to unmarried minors through such means as window displays and vending machines located in the men's room of truck stops."

Observers noted that the ruling was likely to affect as many as 20 states that had restrictive laws similar to New York's.

Giving contraceptives to minors is not violation of parents' constitutional rights—Distribution of contraceptives to minors by a publicly operated clinic, without notice to their parents, is not a violation of the parents' constitutional right to privacy in family matters, according to the United States Court of Appeals for the Sixth Circuit. The case was *Doe v. Irwin* (1980).

HHS submits teen birth control rule. Health and Human Services Secretary Richard S. Schweiker Jan. 10, 1983, submitted for final approval a proposed regulation that would require federally funded clinics to notify parents when their teen-age daughters were given presecription birth control devices.

The proposed rule had stirred intense controversy after it was issued in draft form in February 1982. HHS received more than 120,000 written reactions from the public, one of the largest responses in the department's history.

The rule would require federally funded clinics to notify parents by mail within 10 days after dispensing prescription birth control devices, including pills, intrauterine devices and diaphragms, to anyone under the age of 18. It would affect an estimated 530,000 teen-agers and 5,000 clinics nationwide.

Schweiker submitted the rule to the Office of Management and Budget for final approval, making only minor changes over his original proposal. If approved by the OMB, the rule could take effect 30 days after being published in the Federal Register.

Schweiker said the rule was needed to "protect the health and safety of minor adolescents who are given prescription birth-control drugs or devices paid for with tax-payer dollars."

The Planned Parenthood Federation of

merica Jan. 10 filed suit in U.S. district court in Washington, D.C., seeking to block implementation of the proposed regulation. The suit argued that the rule would violate the consitutional right of privacy and that it was contrary to federal birth control law. Planned Parenthood President Faye Wattleton called the proposed regulation "an outrage" and said the public's response to it had been overwhelmingly negative.

Rep. Henry A. Waxman (D, Calif.) chairman of the House Energy and Commerce Committee's subcommittee on health and environment, Jan. 14 called on the OMB to delay action on the proposed rule until Margaret M. Heckler took office as secretary of HHS. Heckler, nominated by President Reagan to succeed Schweiker, had expressed opposition to the rule while she was a member of Congress.

Waxman Jan. 10 had joined Planned Parenthood and other birth control organizations in criticizing the reorganization of HHS's family planning program. A Reagan administration spokesman that day had confirmed that Marjory Mecklenburg, author of the parental notification rule and an outspoken opponent of abortion, had been named deputy assistant secretary for population affairs and that the department's Office of Family Planning had been put under her jurisdiction.

Teen-age birth control rule blocked. A federal district judge in New York City Feb. 14 blocked implementation of a Reagan administration rule that would require federally funded clinics to notify parents after giving prescription birth control devices to teen-agers.

Judge Henry F. Werker ruled that the Health and Human Services Department regulation, scheduled to take effect Feb. 25, was invalid because it "contradicts and subverts the intention of Congress." He pointed to a 1978 amendment to Title 10 of the Public Health Service Act, in which Congress had mandated federal support for teen-age birth control programs in order to

counter the "critical" problem of teen-age pregnancy.

Werker, ruling on suits brought by New York State and its Department of Health and by the Medical and Health Research Association of New York Inc., issued a temporary injunction blocking the rule until a trial could be held on the suits. He said the rule would lead to "increased adolescent pregnancies," cause doctors to violate "patient confidentiality" and mean that "many maladies, including venereal disease, will not be prevented, detected or treated."

"The court finds that, based upon the record before it, the regulations constitute a blatant disregard for one of the main purposes" of the federal birth control law, Werker, said. "Unless a trial on the merits discloses information that is drastically to the contrary, the regulations cannot be upheld."

2nd Judge Blocks Birth Control Rule. A federal district judge in Washington, D.C. Feb. 18 issued a temporary injunction blocking implementation of a Health and Human Services Department rule that would require federally funded birth control clinics to notify parents after providing prescription contraceptives to persons under the age of 18.

The ruling followed a similar injunction issued in New York City Feb. 14 by federal district Judge Henry F. Werker.

Ruling on suits brought by the Planned Parenthood Federation of America and the National Family Planning and Reproductive Health Association, Judge Thomas A. Flannery reached the same conclusion as Werker: that the regulations would violate Title 10 of the Public Health Services Act, in which Congress had authorized federal funding for family planning services.

Flannery ruled that the regulations which had been scheduled to take effect Feb. 25, would have deterred teen-agers from using contraceptives and that "as a result of these regulations, substantial numbers of adolescents will become pregnant and will either elect abortion or suffer the consequences of unwanted pregnancies.''

Population Policy and Birth Rate

Demographer disputes 'ZPG' theory. Conrad F. Taeuber, associate director of the Census Bureau, took issue Jan. 13, 1971 with the view that zero population growth (ZPG) was necessary to conquer the nation's social and environmental problems. In a speech delivered at Mount Holyoke College (South Hadley, Mass.) and released in Washington, Taeuber said a "lower rate of growth is not an automatic solution to the problems which confront us.''

Taeuber said "our population problem is one of tackling the agenda for improvement of our total environment" and that a lower rate of growth "would be only one element in the programs which need to be developed." Taeuber, who supervised the 1970 census, said three fourths of the counties in the nation were net "exporters" of people in the 1960s, suggesting that distribution of population was more important than the nationwide growth.

"Pollution, high crime rates, transportation problems and other social ills are not primarily a result of our rate of population growth,'' he said.

Taeuber said the nation's population increased 13% in the '60s while the total volume of goods and services grew about 60%. He said the population grew 63% between 1930 and 1968—a period during which petroleum consumption increased 300% and natural gas nearly 900%. Taeuber concluded, "changing standards and habits, in activities, technology and the style of life have much more to do with the accumulation and disposition of waste materials and pollutants than does the number of persons involved.''

National population policy sought. A new coalition to support a national policy of zero population growth (ZPG) was announced in Washington Aug. 10, 1971 by Milton S. Eisenhower, interim president of Johns Hopkins University, and Joseph D. Tydings, former Democratic senator from Maryland.

The Coalition for a National Population Policy, to be chaired by Eisenhower and Tydings, included environmental and family planning organizations and such individual sponsors as United Auto Workers President Leonard Woodcock and Roy E. Wilkins, president of the National Association for the Advancement of Colored People.

The new organization backed legislation introduced in the Senate June 2 and in the House Aug. 3 to declare a U.S. policy of achieving population stabilization by voluntary means. The resolutions, sponsored by Sens. Alan Cranston (D, Calif.) and Robert Taft Jr. (R, Ohio) and Reps. Morris Udall (D, Ariz) and Frank Horton (R, N.Y.), had the backing of 33 senators and 25 representatives.

A goal of the coalition would be a voluntary limit in family growth to an average of 2.1 children per family versus the current 2.6. Tydings said that even if the 2.1 goal were achieved immediately, there were so many young in the country that it would take 70 years to stabilize the population. At the current growth rate, he said, the population would increase from the present 208 million to 300 million by 2001.

The coalition planned to press for full funding of the $382 million authorized by the 1970 Family Planning Services & Population Research Act. Tydings said Congress had appropriated only $38 million for research and $80.9 million for services.

Tydings critized the federal tax structure, which he said "encourages very large families and discriminates and penalizes childless couples and the unmarried.''

MIT study asks end to growth. "The Limits of Growth,'' a study of current world production and population trends financied by the Club of Rome, predicted a catastrophic world economic and population decline in the next century, unless production and consumption habits were put under deliberate international control.

The study, conducted at the Massachusetts Institute of Technology (MIT) and set for publication in March 1972, centered on a computer model of the interrelations between such economic factors as population, natural resources, industrial and food production, and pollution.

If current trends continued, the report said, growing population and rising demand for production would deplete the dwindling supply of natural resources, including arable land. Recovery of resources would become far more expensive, leaving less capital to replace aging productive capacity, eventually causing a decline in production. This would in turn devastate the population through lack of food and adequate medical services, both of which require heavy investment of capital goods.

Various alternative sets of trends were fed into the computer, but zero population growth alone, even combined with new resource discovery, would only postpone the day of reckoning. A stable world economy with minimally adequate living standards would require "a Copernican revolution of the mind" away from growth and wastefulness.

Specifically, the report called for a halt to population and industrial growth, a reduction in pollution, an increased use of recycling, the production of lasting, repairable goods, and an emphasis on services such as recreation and education rather than consumer goods.

The study was directed by MIT professor Dennis L. Meadows, at the request of the Club of Rome, an international group of business and economic leaders.

Criticism of the study, reported Feb. 26, included charges by economists that the computer model bore little resemblance to complex reality, and that the study ignored possible new technological breakthroughs in energy and food production and in pollution control.

Fewer children born, predicted. Further indications of a long-term decline in U.S. population growth emerged with a Feb. 16, 1972 Census Bureau report on the number of children that married women expected to bear, and a report March 1 of a 6% drop in the 1971 fertility rate.

The Census Bureau report found that the average number of children expected by married women between 18 and 24, surveyed in 1971, had declined to 2.4 from 2.9 in 1967, and from 3.2 in 1955. Taking into account unmarried women, the Bureau estimated an overall expectation rate of 2.2, approaching the replacement level of 2.11, which if maintained for 70 or 80 years would result in zero population growth (exclusive of net immigration). By the year 2,000 the current finding would indicate a U.S. population total of 280 million, 25 million fewer than a 2.9 rate would produce.

The Bureau attributed the decline partly to a rise since 1960 in the average age of women at marriage, from 20.3 to 20.9, and in the proportion of women ages 20–24 who were single, from 28% to 37%. Among young married women, the two-child family was close to the norm, with 64% expecting two or fewer children in 1971, up from 44% in 1967.

The National Center for Health Statistics, it was reported March 1, said the 1971 fertility rate had declined to 82.3 births per 1,000 women ages 15–44, down from 87.6 in 1970, resulting in a 4%, or 159,000 drop in total births to 3,559,000. The fertility rate was the lowest recorded since 1940, and was nearly 50% below 1955, the peak post-World War II year.

Among the reasons for the population slowdown cited Feb. 16 by Charles F. Westoff, executive director of the U.S. Commission on Population Growth, were the use of contraceptives, liberalization of some abortion laws, "environmental ideology" and unemployment. Other experts cited the increased female role in the work force and the "marriage squeeze," or shortage of men born in the 1930's and early 1940s to marry women born in the subsequent "baby boom."

Birth rate drop continues. The National Center for Health Statistics reported March 1, 1973 that all indices of U.S. population growth had fallen in 1972 and that the crude birth rate had fallen to a record low.

The crude birth rate, the number of births per thousand population, dropped to 15.6 in 1972 from 17.3 in 1971, itself a record low. Total births dropped to 3,256,000, 9% fewer than the previous year, despite an increase of 878,000 women of child-bearing age, 15-44. It was the lowest total since 1945.

Total fertility, the average number of children born to each family, declined from 2.28 in 1971 to 2.03 in 1972, and fell further to 1.98 in the last six months of 1972.

Total U.S. population grew at a rate of .78% in 1972, the lowest rate since 1945, and less than half the rate of 1.83 in 1956, the peak post-World War II year.

A Census Bureau expert attributed the birth rate decline to the older average age of women at their first marriage, an increase in divorce, a rapid increase in the number of working women, increasing use of contraception and liberalization of abortion laws, which in itself might have accounted for about one-fourth the decline in the number of births.

Fertility rate at record low. The total fertility rate, a statistic compiled by the U.S. Census Bureau to help indicate whether the future population would decline or grow, was reported May 25, 1975 to have hit a new record low. It was the third consecutive year that the birth rate was below the replacement level.

The total fertility rate for 1974, projected onto the female population, meant that every woman would have an average of 1.86 children. The previous record low was 1.90 in 1973.

Campbell Gibson, the analyst who prepared the report, said it was still too early to tell whether the drop foreshadowed a long-term decline in the birth rate. The relatively sudden drop in the statistic suggested

postponement, rather than abandonment of child-bearing, he said.

Gibson pointed out, however, that none of the recent figures reflected the full impact of this recession. Unemployment and reduced income did, traditionally, encourage lower birth rates. But Gibson noted that the number of women of childbearing age, in relation to the general population, was larger than usual because of the post-World War II baby boom. Normally, that would mean a second baby boom when these women began their families, he pointed out.

The impact of that development had already been muted by improved methods of contraception, a tendency toward marriage and child-rearing at later ages, changes in the role of women and a general concern with environment and overpopulation, Gibson said.

But even if the current birth rate decline were sustained, Gibson noted, "we would be unlikely to hit zero population growth anytime before the year 2000."

The U.S. birth rate declined in 1975 for the fifth straight year.

The provisional natality report from the National Center for Health Statistics said the 1975 birth rate was 14.8 births for 1,000 population, down about 1 per cent from 1974's rate of 14.9.

The fertility rate was 66.7 births for 1,000 women aged 15-44 years, a decline of about 2% from 1974. The fertility rate of decline had slowed from an average of 7% a year between 1970 and 1973 to about 2% between 1973 and 1975.

There were an estimated 3,149,000 live births in 1975, about 1% below 1974's 3,159,958.

Teen contraceptive use effective. An estimated 680,000 premarital pregnancies annually were avoided through the effective use of contraceptives by teen-agers, according to a survey reported June 7, 1978 by doctors at Johns Hopkins University.

The results of a 1976 survey published in Family Planning Perspectives also found that 313,000 additional pregnancies in the U.S.

could have been prevented if contraceptives were used consistently.

The data indicated, the publication said, that teen-agers were "not using abortion as a substitute for contraception." More of those who terminated a pregnancy by abortion had used contraceptive measures than those who were married.

The survey also showed that 41% of teen-agers had premarital intercourse. The regular users of contraceptives faced an 11% chance of becoming pregnant, as compared with 58% for those who did not use birth control methods.

Religious Views

San Juan clergy backs birth curb. The Most Rev. Luis Aponte Martinez, Roman Catholic archbishop of San Juan, Puerto Rico, Feb. 5, 1970 announced conditional approval by the hierarchy of a government-sponsored birth control program. Aponte clarified the clergy's position Feb. 7 by saying the church would cooperate in instructing the public on family planning and Puerto Rico's population explosion, but would oppose any massive propaganda campaign on contraceptives. The clergy's action came in response to a plea by Gov. Luis A. Ferre Jan. 14, which had called for an island-wide formal voluntary program of family planning orientation and services.

U.S. priests oppose birth edict. According to a study sponsored by the U.S. Roman Catholic hierarchy, a "substantial segment" of the priests in the U.S. believed that Pope Paul VI's 1967 encyclical against artificial birth control did not represent a "legitimate exercise" of his authority.

The New York Times reported Aug. 8, 1971 that this study of 5,000 active priests, 800 priests who had left the ministry and 250 bishops was circulated among U.S. bishops the previous week. The survey was conducted by the National Opinion Research

Center under the direction of the Rev. Andrew Greeley.

The 400-page study found that 36% of diocesan priests believed that issuance of the encyclical was a "competent and appropriate use of papal teaching authority," 18% that it was within the Pope's authority but was inopportune, 33% that it was a misuse of papal authority because the Pope "failed to act with sufficient collegiality," 9% that it was beyond papal competence because the Pope "cannot impose concrete universal directives of the natural law," and 4% had no opinion.

Among the bishops surveyed, 72% regarded the encyclical as "competent and appropriate" and 25% expressed reservations. The report said 54% of the major superiors of religious orders believed the encyclical was either inappropriate or a misuse of authority; 42% gave their full approval.

Catholic rates drop. A report resulting from the 1970 National Fertility Study showed that the number of children produced and planned by Roman Catholic families in the U.S. was approaching the figures for non-Catholics, and that both were declining, it was reported May 29, 1972.

The study, funded by the National Institutes of Health and based on a sampling of 5,600 married women of childbearing age, found that Catholic women aged 20–24 in 1970 wanted to bear an average of 2.75 children, down 20% from 3.45 in 1965. Non-Catholic women in the same age group wanted 2.35 children, down 9% from 2.57 in 1965.

Charles F. Westoff, one of the Princeton University demographers who conducted the study, said the figures indicated that "Catholics are becoming more and more like other parents in their use of the pill and other contraceptive devices."

Catholics use birth control—A report published in the Jan. 5, 1973 issue of Science magazine by the 1970 National Fertility Study showed that 68% of white, married Catholic women aged 18–34 were using birth control methods proscribed by their church.

The defection rate was greatest among younger Catholic women (74% for those 30 and younger), although the use of birth control methods other than rhythm had increased from 30% in 1955 and from 51% in 1965 for the entire age group.

College educated women showed the largest measure of nonconformity with church teachings—between 1965 and 1970, their use of birth control increased from 40% to 65%.

The New York Times had reported Dec. 30, 1972 that the fertility study appeared to confirm previous reports released in May 1972 indicating that the average family size for Catholic women had declined from 3.45 children in 1965 to 2.75. The national figures showed a decrease from 2.57 to 2.35 children.

Vatican position reaffirmed. Pope Paul VI March 29, 1974 reaffirmed the church's unequivocal opposition to birth control in a message delivered during an audience for United Nations officials. The Vatican also published the pope's prepared text, which cited his 1968 document, "Humanae Vitae."

A confidential Vatican document outlining a church campaign against governments and international agencies (widely believed to be U.N. groups) supporting birth control efforts had been made public March 11 by church sources opposed to the Vatican position.

The action, and several other unauthorized releases of internal church papers, prompted the Vatican to tighten security measures March 14. A three-page instruction book was published detailing a lengthy list of subjects given pontifical secret (or top secret) classification in an effort to prevent news leaks and limit inquiries. Punishment for violators ranged from reprimand to excommunication. According to the Vatican, the pope had personally approved the new regulations.

Fertility rates decline—Since the early 1960s fertility rates among married white women in the U.S. had dropped dramatically for all religious groups. However, the decline was considerably greater among Catholics,

a study made public April 15, 1978, showed. The report was released by the Office of Population Research at Princeton University.

The statistics confirmed that by 1975 the average family reproduction rate had reached a level that would result in 2.2 children, with virtually no difference between Catholics and non-Catholics.

In 1955, 80% of the nation's Catholic women had conformed to the church's prohibition against any contraceptive method other than the rhythm method, which gave them the highest fertility rate of any group, an average of four children each.

In 1975, 90% of those who had been married less than five years were using contraceptive methods not approved by the Catholic Church.

The Pill

Introduction

The development of oral contraceptives—"the pill"—had been hailed by advocates of population control as a nearly ideal weapon in the campaign against unwanted births. The U.S. Food & Drug Administration (FDA) disclosed May 9, 1960 that it had issued its first approval of a birth-control pill's safety. The first accepted pill, G. D. Searle & Co.'s Enovid, had received FDA approval after a four-year test involving 1,500 women. Other birth-control pills were soon also accepted.

But disquieting reports began to surface to indicate that "the pill" wasn't always effective and wasn't always safe. By Aug. 3, 1962, the FDA had announced its intention to investigate the possible relationship between Enovid and the deaths of several women who had used Enovid or the British version of Enovid (Conviod). A number of cases of thrombophlebitis had been reported among Enovid users.

Physicians, researchers and the FDA have

reached no conclusions about the safety risks of the Pill. Sequential oral contraceptives were withdrawn from the market in 1976, after studies showed an increased risk of cancer of the uterus. However, other types remain on the market, despite periodic warnings of increased incidence of cancer, heart attacks and blood clots among Pill users. The decision to use oral contraceptives remains to be made between the individual and her physician; the physician's advice is often based on a woman's individual and family history of cancer and heart disease.

Birth-control pill caution urged. The Food & Drug Administration asked the nation's doctors Jan. 19, 1970 to familiarize themselves with the risks involved in the use of birth control pills and to explain to their patients the potential long-range side effects of the pills. The FDA sent letters to 381,000 hospital administrators and physicians, asking them to keep informed about the latest information linking birth control pills to blood clotting problems.

The letters, signed by Commissioner of Food and Drugs Charles C. Edwards, also urged the doctors to study the FDA's newly revised pill labeling system which cited the risks of thromboembolic (blood clot) problems in the use of the pills. The revised system was inaugurated in September 1969 after the FDA's Advisory Committee on Obstetrics and Gynecology had conducted a full review of the pills' potential hazards.

"In most cases a full disclosure of the potential adverse effects of these products would seem advisable, thus permitting the participation of the patient in the assessment of the risk associated with the method," the letter said.

U.S. gets British data—The U.S. Department of Health, Education & Welfare received data from British medical authorities that linked the use of certain birth control pills to potential blood-clotting problems.

The British study, made public in December 1969, reported that there was a greater risk of blood clot problems in birth control pills with a relatively high content of estrogen than in those with a low estrogen level. All birth control pills contain synthetic estrogen, a female sex hormone, and progestogen, another synthetic hormone, to prevent ovulation, and if it occurs, to stop implantation of a fertilized egg on the uterus wall.

The British study panel reported finding an abnormally high correlation between the incidence of thromboembolisms (blood clots) and the use of birth control pills composed of more than 50 micrograms of estrogen. When the British study was made public, many British women switched to pills with a lower level of estrogen. Many British companies voluntarily withdrew from the market pills that had an estrogen content of more than 50 micrograms.

Several leading U.S. physicians estimated that nearly half of the 8.5 million American women using birth control pills took pills composed of more than 50 micrograms of estrogen, either in combination or in sequence with progestogen.

British study of pill safety. G. D. Searle & Co. May 22, 1974 released a preliminary report on a large-scale British study of the effects of using oral contraceptive pills. Financed by Searle, the study by the Royal College of General Practitioners was begun in 1968 and involved 46,000 British women.

According to the report, users of the pill faced distinct, though rare, health risks. Thrombophlebitis, blood clots in the legs, was found to be 5-6 times more prevalent among users than nonusers. Users exhibited a rate of high blood pressure twice that of nonusers. Oral contraceptives were also linked to higher than normal incidences of chicken pox and other viral infections such as stomach flu. This, the report said, suggested that the pill suppressed residual viral immunity from childhood.

On the positive side, the report indicated that oral contraceptives could reduce menstrual disorders, iron-deficiency anemia, premenstrual tension and benign cysts of the breast.

The report said the study had found among users a higher occurrence of lung blood clots, coronary artery disease and cervical cancer, but it said that the incidence of these conditions was too "small to justify any conclusions."

Senate hearings on 'the pill.' At Senate subcommittee hearings, which opened Jan. 14, 1970, prominent physicians disagreed on the potentially dangerous side effects of birth control pills. Sen. Gaylord Nelson (D, Wis.), chairman of the Monopoly Subcommittee of the Senate Select Committee on Small Business, said he had called the hearings to question whether the pills' manufacturers had deliberately under-emphasized the risks involved in using birth control pills.

Dr. Hugh J. Davis, a Johns Hopkins specialist in birth control devices, told the senators Jan. 14 that he feared that birth control pills may cause breast cancer that would remain undetected for years. Dr. Davis questioned whether it was wise to have "millions of Americans on the pill for 20 years and then [we] discover it was all a great mistake?" About 8 ½ million American women were reported using birth control pills.

Dr. Roy Hertz, of the Population Council and Rockefeller University, agreed with Davis. Hertz testifed Jan. 15 that only two facts about birth control pills had been substantiated: the pill's high degree of effectiveness in preventing pregnancy and the pill's ability to cause blood clotting problems. Hertz said all doctors prescribing birth control pills should treat each patient as though she were part of a research program. He advocated such safety measures, he said, because too many important questions about the pill's long-range side effects remained unanswered. Hertz also cited examples of laboratory experiments in which animals treated with synthetic hormones similar to those found in the pills developed certain strains of cancer.

Dr. Robert W. Kistner, a specialist in research and treatment of illnesses related to the female reproductive system at the Harvard Medical School, disagreed with Davis and Hertz. Kistner said animals treated with birth-control hormones in laboratory experiments had produced a protective effect against cancer-producing agents. Among the patients at the Boston Hospital for Women, Kistner said, there had been no appreciable increase in the incidence of pre-cancerous conditions in the female cervix between 1964 and 1969 despite an increase in the number of women using birth control pills.

A third physician to testify Jan. 15 said the manufacturers of birth control pills had failed to inform doctors about the true risks of the pill. Dr. Edmond Kassouf said manufacturers were still distributing information that failed to say anything about current data linking such pills to blood-clotting problems. He said risks were often distorted or minimized and in some cases denied by the pills' manufacturers.

The Senate subcommittee resumed its proceedings Feb. 24 and heard a New York obstetrician link "panic" and "unwanted pregnancies" to the publicity generated by the hearings.

Dr. Elizabeth Connell, an associate professor of obstetrics and gynecology and the first women to testify at the hearings, said "we are just beginning to see the first of the pregnancies of women who panicked in January, stopped using their pills and did not seek or use another means of birth control." Dr. Connell added that in New York some doctors were performing abortions on women who became pregnant since the subcommittee began investigating potential health hazards linked to the pill's use.

A second physician who testified Feb. 24 was Dr. Phillip Ball, who urged a five-year moratorium on the use of oral contraceptives because doctors "have been all wrong about birth control pills." Dr. Ball told the senators that he had refused to prescribe the pills for four years because of harmful side effects, including psychological changes in the users.

The director of the Planned Parenthood-World Population testified Feb. 25 that for all their supposed complications, birth control pills remained the most effective safeguard against "one of the gravest socio-medical illnesses—unwanted pregnancy." Dr. Alan Guttmacher said the potential side effects were secondary to the medical and social dangers of an unwanted pregnancy.

Dr. Guttmacher told the senators that the hearings on the safety of the pill had spread "unwarranted and dangerous alarm" throughout the world.

Doctor changes stand on pill. Dr. Robert W. Kistner, a professor of obstetrics and gynecology at Harvard Medical School, who had spoken out against critics of oral contraception and synthetic estrogens, Jan. 10, 1976 retracted his earlier statements on the subject.

Kistner acknowledged in an interview with the Washington Post that his statements regarding the safety of birth control pills and the use of estrogens in the treatment of menopause-related afflictions "cannot be substantitated." Kistner also said that he had given up research on hormonal agents seven or eight years ago and that he did not want to be known as an authority on the subject any more.

Pill warning. The federal govenment announced April 7, 1970 that it had accepted a compromise warning statement which would accompany all sales of birth control pills.

Three earlier versions of the statement cautioning women about the potential hazards of the pill had evoked strong opposition from some physicians and firms that manufactured oral contraceptives.

Secretary of Health, Education and Welfare (HEW) Robert H. Finch said the statement would be published in the April 8 edition of the Federal Register to allow comment from interested parties. (This was the initial step in making such a warning a required part of birth control pill packages.)

The new statement accepted by the government was shorter and less emphatic about the potential dangers of the pills than the others.

The warning, as revised, was inserted in the pills' packages beginning Sept. 9.

The FDA also required that physicians be provided with an 800-word brochure that reported the pills' possible side effects in detail. The pamphlet was written by the American Medical Association (AMA). It was left up to the physician to decide whether his patients received a copy.

The message said in part: "Do not take this drug without your doctor's continued supervision. Oral contraceptives are powerful and effective drugs which can cause side effects in some users and should not be used at all by some women. The most serious known side effect is abnormal blood clotting, which can be fatal."

The FDA had sought to have a 600-word warning statement carried in the pills' packages, one that FDA officials regarded as more forthright in warning women of the possible side effects of the pills, but the statement was cut after the medical profession and some pharmaceutical houses that manufactured the pills complained about the longer warning.

2 pill brands discontinued. Two large pharmaceutical houses Oct. 23, 1970 voluntarily discontinued the production of two brands of birth control pills whose chemical ingredients might have contributed to tissue changes in dogs. The action taken by Eli Lilly & Co. and the Upjohn Co. was made public by the Food and Drug Administration (FDA).

FDA Commissioner Dr. Charles C. Edwards Oct. 23 called the halt in production of the two brands of oral contraceptives "the only prudent course." At the same time Edwards said that there was no cause for alarm among women taking the pills.

The Eli Lilly product was marketed under the name C-Quens. Upjohn used the trade name Provest.

Edwards said that women using either of the two pills should continue to do so until their physicians told them otherwise.

The FDA had required continuing studies of the active chemicals in birth control pills and it was in one such study that dogs developed noncancerous nodules in their breasts when treated with large doses of two chemicals. One of those chemicals was an active ingredient in Provest. The other chemical was part of the makeup of C-Quens. The chemical in Provest was identified as medroxyprogesterone acetate, while the chemical in C-Quens was chlormadinone acetate.

Oral contraceptive recalled. Modicon, an oral birth control pill manufactured by Ortho Pharmaceutical Corp., was being voluntarily removed from the market, it was reported Oct. 14, 1975. The company, a Johnson & Johnson subsidiary, said a routine check of pills, had found reduced levels of estrogen, the active ingredient, in a small number of pills. However, the company emphasized that the move was only a precautionary one, pointing out that it was "not known if this reduction in estrogen lowers contraceptive effectiveness."

Ortho said that about 150,000 U.S. women, 1.5% of those "on the pill," took Modicon. The company advised women taking Modicon to continue taking it along with a supplemental contraceptive until their doctors would prescribe a new oral birth control pill.

A spokesman for the drug company said the problem appeared to be related to a chemical reaction between Modicon's estrogen, called ethinyl estradiol, and a red dye in the pill. Although several other companies used the same type of estrogen in some of their oral contraceptives, they were not considering recalling their pills. They discounted the Ortho findings in relation to their pills, explaining that theirs contained different dyes from those of Modicon.

Sequentials withdrawn. At the request of the Food and Drug Administration, three major drug companies had stopped the marketing and distribution of sequential oral contraceptives, it was reported Feb. 25, 1976.

The discontinued birth control pills were Oracon, made by Mead-Johnson Company Ortho-Novum SQ by Ortho Pharmaceuticals, and Norquen by Syntex Laboratories.

The FDA said it asked the drug companies to withdraw the pills because of new studies strongly suggesting that sequential pills posed an increased risk of cancer of the uterus.

An estimated two week's supply of the pill on the market was not recalled, the agency said. The sequential pills were used by 5%–10% of the 10 million American women who took oral contraceptives.

Birth control pill adds risk to smokers. The combined effect of birth control pills and cigarette smoking significantly increased the death rate among women over the age of 30, according to a report released March 30, 1977 by the Population Council, a private research group. The analysis was based on British and American studies that already had indicated that among women over 40, pill use greatly increased the risk of heart attack, stroke and death. The new findings were the first to distinguish smokers from other women.

The new data suggested that for women over 30 who smoked heavily (defined as over 15 cigarettes a day), the pill was the most dangerous contraceptive method and was more hazardous than pregnancy and childbirth.

Dr. Anrudh K. Jain, who prepared the report, called the combined effect of the pill and cigarette smoking "synergistic," meaning that the death rate among women who smoked and took the pill was higher than the combined death rates of smokers and pill users. One factor multiplied the effects of the other, a common phenomenon with certain substances such as barbituates and alcohol.

Among women aged 40 through 44 who took the pill and smoked, the death rate from heart attack was 62 per 100,000. For nonsmokers who used the pill, the heart attack death rate was 11 per 100,000; for those who smoked but did not use the pill, the rate was 16 per 100,000.

Higher mortality rates similarly applied to women in their 30s, who had a death rate of 10.2 per 100,000 among smoking pill users.

Jain's findings suggested that even for women in their 20s who smoked heavily, oral contraceptives could be the most dangerous form of birth control.

Pill warning for doctors. The Food and Drug Administration said April 8, 1977 that doctors and druggists had to be told that birth control pills could cause birth defects, tumors, blood clots and, in women over 40, heart attacks. The action, directed at manufacturers of the pill, put into effect a December 1976 FDA order.

The warning would be included in "physician labeling," information for doctors and pharmacists that was included with the pill and governed advertising claims drug companies could make.

The new labeling described the pill as the "most effective method of contraception" except for sterilization. It identified potential hazards and necessary precautions for use of the pill. The FDA said it was studying a proposed requirement that women who purchased the pill receive a brochure containing the same information.

Birth Control Danger

Introduction

The dangers presented by contraceptives, including the Pill (see previous section), should be considered in conjunction with the chapter entitled "Drugs," because the issues are the same. With regard to contraceptives other than the Pill, however, the issues of product liability and access tend to merge once a non-pharmacentical contraceptive device is marketed with accompanying claims of safety; legal claims to damages for resulting injuries often assert that manufacturers knew or should have known of the device's dangers, and thus should have withdrawn it from the market.

"Morning-after" pill. A senior physician at the University of Michigan Health Service Oct. 25, 1971 made public findings that a "morning-after" birth control pill had safely prevented pregnancy in all 1,000 women of child-bearing age involved in a university study.

Dr. Lucile K. Kuchera described the study and her results in an article published in the Journal of the American Medical Association.

The pill used in Kuchera's experiment consisted of a synthetic estrogenic substance called diethylstilbestrol (DES), a hormone substitute used to relieve several female ailments.

In Kuchera's study, no pregnancies occurred among the 1,000 women, most of them co-eds, although almost all had had sexual intercourse without using contraception at a time when they would be most fertile. Calculations indicated that at least 20 to 40 of the women would have become pregnant if they had not used the drug.

Dalkon Shield linked to death of 4. Another birth-control device was described in 1974 as possibly dangerous. A. H. Robbins Co., a pharmaceutical manufacturer, informed 120,000 doctors in a letter dated May 8 that the Dalkon Shield, an intrauterine contraceptive device (IUD) made by Robbins, had been implicated in the deaths of four women, who had become pregnant while using the Dalkon Shield.

The Robbins letter stated that the company had learned of 36 septic abortions among women who became pregnant while using the IUD. Septic abortions were spontaneous abortions that sometimes caused a uterine infection called septicemia, a widespread blood infection. The four deaths cited in the Robbins letter were from septicemia.

As a result of the Robins letter, the Planned Parenthood Federation of America May 23 ordered its 700 affiliated birth control clinics to stop dispensing the Dalkon Shield and directed the clinics to inform its current users of the device of its potential dangers.

Robbins said 2.2 million women had been fitted with the Dalkon Shield since it was first marketed in 1970.

The Food & Drug Administration (FDA) June 28 ordered a ban on the manufacture and sale of the Dalkon Shield, and an FDA advisory committee recommended Aug. 22 that the ban continue until controlled trial experiments demonstrated that the shield was as safe as other IUDs. At a public hearing Aug. 21, the FDA said it had learned of 11 fatal and 209 nonfatal septic abortions among the women fitted with the shield.

But the FDA Dec. 20 ended the Moratorium on the sale of the Dalkon Shield. It said the manufacturer of the device had agreed to register all new users of the shield, as well as follow their progress. Data to be reported to the FDA by Robbins was to include the number and kind of adverse reactions, the rate at which the device was expelled by women and other details.

In October, an FDA advisory panel of medical experts had concluded that the Dalkon Shield didn't pose greater risk to women than other intrauterine contraceptives.

Dalkon IUD user wins suit, controversy grows. A jury in Wichita, Kan. awarded Connie L. Deemer $85,000 in damages against the A. H. Robbins Co. in connection with her use of the Dalkon Shield, it was reported Feb. 8, 1975. She said that the device caused a perforation in her uterus and failed to prevent pregnancy. The case was the first of its kind to go to trial but was one of many similar cases pending against Robbins. (Robbins reported Oct. 20 that it had paid $1,548,000 to settle litigation, legal fees and other expenses from the various cases.)

The FDA advisory committee had discovered that the shield's multifilament string or "tail" could draw bacteria up into the uterus, and Robbins announced Jan. 20 that it was recalling all unused domestic stocks of the shield and would not return them until a new mono-filament tail had been developed.

The FDA, in a Senate hearing Jan. 28, pledged to control testing of the revised model in order to obtain reliable data on its safety. The promise was partly in response to complaints by the advisory panel, and the resignation of one of its members, that the agency had not done enough to control the testing of the new model. It was reported Jan. 21 that the Planned Parenthood Foundation of America and the U.S. Agency for International Development were permanently discontinuing distribution of the shield.

Robbins then announced Aug. 8 that the Dalkon Shield would not be returned to the market. The manufacturer said that it believed the shield was "safe and effective" when properly used but felt that, because of unfavorable publicity, reintroduction of the device would be "difficult, if not impossible."

IUD's raise abortion death risk. The death rate from septic abortions was 50 times higher among women who continued to wear intrauterine devices (IUD's) after becoming pregnant than among those who used other methods of birth control, according to a study released by the Center for Disease Control Nov. 18, 1976.

The findings were derived from a survey of spontaneous abortion deaths in the U.S. between 1972 and 1974. The mortality rate among pregnant women who did not use the IUD was 0.28 per 100,000. In contrast, 14.8 deaths per 100,000 occurred among pregnant women who used the IUD.

FDA orders IUD labeling. Manufacturers of intrauterine birth control devices would be required, effective Nov. 7, 1977, to make brochures describing the potential risks and side effects of the IUD available to all women considering that method of contraception, the Food and Drug Administration announced May 6. The federal agency, which had originally proposed the regulations in 1975, also ordered uniform labeling for physicians that would include information on use of the IUD and dangers in prescribing it.

The FDA order required that doctors give their patients the opportunity to read the brochure before insertion of an IUD. Women could then evaluate rates of effectiveness and rates of adverse reactions.

Depo-Provera used in Tennessee. A Tennessee health official admitted Feb. 21, 1973 that his office allowed the distribution of

Depo-Provera as a contraceptive for clinic patients and the mentally retarded. The Food and Drug Administration (FDA) had not approved use of Depo-Provera in the U.S. as a contraceptive because it had produced breast cancer in dogs and because scientists believed use of the drug needed more study.

The FDA had approved the drug for use in the treatment of pre-cancerous inflammation of the uterus and terminal cancer of the uterine lining. Used as a contraceptive, Depo-Provera would be injected for protection from pregnancy for up to three months.

Dr. Robert Hutcheson Jr. of the Tennessee Health Department said studies on Depo-Provera in other countries convinced state officials to use the drug in special cases where neither interuterine devices nor oral contraceptives would work. Hutcheson said Tennessee health officials had the same information as the FDA, "but they came to a different conclusion."

Hutcheson said all patients were told of possible harmful side effects. However, Anna Burgess, 21, of Cumberland County, Tenn., testified before a Senate health subcommittee hearing Feb. 21 that the State Welfare Department urged her to take Depo-Provera and at no time told her of possible bad effects or that the FDA had banned the drug as a contraceptive.

Upjohn Co., sole maker of Depo-Provera, stopped shipments of the drug to Tennessee when it found it was being used as a contraceptive, it was reported Feb. 21.

The FDA then approved limited use of Depo-Provera as a long-term contraceptive Oct. 10, but it ordered that patients be provided with detailed information of its risks.

Sterilization

Introduction

Voluntary sterilization has become an uncontroversial form of birth control for married couples who had their desired number of children. The legal issue that tends to arise from such voluntary sterilizations is whether a physician who does not properly perform the procedure is liable for the costs of pregnancies that may result or for the upkeep of the child (see Wrongful Birth/Wrongful Life).

Most of the legal questions that arise from use of sterilization as contraception involve problems of consent, typically in two situations. Mental incompetents who can neither control their behavior nor care for children have been sterilized by their guardians who fear that pregnancy will result. If it later becomes possible for people sterilized under these circumstances to lead normal lives, problems of liability may arise. The legal issue here is similar to that in cases involving medical treatment of terminally ill incompetents and other informed consent cases (see Death & Dying and Ethical Issues & Health Care).

Legal questions also arise when sterilization is made a condition for hazardous but well-paying jobs, or services such as government-funded medical treatment.

In resolving these issues, courts have applied privacy cases as precedent: in question is the extent of the constitutionally recognized right to privacy, i.e. freedom from government intervention, in matters pertaining to the family and to children. The same legal principle is involved in abortion cases (see Abortion).

Rise in sterilizations. The Association for Voluntary Sterilization, a New York-based organization that kept records on the number of Americans who underwent voluntary sterilization, reported March 21, 1970 that the rate of requests for such operations was growing by over 100,000 each year.

The association also reported that nearly 75% of those who requested the operations were men. The male sterilization procedure was known as vasectomy. Five years previously, it was reported, almost all of the requests came from mothers with oversized families. The association reported that the number of requests it received for referral had quadrupled, from 825 in 1966 to 3,707 in 1969.

Another association reporting a significant increase in the number of callers seeking information about sterilization operations was the Margaret Sanger Research Bureau in New York. The bureau's manager March 21 said the group, which performed the operations for men, was "booked through the end of May." She said the association was planning to expand its facilities to accommodate nearly five times the number of operations it could presently handle in a week. The manager said the expansion was intended "to try to meet at least some of the demand."

Individual doctors, not associated with the Sanger Bureau or the Volunteer Association, also reported a rise in the number of requests for sterilization operations.

Sterilization program curbed. U.S. District Court Judge Gerhard A. Gesell ruled in Washington March 15, 1974 that rules proposed by the Department of Health, Education and Welfare (HEW) to cover federally-financed sterilizations of poor persons were "arbitrary and unreasonable" and failed to give sufficient protection to minors and mentally incompetent persons.

HEW had been attempting to draw up regulations because of disclosures of sterilization of retarded minors in federally-aided clinics and, as Gesell noted in his decision, evidence that welfare recipients had been threatened with loss of benefits if they refused sterilization.

The proposed rules said that legally competent adults must give "informed consent" to sterilization, and that minors and mental incompetents must give written consent approved by a third party in their behalf.

Ruling in a suit filed by the National Welfare Rights Organization, Gesell said that neither minors nor mental incompetents could meet a standard of voluntary and truly informed consent, and that the "will of an unspecified representative" could not be imposed in a matter as serious as sterilization.

Gesell also said that the consent procedures involving competent adults must be amended to require that persons be informed that no federal benefits could be withdrawn because of a failure to accept sterilization.

Noting that in recent years 100,000-150,000 low-income persons had been sterilized annually in federal programs, Gesell said the matter was of major national significance. Government, including Congress he said, should "move cautiously" to set regulations in "one of the most drastic methods of population control" which could irreversibly deprive unwilling or immature persons of their rights.

New sterilization technique reported. A new surgical technique for female sterilization that could be done in 15 minutes under local anesthetic was reported Feb. 10, 1975 to have been developed by Dr. InBae Yoon, assistant professor of gynecology and obstetrics at Johns Hopkins University. The operation, which was considered safer than more conventional sterilization operations, required the patient to stay in the hospital for only a few hours. It entailed a minor incision and the placement of a ring to close off the fallopian tubes. The procedure had already been performed on 1,050 patients in the U.S. and abroad.

MDs liable for vasectomy failures. The Michigan Court of Appeals ruled May 23 that doctors were liable for costs and suffering of pregnancies that resulted from botched vasectomies. They were held not liable for "wrongful life" or the rearing of the child (see Wrongful Birth/Wrongful Life).

Married sterilization rises—Use of surgical sterilization among married couples rose about 25% between 1973 and 1976, the National Center for Health Statistics reported April 15, 1978.

In the age range for wives from 15 to 44, more than 28% of either spouse had undergone sterilization by 1976. Among white couples in which the wives were 30 to 34, the 1976 figure was 44%.

Use of the pill, or oral contraceptives, fell

to 22.3% during the same period for all women, and to 11.8% for women 30 to 44.

A separate study, issued by the George Washington University Medical Center April 15, showed sterilization as the most widely used form of contraception in the world. Over 80 million couples world-wide used sterilization for birth control, compared with 55 million who used the pill.

4,400 sterilized in Va. state hospitals. More than 4,400 patients in five Virginia mental institutions were sterilized, sometimes without their knowledge or consent, during a 48-year-long program to eliminate future social misfits, state officials said. Feb. 23, 1980.

Although the sterilization program was ended in 1972, the exact number of persons treated under the program was still uncertain, state officials said.

Nearly all were white and included both men and women, officials said. Among those sterilized were persons then considered "feeble-minded" and "antisocial." Also included in the program were unwed mothers, prostitutes, petty criminals and children with disciplinary problems.

Most of the documented cases occurred at the Lynchburg Training School and Hospital, one of the largest mental health facilities in the U.S., where some 4,000 persons were sterilized. Officials cautioned, however, that the figure covered only part of the period that the program was in effect.

The sterilization program was apparently stopped in 1972, state officials said, when the state Board of Mental Health and Retardation banned the practice. Two years later, state laws were amended to prohibit state hospitals from performing involuntary sterilizations without first securing court permission.

The Virginia program, upheld in a landmark 1927 U.S. Supreme Court decision, had stemmed from a now discredited theory, called eugenics, that the human race could be improved by the breeding of genetically acceptable people. Eugenics advocates had maintained that mental retardation, criminal behavior and other behavior considered deviant could be eliminated by preventing the "feeble-minded" from reproducing and passing on these traits.

Judge immune in sterilization case. The Supreme Court March 28, 1978, ruled, 5–3, that an Indiana judge who had approved the sterilization of a 15-year-old girl was immune from a damage suit arising from that action. The decision in *Stump v. Sparkman* broadened the concept of judicial immunity previously upheld by the high court in landmark rulings in 1872 and 1967.

The case concerned an Indiana woman who petitioned DeKalb County Circuit Court Judge Harold D. Stump in 1971 to have her teenage daughter sterilized. (The mother claimed that her daughter, Linda Kay Spitler, was both retarded and sexually promiscuous.) Judge Stump signed the petition without holding a hearing on the matter.

Spitler was sterilized without her knowledge or consent. (She left the hospital believing she had received an appendectomy.) She did not realize she could not bear children until after she had married in 1973. Her husband sued her mother, her mother's attorney, Judge Stump and the hospital.

The U.S. District Court ruled that Stump, as a government official, was the only one who could be sued in the case. However, the same court subsequently held that the judge could not be sued for performing a judicial function.

The 7th U.S. Circuit Court of Appeals reversed the lower court, arguing that Stump had not "acted within his jurisdiction." The appeals court said the judge had forfeited his immunity by failing "to comply with elementary principles of due process."

The Supreme Court overturned the appeals court. Writing for the majority, Justice Byron R. White maintained that a judge could not "be deprived of immunity because the action he took was in error, was done maliciously or was in excess of authority."

While conceding that there was no law in Indiana to authorize Stump's action, White held that it was "more significant" that there was no Indiana law or judicial precedent in that state to prevent the judge from considering a sterilization petition. White said that Stump's signing of the petition constituted "a judicial act."

In dissent, Justice Potter Stewart contended that Stump's action was "beyond the pale of anything that could sensibly be called a judicial act." Stewart concluded that a judge was "not free, like a loose cannon, to inflict indiscriminate damage whenever he announces that he is acting in his judicial capacity."

Justices Thurgood Marshall and Lewis F. Powell Jr. endorsed Stewart's dissent. Powell also issued a separate opinion protesting the fact that Spitler and her husband had been deprived of any legal recourse by the ruling.

Justice William J. Brennan Jr. did not take part in the decision.

HEW Sterilization Regulations. The Department of Health, Education and Welfare issued regulations for federal funding of sterilization procedures, effective February 6, 1979. The regulations require: advice about alternative forms of birth control and explanation of the sterilization procedure, both in language the patient understands; a mandatory waiting period between consent and surgery of at least 30 days but not more than 180 days; use of an HEW-approved consent form.

Consent is invalid if obtained from a person in labor or childbirth, seeking an abortion, or under the influence of alcohol or drugs. No federal funds may be used for sterilization of persons under 21, persons institutionalized in mental hospitals or prisons, or mental incompetents.

Similar regulations were promulgated in 1981 by the California Department of Health Services.

Court rule on sterilization of incompetents. The Massachusetts Supreme Judicial Court held that the Massachusetts statute prohibiting involuntary sterilization should not work "to deny incompetent individuals

the same procreative choices which competent persons may exercise."

In the case *In the Matter of Moe* (Mass. 1982), the mother of a mentally retarded woman sought a probate court order to allow sterilization of her daughter, who lacked the legal capacity to consent to the procedure herself. Consistent with its precedents in *Saikewicz* and *Spring*, the Massachusetts high court held that, because of the intrusive and irreversible nature of the treatment, a parent could not consent to her incompetent child's sterilization without a court order. The court further stated that the probate court should apply the doctrine of substituted judgment in approving such procedures. That doctrine requires that the courts base its decision on what it believes the incompetent person would choose if competent, and not necessarily on what would be the "best" decision. Thus, the Massachusetts court explicitly rejected the "best interests" test applied in other states, such as New Jersey.

The Supreme Judicial Court further emphasized that only the ward's interests should be considered. "Neither the convenience of the state nor the interests of parents are material to the ultimate decision to be made." The court also established the standard of proof required by the petitioner to be a preponderance of the evidence. A higher standard of proof such as beyond a reasonable doubt, the court explained, might tend to result in the denial of the incompetent's right to seek sterilization. One justice dissented from the court's decision, stating that the "very condition of incompetence makes the doctrine of substituted judgment a cruel charade." The court's criteria for making such decisions, he claimed, were biased in favor of sterilizing incompetent persons.

A California appeals court ruled in 1978 that the state courts have no inherent authority to order the sterilization of a mentally incompetent person, even where the operation would serve the person's best interests and the guardian consents. The case was *Guardianship of Tulley*. The effect of the court's ruling is that a statute would be required to authorize courts to order sterilizations of incompetents.

The Washington Supreme Court ruled in 1980 that state courts have inherent authority to order sterilization of mental incompetents, even absent statutes providing such authority. The court specified the procedure to be followed by lower courts when considering petitions for sterilization orders: the judge must find by "clear, cogent and convincing evidence" that 1) the person is unable to make the decision regarding sterilization independently; 2) the person is likely to engage in sexual activities resulting in pregnancy and is permanently unable to care for a child; and 3) no other method of contraception exists. The case was *In re Hayes*.

The Supreme Court of New Hampshire reached a similar conclusion in *In re Penney* (1980).

The United States Court of Appeals for the Fourth Circuit held in 1977 that a physician did not violate the privacy, due process or equal protection rights of his poor patients by conditioning treatment upon consent to sterilization if they were delivering their third living child. Despite the physician's receipt of Medicaid funds, the court ruled that this did not mean his actions constituted implementation of his "personal economic policy" under color of state law. The case was *Walker v. Pierce*.

In 1979 the Supreme Court of Montana held that a nurse-anesthetist's right under the state's "conscience statute" to refuse to participate in a sterilization operation outweighed the hospital's business necessity. The court ruled in *Swanson v. St. John's Lutheran Hospital* that the hospital's dismissal of the nurse was illegal.

The Supreme Court in 1982. Refused to block an appellate court appeal by a union of a decision upholding a so-called "fetus protection policy" adopted at an American Cyanamid plant in West Virginia in 1977. Under that policy, female employees between the ages of 16 and 50 working with toxic chemicals were given the options of either undergoing voluntary sterilization or accepting transfers to lesser paying jobs in safer parts of the plant.

The Oil, Chemical and Atomic Workers International Union had challenged the policy as a violation of the Occupational Safety and Health Act, but a federal district court dismissed the suit. American Cyanamid had then asked the Supreme Court to intervene to prevent an appeal to a higher court. The case was *American Cyanamid v. Oil, Chemical and Atomic Workers International Union*.

Birth Issues

Wrongful Birth/ Wrongful Life

The development of amniocentesis and other predictive tools, along with the increased use of sterilization by couples who do not want to have more children, have led to new legal theories of injury involving the birth of unplanned or deformed children. The most common of these new actions are "wrongful birth" and "wrongful life." Wrongful birth most commonly involves a negligent act by a physician which results in the birth of a child which the parents did not intend. The damages available in such an action range from the expenses involved in the pregnancy and delivery, compensation for the parents' mental and physical pain and suffering and loss of consortium, to the costs of raising the child. Similarly, wrongful life usually involves a negligent act by a physician resulting in the birth of a deformed or "defective" baby. The damages are similar, tending to include life-long costs of special care needed by the child.

The courts' reaction to wrongful birth and wrongful life actions have been varied over the past several years. The cases below demonstrate the range of opinions concerning these issues.

In the 1977 case of *Bennett v. Graves* (Ky. 1977), the Kentucky Court of Appeals held that a physician who had performed a tubal ligation on a female patient was not liable for the subsequent birth of another child.

The court found that, although performed properly, there was a recognized low failure rate for the operation. The court regarded as especially significant the fact that the plaintiff had signed a surgical consent form acknowledging that the results of the procedure were not guaranteed.

The following year, the Alabama Supreme Court, in the case of *Elliott v. Brown* (Ala. 1978), ruled that a child born with severe birth defects could not sue the physician who allegedly performed a negligent vasectomy on the child's father. The court held that there was no legal right not to be born. Therefore, there could be no cause of action for wrongful birth against the physician unless the plaintiff alleged that some preconception act by the physician caused the deformities. [Compare the cases on prenatal injury, below.]

The New York Supreme Court's Appellate Division, in the 1980 case of *Sorkin v. Lee* (N.Y. Sup. Ct. A.D. 1980), held that a physician who negligently performed a vasectomy may be liable to the parents of a healthy baby fathered after the operation. In such a case, the court held, damages will be limited to the costs of raising and educating the child since "abortion was a legitimate medical option." Though not requiring the parents to mitigate their damages by seeking an abortion, the court stated that "their decision should not affect the physician's potential liability."

Prior to the *Sorkin* decision, however, the

New York court had a different reaction to a case involving the birth of a deformed child. In *Karlson v. Guerinot* (N.Y. Sup. Ct. A.D. 1977), the Appellate Division held that the parents of a deformed child could recover damages from their physician for their mental anguish and physical pain and suffering associated with the birth. The physician had negligently failed to inform the mother of the likelihood that the child would be deformed. Thus, unlike the parents in *Sorkin*, this couple did not have sufficient information to know that abortion was an option. The court further held, however, that the child did not have a cause of action for wrongful life.

The following year, the New York Court of Appeals, the state's highest court, unanimously rejected two claims for wrongful life. In the companion cases of *Becker v. Schwartz* and *Park v. Chessin* (N.Y. Ct. App. 1978) two deformed babies were born after their physicians negligently failed to advise their parents of the likelihood of birth defects indicated by their family histories. The court did, however, allow damages measured by the cost of necessary care and treatment for the children.

In 1979 the New Jersey Supreme Court upheld a cause of action for wrongful birth brought by the parents of a child born with Down's Syndrome. The parents claimed that their physician had negligently failed to inform them of the availability of amniocentesis, by which the parents could have learned of the child's defect in time to have an abortion. In its decision in *Berman v. Allen* (N.J. 1979), the New Jersey high court held that the parents' damages were limited to their emotional distress, but did not include the child's medical or educational expenses. The court rejected the child's claim for wrongful life, holding that requiring the physician to pay for the child's support would "disavow the basic assumption upon which our society is based."

The Alabama Supreme Court in 1982 changed its position from that in *Elliott* (see

above). In *Boone v. Mullendore* (Ala. 1982) the court held that a woman whose sterilization procedure had been improperly performed could sue her physician after the birth of a healthy child following the operation. The Alabama court limited those damages to the mother's mental and physical pain and suffering, and the couple's loss of consortium. The court refused, however, to award recovery for the costs of raising the child, stating that the "birth of a healthy child, and the joy and pride in rearing that child . . . far outweighs any economic loss that might be suffered by the parents."

In contrast to these decisions is that of the Minnesota Supreme Court in *Sherlock v. Stillwater Clinic* (Minn. 1977). There the court held that the parents of a healthy child born after an unsuccessful vasectomy performed on the father, had a cause of action for wrongful conception against the father's physician. The court held that the damages included not only the expenses associated with the pregnancy and delivery, but also "the reasonably foreseeable costs of rearing [the child], subject to an offset for the value of the benefits conferred to them by the child." The Minnesota court rejected the claim that the joys and benefits of raising a child outweigh the economic costs.

In 1981, two years after the *Berman* decision (see above), the New Jersey Supreme Court changed its position in *Schroeder v. Perkel* (N.J. 1981). In that case, physicians had been treating a child for four years without diagnosing her illness as cystic fibrosis, a hereditary disease. The court held those physicians liable to the parents for the costs of caring for a second child born to the parents before they learned of the genetic disorder in their first child. Although treating the child, the physicians owed an independent duty to her parents to disclose the nature of her illness, and would be liable for the foreseeable results of their negligent failure to disclose. Given that the first child's parents were of child-bearing age, it was foreseeable that they would have a second

90

child absent information regarding the hereditary nature of the first child's illness. "It would be unreasonable," the court said, "to compel parents to bear the expense of medical treatment required by a [second] child and to allow the wrongdoer to go scot-free."

In the 1982 case of *Ochs v. Borelli* (Conn. 1982), the Connecticut Supreme Court held that the parents of a child conceived after an improperly performed sterilization procedure may recover damages from the negligent physician. Those damages, the court held, may include the expenses of raising the unplanned child to its majority, as well as the parents' mental and physical anguish. As did the Minnesota court in *Sherlock*, the Connecticut high court rejected the position that "the birth of a child is always a blessing to its parents and that this benefit must, as a matter of law, totally offset concomitant financial burdens."

Surgeon liable for wrongful birth. A surgeon who had unsuccessfully performed a sterilization on a woman was liable for the costs of raising her child, the Supreme Court of Connecticut ruled unanimously June 3, 1982.

Carol Ochs had filed the "wrongful birth" suit against Dr. Anthony P. Borelli when a 1973 sterilization operation had failed to prevent her from becoming pregnant. She gave birth to a child less than two years after the operation.

The State Supreme Court upheld a lower court award to Ochs of $56,375 for expenses that would be incurred in raising the child. Ochs had also been awarded another $49,985 for pain and suffering and for medical expenses, includng the cost of a second sterilization.

Borelli had agreed to pay the medical expenses but had challenged the propriety of paying the cost of raising Ochs' child.

"We may take judicial notice of the fact that raising a child to maturity is a costly enterprise, and hence injurious, although it is an experience that abundantly recompenses most parents with tangible rewards," the court's opinion stated.

Preconception Injury

Similar to the actions for wrongful birth and wrongful life are cases brought by the parents of deformed children alleging that some preconception injury to the mother caused the deformity. The two cases below are representative.

In *Bergstreser v. Mitchell* (8th Cir. 1978), a federal appeals court held that under Missouri state law, injuries to a baby resulting from a preconception tort against the mother would give rise to a claim by the child. In this case, the plaintiff claimed that the defendant physician had negligently performed cesarean section on the plaintiff's mother in 1972. Damage from that earlier procedure allegedly caused a rupture of the uterus during a 1974 pregnancy, necessitating the plaintiff's premature birth by emergency cesarean section, resulting in the plaintiff's permanent brain damage.

In contrast, the New York Supreme Court's Appellate Division, relying on its 1978 decision in *Park v. Chessin* (see above), held that a child has no cause of action against a physician for injury resulting from a preconception tort against its mother. In *Albana v. New York* (N.Y. Sup. Ct. A.D. 1981) the court held that a child born with brain damage had no claim against a physician for allegedly negligent treatment of its mother prior to the child's conception.

Fetus given a right to sue. A federal judge in Connecticut ruled July 7, 1982, that a fetus had the right to join its mother in suing a police department in a brutality case.

U.S. District Judge T. Emmet Clarie of Hartford was the first federal judge to recognize a fetus as an independent person. He further held that both the fetus and its mother had equal right to bring suit under the Civil Rights Act of 1871.

91

The suit had been filed by Rosalee Douglas of Hartford. Douglas maintained that in July, 1981, when she was 5½ months pregnant, she had been beaten by a police officer who was investigating a car theft. She claimed that a second officer had stood by and watched the beating.

Douglas had filed suit against the Hartford Police Department and both officers, on behalf of herself and her fetus. She was seeking $250,000 in damages.

Douglas had given birth to a son, Paul, in October 1981.

Surrogate Mothers

Use of Surrogate Mothers Involves Complex Legal Issues

Advances in the science of artificial insemination, coupled with a shortage of infants available for adoption, have produced a brand-new potential "industry": surrogate motherhood. A May 30, 1980 article in the *Boston Globe* noted the increasing use of surrogate mother arrangements by childless couples in recent years.

Many couples are unable to produce their own children, due to the wife's physical incapacity or career pressures. Adoption procedures are often slow, expensive, and offer couples little choice regarding the age and hereditary make-up of the child. As a result, many couples seek to hire a woman capable of childbearing, and have her artificially inseminated with the husband's sperm as a surrogate biological mother for the couple's child, and pay the surrogate mother anywhere from $4,000 to $15,000 for her services.

There are many potential legal problems with surrogate mother arrangements. In April 1981, a surrogate mother in California went to court to keep the child she had borne under a contract with the child's father. An out-of-court settlement gave her custody of the child. In January 1983, a Michigan woman sued a New York man who had offered her $10,000 to serve as a surrogate mother for his child. The man denied fatherhood of a child who was born with a birth defect. Tests showed that, indeed, he was not the father. The surrogate mother claimed that she and her husband had conceived the child due to improper instructions regarding abstention from intercourse preceding artificial insemination.

A Note in the *American Journal of Law & Medicine*, Fall 1981, observed that questions may exist concerning the legality and enforcability of surrogate mother contracts. The Note concluded that such arrangements are legal, and should be enforceable. It suggested, however, that legislation is necessary to establish the rights and obligations of the parties to surrogate mother contracts in order to protect the parties from misplaced assumptions and liabilities.

Death and Dying

Introduction

Medical advances have brought into question the very fact of death. Routine use of respirators during emergency life-saving efforts has made the traditional criteria of death, cessation of respiratory and circulatory function, less effective as a standard. The prospect of keeping people technically "alive" until new cures are found may be philosophically attractive to some, but at some point costs to society begin to outweigh benefits. Moreover, many people do not want to be maintained on life-support systems when they can no longer function as autonomous, conscious individuals, or when continued survival means increasing pain. Therefore new definitions of death and new standards of consent to treatment have been explored.

Definition of Death

The difficulty of definition. A "discursive" definition of the term "death" was prepared by the staff of the U.S. House Commerce Committee's Subcommittee on Health and the environment. The definition: *death*—a permanent cessation of all vital functions; the end of life (often called mortality). A simple concept whose actual occurrence medicine has made very difficult to define and measure. A consensus appears to be forming that death occurs when all measurable or identifiable brain functioning (electrical or any other kind) is absent for over 24 hours.

The problem of definition had been discussed by Dr. Eliot Corday in the May 7, 1970 issue of the Hospital Tribune. "Already, in view of the known resuscitative methods and life-support systems that may revive a patient from apparent death," he wrote, "the public has begun to question the criteria by which a live heart is removed from a dead donor."

Corday warned that the medical profession appeared "to be moving toward a double standard. One standard would be to accommodate the transplanters—certifying that death has occurred when there are no reflexes and the EEG trace is linear—in other words, cerebral death. The other standard for the everyday practice of medicine would be to continue to accept the age-old definition of death as the irreversible cessation of perceptible heartbeat and respiration. And today this may have to imply that cardiac resuscitation, assuming it was available, had been attempted and failed—a question that has come up in at least one court case."

Corday recalled that a Harvard ad hoc committee had drafted a definition of irreversible coma. The criteria would include: maintenance of respiration only by artificial means and inability to maintain spontaneous respiration when artificial means are with-

93

drawn; no awareness of externally applied stimuli; no spontaneous muscle movement or reflexes; a flat EEG. These criteria had been generally accepted as justifying a diagnosis of cerebral death and thereby permitting the removal of organs, but Corday noted that "some transplant surgeons, however, have declared cerebral death while spontaneous respiration was still present."

Similar criteria were adopted in 1968 by 24 surgeons, immunologists, neurologists and heart specialists who met in Geneva on the call of the Council for International Organizations of Medical Science, under the aegis of the World Health Organization and UNESCO. These conferees insisted on two further criteria, Corday recalled: "(1) the donor's heart must be in perfect condition at the time of removal; (2) an immunological examination should be made before the operation to determine the compatibility of donor and receiver." The addition of these two requirements could indicate that some question remained in the minds of conferees as to the adequacy of the criteria they were accepting and that they were proposing to balance the desirability of saving another's life against the uncertainty over whether the potential donor had actually died. Corday noted that the scientists had added still another requirement— that "two independent teams should be deployed in heart transplant operations, one to establish the donor's hopeless condition, the other to perform the operation."

Corday held that there was still "need to determine whether there is adequate evidence that the moment of death may now be advanced to coincide with brain death, though cardio-respiratory activity is spontaneous."

4 MDs cleared in transplant case. Four doctors—three transplant specialists and a state medical examiner—were acquitted May 25, 1972 by a jury in Richmond, Va. of wrongdoing in removing the heart of a 56-year-old man for a transplant operation although under the legal definition of death he was still alive.

The jury set a precedent in allowing the medical definition of death to take precedence over the legal definition. Most medical authorities regarded a person as no longer alive if the brain was dead even if other life systems could be kept going by mechanical means.

At issue in the trial was whether Drs. David Hume, Richard Lower and David Sewell, members of a transplant team, ended the life of Bruce O. Tucker May 25, 1968 so they could use his heart in a transplant operation. The fourth doctor named in the suit was Dr. Abdullah Fatteh, the state medical examiner, who released Tucker's body for the transplant team's use.

Legal definition of death at issue. An Oakland, Calif. superior court jury convicted Andrew Lyons of involuntary manslaughter May 24, 1974 despite his contention that his victim, whose brain-wave activity had stopped, had not died until surgeons removed his still-beating heart for transplant into another person.

Dr. Norman Shumway, one of the surgeons involved in the case and a heart-transplant specialist at Stanford University in Palo Alto, Calif., testified at the trial May 19 that irreversible cessation of brain activity, rather than an end to heartbeat, was the best way to legally determine death. (The recipient of the manslaughter victim's heart died a month after receiving it.)

AMA for postponing definition law. In an action Dec. 3, 1974, the House of Delegates of the American Medical Association adopted a resolution calling on state medical societies to ask legislatures to postpone enactment of statutes defining death. Calling statutory definition "neither desirable nor necessary," the delegates said death should "be determined by the clinical judgment of the physician." The "permanent and irreversible cessation of function of the brain" was suggested as a possible clinical criterion for death.

Definition complicates slaying. Walter Burton Carey 3rd, a 27-year-old ex-convict, pleaded innocent Dec. 7, 1976 to charges of second-degree murder, murder in the commission and furtherance of a felony and first-degree robbery in the slaying of an Islip, N.Y. high school student.

Carey was accused of killing Karen Ann Pomroy, 17, in a Nov. 29 robbery. Pomroy had been found unconscious, her skull partially crushed, that afternoon on the grounds of Islip High School. She was operated on that evening at Southside Hospital in Bay Shore by Dr. William H. Bloom, a neurosurgeon and the president of the county medical society.

According to Bloom, Pomroy had gone into an irreversible coma on Tuesday, Nov. 30, "with a total absence of reflexes." Bloom said tests revealed blood was not reaching her brain. She was placed on a respirator early Wednesday morning, Dec. 1, and electroencephalograms were administered to measure brain activity. These scans, said Bloom, had shown no brain activity was present. Pomroy was removed from the respirator Thursday, Dec. 2, after her corneas and her kidneys had been removed for transplant with her parents' consent.

(Carey was arrested for assault Dec. 1 and charged with murder Dec. 3. According to papers submitted to the court Dec. 3, he had told a detective, "I grabbed her. I grabbed her pocketbook. She started screaming, and I kept hitting her with a [iron railroad] spike.")

Suffolk Assistant District Attorney Gerald Sullivan Dec. 7 indicated he believed Carey's attorneys would challenge the murder charges on the ground the actual cause of death had been her removal from the respirator, not the blows Carey had allegedly struck. Bloom Dec. 3 said, in his opinion, "brain death" had occurred at approximately midnight on Nov. 30. Pomroy had not been pronounced dead until 3:45 PM, Dec. 2.

Sullivan said the Carey trial would be the first of its kind, since New York State had no legal definition of death. Bills proposing legal definitions had failed to pass in the state legislature.

Uniform death definition urged. A presidential commission July 9, 1981, voted unanimously to urge legislation that would standardize the definition of death for every state. Currently, 23 states recognized only combined heart and respiratory stoppage, while 27 states recognized different degrees of brain death.

The recommendation was made by the President's Commission for the Study of Ethical Problems in Medicine and Biomedical and Behavioral Research. It was established by Congress in 1978.

The disparity in criteria for determining the moment of death created difficult choices for physicians, who often feared legal action should they remove artificial supports that had kept the heart of a brain-dead patient functioning. The commission found that even within the same state the policies of different hospitals varied greatly, some halting artificial respiration in all irreversibly brain-dead patients and others awaiting the cessation of the heartbeat in all cases.

The commission proposed a law that would define as dead "any individual who has sustained either 1) irreversible cessation of circulatory and respiratory functions, or 2) irreversible cessation of all functions of the entire brain, including the brain stem."

The inclusion of the phrase "including the brain stem" made the definition a relatively conservative one, eliminating the far more controversial alternative of equating death with the end of "higher brain" function. The upper brain controlled reason, thought and emotions; the brain stem or lower brain controlled breathing and swallowing.

Patients who had lost all powers of consciousness but retained the lower brain ability to breathe could exist in a comatose state for years. These patients would be considered alive under the proposed definition. The definition would include all those patients, however, who had lost all brain function and were "alive" only in the sense that their heart and lungs were made to function with life support machines.

Both the American Medical Association

95

and the American Bar Association concurred with the commission's definition, which was similar to definitions formulated independently by each of these organizations.

The Commission also released a list of accompanying guidelines to aid physicians in deciding when brain or heart-lung death has occurred. The guidelines stress irreversibility and cessation and suggest that clinical tests be more mandatory.

Washington state high court adopts 'brain death' standard. On October 2, 1980, the Washington State Supreme Court judicially adopted the provisions of the Uniform Determination of Death Act as the legal rule for that state. The Act states:

An individual who has sustained either (1) irreversible cessation of circulatory and respiratory functions, or (2) irreversible cessation of all functions of the entire brain, including the brain stem, is dead. A determination of death must be made in accordance with accepted medical standards.

States adopt brain death as legal definition. The highest courts of Massachusetts, Kansas and Colorado have accepted irreversible cessation of brain function as a proper legal standard of death. Affirming murder convictions, the Supreme Judicial Court of Massachusetts in *Commonwealth v. Golston* (1977) and the Supreme Court of Kansas in *State v. Shaffer* (1978) rejected arguments that the real cause of death was the decision to remove brain-dead victims from respirators. The Supreme Court of Colorado accepted brain death as an alternative to the traditional definition of irreversible cessation of circulatory and respiratory functions, when it upheld a lower court's decision to permit a hospital to remove a battered child from a respirator over the mother's objections. The case was *Lovato v. District Court* (1979).

Choosing Death

Ethical, medical & legal problems. Hearings were held by the Senate Special Committee on Aging Aug. 7–8, 1972 on what the committee chairman, Sen. Frank Church (D, Ida.), said in his opening statement was a subject "sometimes called 'Death With Dignity,' or 'The Right to Die,' or . . . other titles which question the right to prolong life by extraordinary means when all hope for recovery—or in some cases, even for consciousness or lucidity—has vanished."

Church indicated that the advances of medical science had caused the ethical, medical and legal problems being explored by the committee. He said: "At least 80% of the population of this nation now dies in institutions—hospitals, nursing homes, and other facilities of one kind or another. Yet, not very long ago, the largest percentage of Americans died in their own homes. . . . Lingering illnesses, of course, occurred with some frequency, but more often than not there was no practical way of keeping persons alive after they had lost conscious relationship to the world around them. Today, the very institutions and medical talent that have triumphed over many illnesses are also coming under criticism because of the way in which they deal with the terminally ill, or apparently terminally ill, patient."

Alexander Morgan Capron of the University of Pennsylvania School of Law discussed the legal aspects of the subject. He said:

". . . The crux of the problem . . . is whether dignified death is inconsistent with good medical care. There is a pressing need to make clear that these are consistent and indeed that good medical care is a means to achieving a dignified death as well as a dignified life.

"If there is an inconsistency between what medicine ought to be doing and present practices, at least part of the blame can be laid at the door of the law. So far as I know there are no clear and certain answers to such questions as: (1) When can a dying patient choose to cease being treated? (2) Who else can exercise that authority on the patient's behalf? (3) What interests do physicians and the state have in prolonging treatment and what weight do these interests carry compared with others? (4) What action could be taken against a physician who—on his own initiative or at the request of a patient or his relatives—ceased treatment?

"The law's initial answers to these questions are contained in a group of cases that arose from refusals by Jehovah's Witnesses to accept blood transfusions which physicians believed were necessary to save the patients' lives. American courts are divided in their response.

"In one leading case, *In re Brooks Estate* . . . (1965), the Illinois Supreme Court held that a competent adult who steadfastly opposed blood transfusions for her chronic peptic ulcer should not have been compelled to receive blood under a court order. Unfortunately, the appellate court's reasoning is not particularly useful for this discussion because it was grounded in the patient's First Amendment right to free exercise of her religion.

"A number of courts have reached an opposite conclusion. For example, in *application of President and Directors of Georgetown College,* 331 F.2d 1000 (D.C. Cir.), *cert. denied* 377 U.S. 978 (1964), Judge J. Skelly Wright, sitting alone on an emergency appeal, ruled that a hospital was entitled to an order permitting it to administer blood over the patient's objections. While I disagree with the action taken by Judge Wright, this case is still useful for the issues it raises which, aside from the religious factor, seem very similar to those raised in the death with dignity situation. . . .

". . . The creation of an explicit legal right for patients to decline potentially lifesaving treatment presents a second issue discussed in the *Georgetown* case: the court's analogizing of the refusal to be treated with 'self-homicide.'

"Accepting, *arguendo,* that the state has a legitimate interest in prohibiting suicide, I do not believe that this interest or its rationale should be extended to preclude the choice of a dignified death. Suicide concerns the state because it devalues life as much as any form of murder and because the attempts

at suicide so often imperil the lives of other people. The same cannot be said of a dying patient, for he is not rejecting life but only declining further treatment with the recognition that death is inevitable.

"In another case, *John F. Kennedy Hospital v. Heston,* 58 N.J. 576, 279 A. 2d 670 (1971), in upholding the appointment of a guardian to consent to blood transfusions for a Jehovah's Witness who needed an operation for a ruptured spleen, the New Jersey Supreme Court equated refusal to receive blood with suicide and declared that 'there is no constitutional right to choose to die.' Chief Justice Weintraub wrote that, 'If the state may interrupt one mode of self-destruction, it may with equal authority interfere with the other.' He then continued with *obiter dictum* which is highly relevant to this discussion: 'It is arguably different when an individual, overtaken by illness, decides to let it run a fatal course. But unless the medical option itself is laden with the risk of death or of serious infirmity, the state's interest in sustaining life in such circumstances is hardly distinguishable from its interests in the case of suicide.' . . ."

Dr. Arthur E. Morgan, former president of Antioch College, testified:

"In many cases, continued living is an unalloyed liability, giving none of the values of life to the person involved. However, the decision to cease living should have legal consideration before action. Even the decision of the person himself may have been induced against his own judgment, simply by acquiescence. Should it not be social custom in matters of life and death that a legal verdict be required? Quite commonly the issues will be so clear that legal determination will be little more than a form. Furthermore, in cases where the person chiefly involved may be largely without self-determination, a legal and social judgment would seem to be sound public policy.

". . . [T]he real burdens sometimes placed upon others by the necessity of caring for persons for whom life has lost all meaning, or for the hopelessly aged or infirm, must also be considered. There are diseases and disabilities characterized by disorganization of the brain . . . which lead to permanent and irrecoverable and complete loss of intelligence and awareness which lasts through life, sometimes 20 or 30 years or more. In many instances the care of such cases through the years monopolizes family activities and attention with no relaxation and the certain prospect of no recovery. The necessary continuance of life in such cases often represents unrelieved tragedy for the responsible individuals or families, or the waste of institutional facilities. Experienced and representative physicians hold that this class of totally incurable disability has called long and loudly for relief which up to the present has been denied. . . .''

Dr. Laurance F. Foye Jr., education service director of the Veterans Administration, offering a dissenting opinion, said:

"A number of complex problems are encompassed by the popular but obscure phrase 'death with dignity.' These include the hopeless case, prolongation of suffering, active and passive euthanasia, the 'right to die,' and the 'living will.' Essentially, these are all medical problems relating directly to the responsibilities and decisions of the physician in his relationship with his patient. Rational consideration of these questions is unfortunately and customarily confused by opinions based upon misconceptions and emotion.

"A recent newspaper article on this problem clearly demonstrated and contributed to the confusion by quoting priests, rabbis, theologians, the pope, a state governor, a poet and several physicians. It is a disturbing observation that, to my knowledge, every religious spokesman on this subject has come out in favor of passive and occasionally active euthanasia in hopeless cases. . . .

". . . [W]e must not equate incurability with hopelessness. Diabetes, emphysema, practically all heart disease, baldness and flat feet are incurable but rarely hopeless. While approximately one-third of cancer patients can be cured of their disease, the remaining two-thirds are today incurable. The incur-

able cancer patient may live three month . . . or 30 years with his disease, possibly earning a living, raising a family, and enjoying life during this period. He may or may not require treatment along the way, and he may or may not die of this incurable disease These statements are generally true of all incurable diseases. . . .

"Every physician can . . . describe a number of patients for whom he predicted a rapidly fatal outcome saying, 'I knew they were going to die'—and was wrong. The patient who was told by his doctor that he had six months to live but is alive years later is legendary. Thus, since the practice of any form of euthanasia, active or passive, can only be justified by certainty of outcome and we can't be certain for any specific patient, we dare not authorize or practice euthanasia. If a physician withholds maximum effort from patients he considers hopelessly ill, he will unavoidably withhold maximum effort from an occasional patient who could have been saved. Patients will die because of the physician's decision not to treat actively. This approach and concern cannot be fostered or condoned, legally or otherwise.

"Typically, at this point in the discussion, the proponent of euthanasia then describes in detail a patient being kept alive 'uselessly' with tubes and machines and urges that the machines be turned off and the tubes removed 'so the patient can die peacefully and with dignity.' Neither I nor anyone else knows how to decide when being alive becomes 'useless'; I can only point out that 'tubes and machines' are used because they save lives, relieve symptoms and permit many patients to survive critical stages of an illness. Since it is usually a serious life-threatening problem that calls for these measures, they don't always work, and . . . some patients will die. One cannot then say, because such a patient dies, that these measures were a waste of time . . . since when they are initiated it is not known in which patient they will be successful.

"The statement made by noted clerics that the physician is not obligated to use 'heroic or extraordinary' means in a 'hopeless' case now becomes meaningless, since we can't be certain the case is hopeless, and it is precisely in such critical cases that 'extraordinary' measures must be considered and may be effective. . . .

"The 'living will,' a document in which the patient permits and instructs his physician to let him die if his condition is hopeless, really solves nothing but does create problems of its own. The danger is that relatives, deciding for any number of reasons that active treatment should be stopped, will attempt, with or without legal support, to prevent the doctor from continuing his lifesaving efforts, or that the doctor will find that the existence of such a document will be one 'reason' to terminate his active treatment. . . .

"The 'right to die' concept implies that, if our death is certain and immediate we have the 'right' to make it even more immediate. The now obvious fallacy is that the patient or the doctor can know when death is certain. . . . We must never forget that on occasion patients, their families, and their physicians will conclude that a disease has reached the hopeless stage and death is imminent—and be wrong. If they can stop treatment on the basis of their hopelessness, the prophecy becomes self-fulfilling. Whether the patient was going to die or not, their action ensures his death and the physician's confidence in his ability to predict death is dangerously enhanced. . . .

"Finally, what many laymen fear is that the doctor, in a pointless attempt to postpone death, will keep them in agony for long periods of time—the prolongation of suffering problem. A number of studies have shown, and this corresponds to my experience, that the majority of critically or terminally ill patients do not have pain and that those who do can be controlled by the judicious use of pain-killing medicines. . . ."

Dr. Henry K. Beecher of Harvard Medical School told the committee Aug. 8, that "death occurs at several levels: There is cellular death. Human cells can be maintained alive in tissue cultures for years; so we cannot define death as the loss of all vital functions. There is 'physiological' death when the vital activities have ceased; that is, death occurs when integrated tissue and organ functions cease. There is intellectual death, spiritual death and social death. . . . Or to approach the problem with more generality: There is subcellular and cellular life, life of organs, life of the individual and beyond this, life of the individual as a member of the community. However it is phrased, our basic concern is with the presence or absence of physiological life, especially neurological life. The lack of an accepted definition of death handicaps many of the activities within the hospital, the cadaver transplant problem. This is a medicolegal problem; it is also a sociolegal problem. . . ."

Beecher recalled Pope Pius XII's speech on "The Prolongation of Life" before the International Congress of Anesthesiologists Nov. 24, 1957. The pope said that the physician had a duty to use all reasonable ordinary means to restore vital functions and consciousness and to employ such extraordinary measures as are available to him. "But," the pope said, "normally one is held to use only ordinary means—according to circumstances of persons, places, times, and culture—that is to say, means that do not involve any grave burden for oneself or another. A more strict obligation would be too burdensome for most men and would render the attainment of the higher, more important good too difficult. Life, health, all temporal activities are in fact subordinated to spiritual ends. On the other hand, one is not forbidden to take more than the strictly necessary steps to preserve life and health, as long as he does not fail in some more serious duty."

Dr. Walter W. Sackett, a member of the Florida House of Representatives, told the committee Aug. 7 that he considered "euthanasia . . . more closely akin to death with dignity than it is to mercy killing." "Euthanasia means happy death," he continued. "[T]his philosophy is almost unanimously accepted by the general population. I have asked for a referendum on it. I have asked for a constitutional amendment. . . .'' Sackett also said:

''. . . I have been accused by a few rattlebrains, I think, of . . . trying to act like God. Now, when I keep a person such as we have been describing alive, I feel then I am acting like God, and I am being very inhumane to that person by continuing his suffering. . . .

''You talk about there are no diseases that are actually incurable. . . . There are. When the central nervous system is injured, that is permanent. That is forever. When the brain tissue, spinal cord tissue, is injured, that is it. It will never get any better. That is final. There is no return from it. . . .''

Church asked: ''. . . Dr. Sackett, . . . you have said that in your practice of medicine you have let patients die?'' Sackett replied, ''Hundreds of them.'' He estimated that ''75% of the doctors'' do likewise.

California gets right-to-die law. California Gov. Edmund G. Brown Jr. Sept. 30, 1976 signed into law a bill allowing adult patients to make a ''living will'' authorizing their doctors to turn off life-sustaining equipment if, in the judgment of the doctors, the patient was unquestionably dying and the equipment was only serving to stave off the moment of death.

The legislation—the first such to be enacted by any state in the U.S.—required that the ''living will'' be witnessed by two persons who were not doctors and were not relatives of the patient. A doctor who acted under the authority conveyed by such a will could not be held liable for a patient's death that resulted from the disconnecting of life-support equipment. The law—which then went into effect Jan. 1, 1977—also provided that such deaths could not be classed as suicides for the purpose of denying life-insurance benefits.

The bill had cleared the California legislature Aug. 30.

California's Natural Death Act. Doctors reported minimal response to California's

Act, according to the New York Times March 18, 1978. They said that only a small number of their patients had directed them to cut off life-support systems when death was imminent. Precisely how many directives had been signed was not known, but one cancer specialist said only five of his approximately 1,000 patients had signed a directive.

A directive was legally binding only if the patient was certified as terminally ill at least 14 days before the directive was signed. The California law did not cover comatose patients, such as Karen Anne Quinlan, or persons who were suddenly rendered incompetent by a stroke or an accident.

Seven other states had passed ''right-to-die'' laws with varying provisions, the Times reported. They were Idaho, Oregon, New Mexico, Nevada, Texas, North Carolina and Arkansas.

Lifestyle reflected in death view—A panel of scientists and theologians met Feb. 25, 1977, to discuss ''The Right to Die'' and concluded that Americans were experiencing ''rootlessness and isolation, in death as well as in life.'' Dr. Thomas Schelling of Harvard University said that the wish of many Americans to die suddenly with little or no time for preparation reflected the uprooted lives led by increasing numbers of people who were dying far from family and friends.

Burn patients choose to die. During 1975–76, 21 of 24 terminal burn patients admitted to the Los Angeles County-University of Southern California Medical Center elected an earlier death without extensive treatment over life-prolonging procedures. A report on the hospital's ''decision-to-die'' program was published in the New England Journal of Medicine dated Aug. 11.

Severely burned victims' nerve endings were so extensively damaged that for several hours after injury they were lucid and felt no pain. During that time, a doctor informed the patient that survival in cases comparable to their's was unprecedented.

The staff who compiled the report said that relatives of the patients, who ranged in age from 19 to 90, were relieved not to have to make the decision for the victim. Those who decided to die without struggle "then try to live their lives completely and fully to the end, saying things that they must say to those important to them, making proper plans, reparations and apologies."

The three men who opted for maximal treatment in the intensive care unit also died—the longest survivor lived for seven days.

Massachusetts court distinguishes competence from rationality. In a per curiam decision, the Massachusetts Court of Appeals upheld the right of a 77-year old woman to refuse to have life-prolonging surgery. Mrs. Rosaria Candura, a patient at Symmes Hospital in Arlington, was suffering from gangrene in her right foot and lower leg. Although her physician recommended that she have the leg amputated without delay, Mrs. Candura refused to undergo surgery. Mrs. Candura's daughter, Grace R. Lane, subsequently petitioned the Probate Court for Middlesex County for appointment as her mother's legal guardian with authority to consent to the surgery on her mother's behalf. Mrs. Candura appealed the Probate Court's appointment of her daughter as legal guardian.

Citing the Massachusetts Supreme Judicial Court's decision in *Saikewicz,* the Court of Appeals in *Lane v. Candura* (Mass. App. 1978) held that Mrs. Candura had the legal right to refuse even life-saving treatment. The court also reversed the Probate Court's finding that Mrs. Candura was incompetent to make the decision for herself. Noting that the law presumes a person to be competent unless shown to be otherwise, the court criticized the Probate judge's conclusions, which confused irrationality with incompetence. A patient need not consider all the medical alternatives, the Appeals Court said, in order to make a competent decision. Instead, the patient need only be informed and fully appreciate the consequences of her decision. Mrs. Candura's consideration of irrational and emotional factors, such as her

unhappiness since the death of her husband and her desire not to be confined to a nursing home as an invalid nor to be a burden on her children, was not evidence of legal incompetence. "The law," observed the court, "protects her right to make her own decision to accept or reject treatment, whether that decision is wise or unwise."

Artist carries out suicide plan. Jo Roman, a painter and sculptor, committed suicide June 10, 1979, in New York. For 15 months, she had carefully planned the details of when, where and how she would take her life, according to the New York Times June 17 and Newsweek July 2.

Roman had made preparations for her death that included finishing a 250 page book, *Exit House*, in defense of the right to die. She also had a cameraman videotape 19 hours of conversation with family and friends on the subject of suicide. In a posthumous letter on the tape, Roman told them: "By the time you read these lines I will have gently ended my life on the date of this letter's postmark."

Roman also handled her own funeral arrangements. She built a pine coffin, filled it with personal mementos, and wrote her obituary for the New York Times.

After completing these tasks June 10, Roman said good-bye to her family and swallowed 35 sleeping pills and drank champagne.

Roman took her life in this way, it was reported, because she believed that people should decide their own time of death. She had originally chosen 1992, her 75th year, for her own "self-termination." But after doctors had told her she had breast cancer in March 1978, she decided to end her life at age 62 instead.

Roman had undergone 10 months of chemotherapy before ending the treatment. She said she had found it "debilitating," and had not wanted to subject herself or those around her to the "emotional strains and physical ravages of cancer."

Dr. Michael Baden, the chief medical examiner of New York City, had found no evi-

MEDICAL SCIENCE AND THE LAW

dence of cancer beyond Roman's lymph nodes during an autopsy of her body, it was reported June 17. Baden had performed the autopsy in the absence of a death certificate signed by a family physician.

Decision-Making for Terminally Ill Incompetents

Court orders Karen Quinlan be allowed to die. The New Jersey Supreme Court ruled unanimously March 31, 1976 that the mechanical respirator that had kept Karen Anne Quinlan alive for more than 11 months could be disconnected if attending physicians and a committee of hospital officials concluded she would never recover.

"If . . . there is no reasonable possibility of Karen's ever emerging from her present comatose condition to a cognitive, sapient state, the present life-support system may be withdrawn . . . without any civil or criminal liability . . . on the part of any participant, whether guardian, physician, hospital or others," the court said in its 59-page opinion written by Chief Justice Richard J. Hughes.

In so ruling, the court agreed to appoint Joseph Quinlan, Miss Quinlan's adoptive father, as her legal guardian. He was to have "full power with regard to the identity of treating physicians," the court said.

While rejecting arguments by Paul W. Armstrong, attorney for parents Joseph and Julia Quinlan, that the right to seek removal of the respirator was grounded in the constitutional guarantees of freedom of religion and against cruel and inhuman punishment, the court asserted that Miss Quinlan had a "right to privacy" that would allow her to make life-sustaining medical decisions. Moreover, the court held Miss Quinlan had the right to make such a fatal decision "in much the same way" as a woman who decided to terminate a pregnancy under certain conditions.

"We have no doubt," the court said, ". . . that if Karen were herself miraculously lucid for an interval . . . and perceptive of her irreversible condition, she could effectively decide upon discontinuance of the life-support apparatus, even if it meant the prospect of natural death."

However, since she was legally incompetent to make this decision, her father, acting as guardian, should do so, the court ruled.

"If a putative decision by Karen to permit this noncognitive, vegetative existence to terminate by natural forces is regarded as a valuable incident of her right to privacy, as we believe it to be, then it should not be discarded solely on the basis that her condition prevents her conscious exercise of the choice," the court added. (It had been brought out in testimony in the Superior Court trial in 1975 on the Quinlans' request to turn off the respirator that Miss Quinlan had at one time said she would not want extraordinary means used to keep her alive if she were beyond hope of recovery.)

Under the court's ruling, Joseph Quinlan would have to discuss his daughter's condition with her doctors. If they agreed the respirator should be disconnected, his request would have to be submitted to the hospital's "ethics committee or like body" for a ruling on her prognosis. If the committee agreed she had no hope of ever becoming conscious again, the respirator could then be turned off.

The court said, however, that if the attending physicians or the hospital balked at shutting off the respirator, Joseph Quinlan should seek out doctors or a hospital willing to so act.

The court's ruling also noted arguments by Morris County Prosecutor Donald G. Collester Jr. and others that disconnecting the respirator would be criminal homicide. "There is a real and in this case determinative distinction between the unlawful taking of the life of another and the ending of artificial life-support systems as a matter of self-determination," the court concluded.

Lower-court ruling reversed—The decision to authorize the disconnection of the respirator reversed a Nov. 10, 1975 decision f a state Superior Court judge. In refusing er parents' request, Judge Robert Muir Jr. ad cited the fact that, although Miss Quinan had lost all ability to think or function s a normal person, she was still legally and nedically alive and as such retained the right o live.

The legal dispute had begun in September 975, when the Quinlan parents, sure their laughter had no chance of recovery, petiioned the court to have her returned to "her natural state" and "leave her to the Lord" by having the respirator removed. The Quinlans, Roman Catholics, were upheld in their views by their parish priest. The parents had made their decision after Miss Quinlan had been in a coma for seven months and had fallen into an irreversible "persistent vegetative state," according to doctors.

The Quinlans went to court after a request to attending physicians to disconnect the respirator was turned down. Muir left the final decision on use of the respirator with the doctors. He authorized Daniel R. Coburn, a Morristown lawyer who acted as Miss Quinlan's guardian for the court hearings, to continue as the guardian of "her person." Coburn would not be authorized to initiate any new medical procedures but would be available for consultation with the attending physician.

Respirator removed—Miss Quinlan's respirator was removed May 22, 1976, and she continued to breathe without it. Her doctors described her June 3 as being in stable condition.

In their first public statement since the court ruling, Quinlan's doctors—Robert Morse and Arshad Javed—and officials of St. Clare's Hospital in Denville said that Quinlan's treatment was in keeping with "prevailing medical practice and moral constraints" and would be guided "in addition" by "an irreversible tenet to protect life." The doctors had opposed removing the respirator. The statement said that Quinlan would continue to receive "appropriate nutrients and antibiotics to fight infection, along with

other procedures indicated by her condition."

Dr. Joseph F. Fennelly of Madison, N.J. was reported May 30 to be spokesman for a group of seven doctors who had agreed to look after Quinlan as a "chronic care patient." She was moved June 9 from St. Clare's Hospital to the Morris View Nursing Home in Morris Township, N.J.

According to published reports, Quinlan was not connected to a respirator or any other mechanical life-supporting device. Attendant physicians at St. Clare's had over a three-week period weaned her from the mechanical respirator that had been thought needed to keep her breathing. Since removal, she was reported to have been breathing unaided.

According to a report in the June 2 Morristown Daily Record, the parents of Miss Quinlan, Joseph and Julia Quinlan, had begun searching for a facility other than St. Clare's after they and their attorneys had reached an impasse May 18 with hospital officials over future treatment of the comatose woman. The hospital and its doctors, the Daily Record said, had apparently refused to change their position expressed at the 1975 trial on Joseph Quinlan's petition to disconnect the mechanical respirator then thought to be keeping their daughter alive. The doctors and the hospital opposed withdrawal of high calorie nutrients and antibiotics, the Daily Record reported

Following the meeting, the Quinlans attempted to find a local nursing care facility willing to accept their daughter but were apparently turned down a number of times because of the notoriety that would accompany acceptance.

The decision by Morris View, a 375-bed facility operated by Morris County for indigent patients, was presaged in guidelines for admission of comatose patients adopted by the county's welfare board June 3. The guidelines required that a patient be in a coma for at least six months if the condition were the result of trauma or unknown causes and three months from other causes. The guidelines further stipulated that treating physicians and family agree recovery was unlikely and that "aggressive treatment of any acute problem . . . or readmission to a hospital" was inappropriate.

Quinlan's treating physicians at St. Clare's had stated they would have used blood transfusions, and if need be, reconnected the mechanical respirator to fight infections or other problems affecting her.

On June 10, the day after Quinlan's admission to Morris View, a newly formed ethics committee at the county nursing home ruled the 22-year-old woman was in an irreversible coma with no reasonable possibility of recovery to a "cognitive, sapient state." In so finding, the committee set the stage for the withholding of extraordinary means to rescue Quinlan from any medical crisis that might arise. The committee also agreed, however, that "normal" levels of food and antibiotics should be continued.

In a related development, state Attorney General William Hyland said June 10 he believed the state Supreme Court's ruling in the Quinlan case would allow doctors to withhold food and medicine from terminally ill patients to let them die. But Hyland told a news conference this did not mean he thought feeding of Quinlan should be stopped.

Quinlan 'alive' a year off respirator—Karen Anne Quinlan was breathing normally March 31, 1977, a year after the state Supreme Court had ruled that the machine could be turned off. Joseph and Julia Quinlan, who had felt the respirator was preventing their daughter from dying "with decency and dignity," continued to make daily visits to the nursing home where Karen Anne was being fed a high-calorie food formula and receiving antibiotics to guard against infection.

Quinlan, now 23 and weighing about 70 pounds, had gone into a coma on April 14, 1975 after accidentally mixing barbituates and alcohol. Her doctor said her current blood oxygen level was adequate for her

body's limited needs, meaning she coul continue to breathe unassisted. He saic however, that in the event of a respirator collapse, Quinlan would not be placed bac on a respirator.

The Quinlan case continued to generat interest in "right to die" legislation that a lowed individuals to fill out "living wills limiting the amount of medical treatmer they would receive in the event that the became hopelessly terminally ill. Right-tc die bills had been introduced in the legis latures of 38 states in 1977, but to date onl two had been passed and signed into law, i California and Idaho.

Ethics panel backs right to die. A presi dential panel appointed to study the ethica problems associated with medicine issued : report March 21, 1983, recommending tha patients be allowed to discontinue life-sup port treatment, if they so chose.

Morris Abram, a former president o Brandeis University and the chairman of th President's Commission for the Study o Ethical Problems in Medicine and Biomed ical and Behavioral Research, observed tha "the wonders of modern medicine—anti biotics, resuscitation, intensive care, artifi cial kidneys and chemotherapy, for exam ple—mean that for almost every life threatening condition some intervention car delay the moment of death." While at one time most Americans had died at home, now 80% or more died in hospitals, where the presence of life-support technology con fronted patients and doctors with difficult decisions.

The commission's report—titled "Decid ing to Forgo Life-Sustaining Treatment"— sought to provide guidelines on the rights and responsibilities of doctors and patients. The commission did not urge states to enact legislation guaranteeing these rights, Abrams said. The chairman said the commission's report by itself should have sufficient influ ence on court decisions and hospital policy makers to bring about respect for these rights.

(The 11-person commission was made up of doctors, lawyers, theologians and public policy experts.)

The report recommended that patients who were mentally competent should be given full information about their condition and permitted to decide whether they wished to be given special life-support treatment. In the case of patients who were unconscious or incompetent, such decisions should be made by family members or others acting on behalf of the patients. A decision to discontinue the use of respirators, antibiotics or artificial feeding could be taken by family members, the report said, holding that "the law does not and should not require any particular therapies to be applied or continued."

While the commission came out in favor of the right of family members to make decisions on the use of life-support treatment, the report said that a "very strict standard" should be used for decisions on new-born infants with serious defects. Controversy had arisen in particular over babies born with Down's syndrome and who were also afflicted with a block of the esophagus that prevented food from reaching the stomach. Some parents of such babies had not authorized the necessary surgery to remove the esophagus block, and consequently the babies had died. (Down's syndrome was associated with varying degrees of mental retardation.)

The report said that babies with such handicaps should be given the necessary surgery, regardless of the wishes of their parents. The problems connected with Down's syndrome did not justify "failing to provide medically proven treatment."

Although the report took this position, it did not endorse a Reagan administration proposal to deny federal funding to hospitals that failed to provide sufficient life support to infants with severe handicaps. These sanctions, the report argued, "could unjustly penalize the hospital's other patients and professionals" and also "involve government reimbursement officials in bedside decision-making."

Superintendent of Belchertown State School v. Saikewicz (Mass. 1977). On July 9, 1976, the Massachusetts Supreme Judicial Court affirmed a lower court's order to the Superintendent of the Belchertown State School to refrain from administering chemotherapy to a profoundly retarded resident of the school.

In its opinion, issued fourteen months after the decision, the Massachusetts court paid special attention to the facts of the case. Joseph Saikewicz was a 67-year-old retardate who had been institutionalized since 1923. In April of 1976, Saikewicz was found to be suffering from acute myeloblastic monocytic leukemia. Medical experts testified in the Probate Court that chemotherapy was the only possible treatment available. Such treatment was only palliative, not curative, and had only a thirty to forty percent chance of success for Saikewicz. Furthermore, although, left to run its course, the disease would result in a painless death, the chemotherapy would cause the patient great discomfort.

Justice Liacos, writing for the court, noted that an incompetent has the same right to decline treatment as anyone else. In the incompetent's case, however, the State has a greater duty to safeguard that right. This duty has become more complex with the advancement of medical technology. The complexity of options facing modern physicians and their patients presents new choices involving considerations of the adverse effects treatment may have on the patient and those around him. Thus, the court noted, the "best interests" of an incompetent person are not necessarily served by being forced to undergo painful, though potentially life-prolonging, treatment.

Every person, including an incompetent person, "has a strong interest in being free from nonconsensual invasion of his bodily integrity." Balanced against this interest are the State's interests in preserving life, protecting innocent third parties, and maintaining the ethical integrity of the medical profession. However, the court observed, merely determining the proper balance of interests is not sufficient in the case of an incompetent person. While an incompetent person has the same right to self-determination as a competent person, determining what the incompetent's choice would—or should—be requires judicial determination. The Massachusetts court distinguished the simple proxy decision-making process involved in the *Quinlan* decision. Here, the guardian could not simply determine what Joseph Saikewicz would want if he could make the choice, since Saikewicz himself never had the mental capacity to understand the nature of such a decision. The test arrived at by the court involved determining not what an ordinary person might do under similar circumstances, but what a reasonable person in the incompetent's particular circumstances—including the inability to understand the need for the treatment or the reason for the discomfort—would do. The court stressed, however, that it firmly rejected any equation of the quality of life with the value of the life preserved. Applying this formulation, the court upheld the lower court's denial of treatment as appropriate in light of the particular circumstances.

The Massachusetts court specifically rejected the New Jersey Supreme Court's approach in the *Quinlan* case, decided the previous year. "We take a dim view of any attempt to shift the ultimate decision-making responsibility away from the duly established courts of proper jurisdiction to any committee, panel or group, ad hoc or permanent. . . . Rather," the court emphasized, "such questions of life and death seem to us to require the process of detached but passionate investigation and decision that forms the ideal on which the judicial branch of government was created." Thus, for the moment, the Massachusetts courts retained the responsibility for decision-making for the terminally ill incompetent.

In the matter of Spring (Mass. 1980). Three years after the decision in *Saikewicz,* the Massachusetts Supreme Judicial Court, on May 13, 1980, upheld the right of an incompetent's family and physician to decide whether to terminate life-prolonging hemodialysis treatment. The court affirmed its position in *Saikewicz,* holding that incompetent patients have the same right to self-determination as competent patients. That right must be exercised through the "substituted judgment" made on their behalf by a guardian.

The court also restated its belief that the courts must retain "ultimate decision-making responsibility" in such cases. However, it denied that judicial approval was required before life-sustaining treatment could be withheld from a terminally ill incompetent patient. Nevertheless, it approved the guardians' decision "to seek explicit judicial authorization for the proposed course of treatment." The court also warned physicians that they may be held accountable in court should their good faith or standard of medical practice be challenged, and advised them that documented agreement of qualified consultants would be their best defense to any such charges.

Life aid ordered in 'right-to-die' case. A Massachusetts Supreme Court judge Jan. 24, 1980, ordered the resumption of life-sustaining devices for a 78-year-old man whose treatment had been stopped earlier in the belief that he would not have chosen to live.

The man, Earle Spring, a retired pharmacist who was suffering from an incurable kidney disease, had been granted "the right to die" by a lower court at the request of his family. However, a court-appointed guardian later said that Spring had expressed a desire to live.

Spring's family had earlier sought and received a judgment in a Franklin County probate court that Spring was mentally incompetent and incapable of expressing a reliable opinion on whether he wanted to live or die. The family had told the court that they wanted Spring to be able to die with dignity.

Spring had been receiving dialysis treatment three times weekly. Without the treatment, according to doctors, he would die within a month.

After the court had ordered the dialysis treatment discontinued, nurses at the Holyoke Geriatric Center, where Spring was a patient, wrote a letter to a local newspaper, saying that they were "appalled over the recent court decision and we feel helpless and frustrated having to abide by it."

Spring himself reportedly had never told anyone that he wanted to die. Also, a doctor and several nurses who had spoken with Spring said that he seemed rational and said that he did not want to die.

The family, however, had opposed a motion to reopen the case and reconsider the decision to stop treatment. An attorney for the Spring family warned that it could turn the case into a "three-ring circus."

Francis Quirico, the Supreme Court judge who ordered the resumption of the kidney treatment, returned the case to a lower court to decide whether to seek more medical evidence about Spring's mental condition.

N.Y. court upholds right to die without court approval. In an important decision, the New York Court of Appeals, the state's highest court, overruled two earlier decisions of the New York Supreme Court's Appellate Division. Combining the cases of *Eichner v. Dillon* (N.Y. Sup. Ct. A.D. 1980) and *In re Storar* (N.Y. Sup. Ct. A.D. 1980), the Court of Appeals upheld the constitutional right of a terminally ill person to decline life-sustaining treatment.

The court stated that a life-sustaining respirator may be removed from an incompetent patient who, while still competent, made a "clear and convincing" expression of his wish to be allowed to die should he become terminally ill and require extraordinary life-sustaining measures. The New York court also overruled the lower courts in ruling that no judicial or other procedures are required prior to the removal of such life-sustaining care. It pointed out, however, that no other person, including the incompetent's guardian, could make that decision for him, regardless of the circumstances or their interpretation of the incompetent's wishes. Only a clear expression by the patient himself, while competent, would allow the removal of life-sustaining care. The Court of Appeal's decision was delivered under the title of *Eichner v. Dillon*.

Delaware court protects right of incompetent to choose death. On December 31, 1980, the Court of Chancery of New Castle County, Delaware, upheld the right of a former member of the Delaware Euthanasia Education Council to choose to die rather than be maintained in a comatose, vegetative state after an automobile accident.

Prior to her accident, Mary Reeser Severns had expressed her wish that, in the event she should become unable to care for herself, she did not want to be maintained in a vegetative state by any extraordinary measures. Instead, she preferred "to be allowed to die with dignity." Over a year ago, Mrs. Severns suffered severe brain damage in an accident, destroying all cognitive functions. Her husband, as her guardian, sought authority to request the cessation of all extraordinary measures, allowing his wife to die a natural death. He also sought protection from the Chancery Court against threatened criminal action should those measures be withdrawn.

Citing the Massachusetts decision in *Saikewicz* and *Spring*, the Delaware Chancellor upheld the right of an incompetent person, through her guardian, to decline life-prolonging treatment. He further held that, under the circumstances, Mrs. Severns should be allowed to exercise that right. Furthermore, although the Chancellor could not normally enjoin a criminal prosecution, the decision of the Chancery Court allowing the termination of extraordinary life-prolonging measures would provide an adequate legal defense for any persons against any subsequent criminal prosecution based on that termination. The case was *Severns v. Wilmington Medical Center, Inc.* (Del. Chanc. 1980).

Massachusetts court orders parents to provide chemotherapy for son. The Massachusetts Supreme Judicial Court, in July of 1978, upheld a Plymouth County Superior Court's order requiring the parents of Chad Green to allow their young son to undergo chemotherapy treatment for leukemia. The parents had sought reversal of that order so that they could seek laetrile treatments for him instead.

"While recognizing that there exists a 'private realm of family life which the state cannot enter,' " the Massachusetts court held that "family autonomy is not absolute, and may be limited where, as here, 'it appears that parental decisions will jeopardize the health or safety of (their) child.' " Balancing the State's interest in protecting the welfare of children living within its borders against the parents' "natural rights," the court stated that "where a child's well-being is placed in issue, 'it is not the rights of the parents that are chiefly to be considered. The first and paramount duty is to consult the welfare of the child.' On a proper showing that parental conduct threatens a child's well-being, the interests of the State and of the individual child may mandate intervention." Relying on medical testimony regarding the high probability of a substantial cure through chemotherapy, the court upheld the Superior Court's order. The case was *Custody of a Minor, Chad Green* (Mass. 1978).

Six months after the initial decision by the Massachusetts high court, Chad Green's parents renewed their petition for custody. This time, they acknowledged the need for chemotherapy, but wished to supplement that with "metabolic therapy," involving the use of laetrile. Examining the evidence of potential dangers of laetrile treatments, the court affirmed its earlier decision denying the parents custody of their son. "This case," the court observed, "well illustrates that parents do not and must not have absolute authority over the life and death of their children. . . . The position of the parents in this case, however well intentioned, is indefensible against the overwhelming weight of medical evidence."

Euthanasia

AMA & Mercy Killing. Dr. Malcolm C. Todd, elected by the House of Delegates of the American Medical Association June 28, 1973 as the organized physicians' next president, said that day that mercy killings "have their place" in certain "uncorrectable" fatal illnesses. Todd added, however, that doctors should not be forced to make the euthanasia decisions by themselves.

Six months later the House of Delegates Dec. 4 adopted a report reiterating opposition to mercy killing. However, the delegates agreed that a doctor should respect the wishes of a dying patient concerning the amount of medical care he wanted. "The cessation of the employment of extraordinary means of prolonging the life of the body when there is irrefutable evidence that biological death is imminent is the decision of the patient and/or his immediate family," the report said.

Mercy Killer Freed. In practice, juries have often been reluctant to convict and punish people accused of hastening the death of loved ones who were terminally ill and in great pain. For example, in Freehold, N.J. Nov. 5, 1973, a jury accepted a plea of temporary insanity as it decided that Lester Zygmaniak was not guilty of the mercy killing of his brother, George Zygmaniak, who had been severely crippled by a motorcycle accident.

The jury acted in the knowledge that Zygmaniak, 23, admitted putting his brother to death. Zygmaniak had told police that George, 26, paralyzed from the neck down, had pleaded with him to end his suffering.

Poll Favors Choice. A Louis Harris survey made public April 23 indicated that those polled believed by 62%–38% margin that "a patient with a terminal disease ought to be able to tell his doctor to let him die rather than to extend his life when no cure is in sight."

However, the same sample group opposed by 53%–37% euthanasia, under which a terminally ill patient could tell his doctor to put him to death.

Md. nurse freed in mercy deaths. All charges against a Baltimore nurse accused of engaging in the mercy killing of four patients were dropped March 29, 1979 by prosecutors for the state of Maryland. In return, nurse Mary Rose Robaczynski agreed to give up her nursing license and never practice again.

Robaczynski had been granted a separate trial in each case in which she was charged with disconnecting a respirator attached to a comatose patient. She denied unplugging the machine in one case while acknowledging that she had in the other three, maintaining that the patients had already died before she did so.

Robaczynski's first trial ended in a mistrial March 20 after the jurors were unable to agree whether the patient was dead at the time she unhooked the respirator. Authorities attributed the decision in part to the vagueness of the Maryland law defining death, which was the absence of "spontaneous brain function." The jurors reported that they were voting, 10–2, in favor of acquittal and that each had his or her own interpretation of the word "spontaneous."

Treatment denied to terminally ill. A study by Dr. Norman K. Brown and Donovan J. Thompson of the University of Washington, published in the New England Journal of Medicine May 31, 1979 found doctors and nurses often let patients die.

Brown, a physician, and Thompson, a statistician, reviewed the records of 1,256 patients admitted to nine Seattle nursing homes approved by the federal Medicare program. The 190 cases selected for the study involved patients 60 years of age or older who had developed high or continuous fevers.

Of the 190 patients, doctors actively treated 109, of whom 10 (or 9%) died. Active treatment was defined as prescription of antibiotics, hospitalization or both. Such treatment was not ordered for 81 patients, of whom 48 (59%) died. For many of the 81 who had cancer and received pain killers, the fever symptom was only a minor part of the dying process. Although these patients received no antibiotics, they were given oxygen and other drugs aimed at comforting them.

"Nevertheless," the researchers said, "it is likely that their lives could have been prolonged, even if for a short time, with antibiotics and hospitalization."

Brown and Thompson concluded that the decision not to treat some fevers "was part of an intentional plan by doctors and nurses." They found that in some cases the nurse didn't call the doctor to report a fever and that sometimes the doctor had already indicated that a patient should not be vigorously treated.

The two researchers said they hoped their study would encourage physicians, patients and families to discuss the subject of when treatment should be denied, as no single pattern of action was appropriate to deal with all dying people.

Vatican stand on euthanasia. The Vatican June 26, 1980 released a declaration reaffirming its traditional condemnation of euthanasia or "mercy killing," but stated that individuals in certain circumstances had the right to renounce "burdensome" efforts to maintain life for terminally ill patients.

The Vatican statement, *Declaration on Euthanasia*, said that church teachings on euthanasia "retain their full force" and that the new guidelines did not represent any departure from principles laid down by the Second Vatican Council and by Pope Paul VI. However, the statement said that medical advances had raised new aspects on the issue, which the church had never specifically addressed.

The document which was issued by the Sacred Congregation for the Doctrine of the Faith, outlined the problems that arose because of the availability of modern life-supporting techniques and stated that it was not necessary in all circumstances to apply all of the possible remedies. The document said that "it is permitted, with the patient's consent, to interrupt these means where the results fall short of expectations." The document also added that the "reasonable wishes" of the patient's family as well as those of the patient had to be taken into account and that doctors might judge that "the investment in instruments and personnel is disproportionate to the result foreseen."

Defective Neonates

Medical journal publishes report on infant deaths. The October 25, 1973 edition of the *New England Journal of Medicine* contained a study of infant deaths in the special-care nursery of the Yale-New Haven Hospital in New Haven, Connecticut. The study noted that 43 out of the last 299 deaths occurring in the special-care nursery were related to the withholding of special treatment. The decision to withhold life-saving treatment was made by the infants' parents in consultation with physicians at the hospital. In each case, the infants were suffering from severe birth defects, and had little or no hope for a "meaningful" life. The study concluded that, while difficult, such decisions to withhold treatment are often the best course for both the defective infant and its family. The authors of the study also concluded that "[i]f working out these dilemmas in ways such as those we suggest is in violation of the laws, we believe the law should be changed."

Parents of Siamese twins charged with attempted murder. On May 5, 1981, Dr. Robert Mueller and his wife, nurse Pamela Schopp, became the parents of twin boys. What should have been a joyous event, however, began a series of trials and tribulations for the parents: the infants were born as Siamese twins, joined at the waist. They have three legs, and share a lower stomach and bowels. The parents, their family physician, and a nurse have been charged with conspiring to let the twins die by denying them food and medication. On May 13, the state ordered the twins to be transferred from Lakeview Medical Center in Danville, Illinois, where they were born, to Children's Memorial Hospital in Chicago.

At a custody hearing in June, an Illinois state court heard a neglect petition filed against the parents by the State. Testimony from nurses at Lakeview Medical Center revealed that one of the attending physicians in the delivery room ordered a nurse not to resuscitate the gasping newborns. Later, the parents' physician ordered the nursery staff not to feed the twins. Despite these orders, some nurses kept the twins alive with occasional feedings of sugar water and formula. At the end of the custody hearing, Judge John P. Meyer, in an emotion-charged opinion, held the parents guilty of neglect, but not of any malicious or willful wrongdoing. The parents and their physician pleaded not guilty to the state's criminal charges of attempted murder.

Arizona deformed baby's death ruled natural. On January 16, 1981, a Scottsdale, Arizona coroner's jury ruled that a 9-day old girl's death was caused by birth defects. The baby, Angela Gesner, was born December 10, 1980, in Mesa, Arizona, and died nine days later. The baby's physician told the coroner's jury that the baby's deformities, which included deformed limbs and water on the brain, were "incompatible with life." Within a few hours of the baby's birth, the parents and the physician agreed, in writing, to withhold food and water from the newborn. Contrary to the testimony of nurses caring for the baby, the county medical examiner testified that the baby had died from her defects, and did not appear to have been denied liquids.

First U.S. selective birth reported. A successful operation to destroy the defective fetus in a pair of fraternal twins was reported June 18, 1981, in the New England Journal of Medicine. Four months after a procedure was performed to kill the 20-week-old abnormal fetus, in which Down's syndrome had been detected through the use of amniocentesis, the normal twin was born and was reported to be healthy.

The procedure to terminate the fetus was

a difficult one involving many risks: that of damaging the abnormal fetus without killing it, of killing the normal fetus by mistake, or of killing both fetuses. Previous attempts had usually resulted in miscarriages. (The only other successful attempt was reported in Sweden in 1978.)

The termination of the abnormal fetus, carried out at the Mt. Sinai School of Medicine in New York, was accomplished by withdrawing about half its blood through a spinal needle inserted in its heart. The fetus's heart stopped beating immediately. Doctors performing the procedure had used an ultrasound device to locate the two fetuses, but were not sure until test results were received three days later whether they had in fact killed the abnormal fetus rather than its healthy twin.

The report, by Drs. Thomas D. Kerenyi and Usha Chitkara, stressed that the 40-year-old mother had decided she was not willing to care for a retarded child. "The mother desperately wanted to have the normal child but could not face the burden of caring for an abnormal child for the rest of her life," it said, and she "would have chosen to abort both fetuses" had not the operation been possible. The medical school, aware of the potential legal problems in such a case, insisted that she obtain confirmation from New York's Supreme Court of the parents' right to consent to the procedure on behalf of the normal twin, which would be endangered.

Amniocentesis was a prenatal test increasingly performed on pregnant women, especially those over 35, for whom the risks of abnormal pregnancies were greater. It enabled doctors to detect genetic defects by examining a sample of amniotic fluid for defective chromosomes. Older mothers were also more likely to bear twins: "The highest frequency of dizygotic twins occurs between the ages of 37 and 40," according to Kerenyi and Chitkara. Therefore, with the growing use of amniocentesis, it was thought that the detection of one congenitally abnormal fetus in a pair of twins would become increasingly frequent in the future, and that barring legal complications, such selective births would become more common.

Infant care rule implemented. The Reagan administration March 22, 1983 implemented rules designed to prevent federally funded hospitals from denying food or medical care to handicapped infants.

The controversial regulations, issued by President Reagan as an executive order, required all hospitals receiving federal funds to post notices in delivery wards and intensive care and pediatric nurseries stating that, "Discriminatory failure to feed and care for handicapped infants in this facility is prohibited by federal law." In addition, the regulations required establishment of a 24-hour toll-free hotline through which anyone aware of violations of the infant-care requirements could notify federal investigators. Hospitals would be held responsible for actions of individual doctors, and hospitals at which violations occurred stood to lose all federal aid.

The regulations, supported by right-to-life and other conservative groups, had been sparked by the April 1982 death of an infant boy, known as "Baby Doe," in Bloomington, Ind. The infant had been born with Down's syndrome, a blocked esophagus and other medical complications requiring major surgery, and had died after his parents, doctors and a state court had approved a complete cutoff of food and medical care. (Down's syndrome, or mongolism, was marked by varying degrees of mental retardation.)

The American Academy of Pediatrics, the National Association of Children's Hospitals and other groups had filed suit, seeking a temporary court injunction to block implementation of the regulations. Federal District Judge Gerhard A. Gesell March 22 denied their request, but ordered a hearing to be held April 8 to review the issue.

Opponents of the so-called "Baby Doe" regulations argued that the rules were inflexible, that they represented an unwarranted bureaucratic intrusion into decisions that should be left to parents and doctors and that they would lead to confusion and disagreement over the proper course of medical treatment for handicapped infants.

Surgeon General Dr. C. Everett Koop March 19 said the rules were necessary because starvation of handicapped infants, and denial of medical treatment to them, had become widespread. "Letting an infant starve to death is infanticide," he said, "and infanticide is murder."

Judge voids infant care rule. A federal judge in Washington, D.C. April 14, 1983 struck down a Reagan administration rule requiring hospitals to provide food and medical care to severely handicapped infants.

The regulation affected 6,400 hospitals in the U.S. that received federal aid.

U.S. District Judge Gerhard A. Gesell was acting on a suit filed by the American Academy of Pediatrics and other groups opposed to the rule.

Judge Gesell found that the so-called "Baby Doe" regulation had been issued in violation of the Administrative Procedure Act. The law required government agencies to invite public comment before issuing new rules.

Calling the rule "arbitrary and capricious," Gesell invoked the image of the "sudden descent of 'Baby Doe' squads on the scene" while doctors were making treatment decisions. He also said that a primary purpose of the regulation was to "prevent parents from having any influence upon decisions as to whether further medical treatment is desirable" for a handicapped infant.

The Reagan administration had issued the "Baby Doe" rule as a reminder to hospitals of their responsibilities under the Rehabilitation Act of 1973. The law stated that no handicapped person shall be excluded from a federally supported program "solely by reason of his handicap."

In response to the decision, Margaret H. Heckler, secretary of health and human services, said the administration "remains determined to protect the lives of handicapped infants and to assure them their equal right to be given appropriate medical care and nourishment."

Science and
Technology

Introduction

Medical technology developed to preserve lives has been relatively uncontroversial, with the exception of the FDA's unwillingness to authorize some artificial internal organs for human use. Technological advances which make possible the creation of "new" life by processes other than normal conception and birth, however, have drawn objections from religious, lay and even some scientific sources. Recombinant DNA research in particular has raised new legal issues as private industry and academic laboratories attempt to patent new "life"-creating procedures and as people in communities surrounding these laboratories confront the possibility that scientific error may create uncontrollable mutants.

Genetic Research

Complete gene synthesized. Scientists at the University of Wisconsin June 3, 1970 announced the first complete synthesis of a gene, the basic unit of heredity. Although other scientists had used a natural gene to form a new one, the Wisconsin group was the first to piece together a molecule link by link.

The synthesis was achieved by piecing together 77 links of a large yeast molecule. It was accomplished by Dr. H. Gobind Khorana, who won a Nobel Prize in 1968 for work in genetics, and his colleagues after experimenting for nearly five years. Although some scientists said the feat came earlier than expected, others predicted that it would be a long and arduous task to tie the work to manipulation of the hereditary material in plants, animals and man.

A human cell was estimated to have six billion such links as compared to the yeast molecule's 77.

(The gene, the basic unit of heredity, comprises an helixical double strand of deoxyribonucleic acid [DNA]. In any one gene, the sequence of the DNA's chemical subunits determines genetic instructions for a living cell. The sum of coded chemical messages in all the genes of a cell gives it complete instructions, determining what the cell can do and what it can become.)

Gene signal decoded and synthesized—Scientists at the Massachusetts Institute of Technology reported Sept. 10, 1974 that they had synthesized and deciphered the chemical structure governing the turning-on of heredity instructions in a gene.

The MIT team of researchers, headed by Nobel Prize laureate Har Gobind Khorana, reported to the American Chemical Society that it deciphered what it believed to be most or all of the "on" signal for a gene they had succeeded in synthesizing in 1973. Khorana said the team also had learned a significant amount about the "off" signal. The synthesized gene was found naturally in the common human intestinal bacterium Escherichia coli.

Bacterial gene made & implanted—Scientists at the Massachusetts Institute of Technology said Aug. 28, 1976 that they had successfully constructed a bacterial gene, complete with regulatory mechanisms, and had implanted it in a living cell where it functioned normally. The gene synthesis, which would allow scientists to study how genes were controlled, was considered a major step toward understanding the influence of the basic unit of heredity upon the health or illness of the organism.

A tyrosine transfer RNA gene from the bacterium Escherichia coli was produced by assembling from scratch the sequence of its 199 pairs of nucleotides (the four fundamental chemicals of the genetic code). These nucleotides had the chemical names adenine, thymine, guanine and cytosine and were abbreviated A, T, G and C. The synthetic gene was assembled entirely from commercially available A, T, G and C.

The first 52 nucleotide pairs, called the "promoter," started the formation of the gene's product. The next 126 pairs specified instruction for the gene to produce tyrosine transfer RNA, a molecule that transported the amino acid tyrosine to ribosomes (granules containing ribonucleic acid) within the cell. There the tyrosine would combine with other amino acids to make protein molecules. The last 21 pairs, the "terminator," halted the formation of a new molecule. This method of synthesis made it possible to alter specific segments of the nucleotide sequence and thus modify the gene's instructions and function.

The breakthrough technique in genetic engineering, developed by Dr. Har Gobind Khorana, was limited to one species and to modifications in only one gene of that species. It was not considered to hold hazards similar to recombinant DNA experimentation, which involved the transplanting of natural genes from one organism to another.

Dr. Khorana's method also differed significantly from that of a Harvard University group which had synthesized a mammalian gene by chemically reversing the gene-to-product sequence and had derived the gene from the product.

Human cell particle produced in lab. Two New York University scientists disclosed June 1, 1970 that they had produced the first man-made part of a human cell, the lysosome, in a laboratory. The two scientists, Dr. Grazia Sessa and Dr. Gerald Weissmann of NYU's School of Medicine, reported their achievement at a meeting of the International Inflammation Club in Kalamazoo, Mich.

Scientists and research biologists said the feat could open the way to a more detailed study of the body's response to disease and to the inflammatory process that led to arthritis and rheumatism. Other biologists called the achievement "a good thing" and "interesting," but emphasized that it represented only a small step in efforts to reproduce the human cell in the laboratory.

Weissmann said the man-made lysosome had been produced from fatty substances called lipids. These tended to form thin layers, and the process of forming the layers in such a way as to make the lysosome behave in a test tube environment exactly as did its natural counterpart took Weissmann and Sessa five years.

Mammal gene constructed. Four Harvard University scientists had developed the first artificial animal gene, the New York Times reported Dec. 6, 1975.

The scientists, Drs. Argiris Efstratiadis, Fotis Kafatos, Allen Maxam and Thomas Maniatis, achieved the synthesis through a combination of methods for making, in a test tube, complete double-stranded sequences of the chemical DNA of rabbit hemoglobin, a blood component.

One of the techniques used by the Harvard team, reverse transcriptases, was developed by two of three 1975 Nobel Prize winners in medicine, Drs. David Baltimore and Howard Temin.

The synthesis of the rabbit hemoglobin was seen as a major advance in the study of genetics, hereditary diseases and the human genetic evolution.

Scientists urge halt to genetic tests. A committee of scientists endorsed by the National Academy of Sciences urged colleagues throughout the world to observe a temporary ban on certain types of experiments involving genetic manipulation of bacteria (reported July 18, 1974). Such a moratorium should be declared, the ad hoc panel said, because gene-transplantation experiments might accidently increase the resistance of some micro-organisms to drugs or lead to the spread of some types of cancer-causing virus. The panel was made up of researchers in the forefront of developing techniques to isolate particular genes and insert them into living cells.

The group asked that two types of experiments be avoided—the insertion into bacteria of bacterial genes determining resistance to antibiotics and toxin formation, and genes from cancer-causing or other kinds of virus. The committee also suggested that experiments involving insertion of animal genes into bacteria should "not be undertaken lightly," given that many types of animal cells contained genes common to certain tumor viruses. Conceding that its recommendations would "entail postponement or possible abandonment of certain types of scientifically worthwhile experiments," committee members requested that their colleagues observe the ban until a conference could be convened in 1975 to assess potential hazards.

The panel especially urged caution in experiments with the bacterium Escherichia coli (E. coli,) which was commonly found in the human digestive tract. A genetically hybrid E. coli, the committee warned, "might possibly become widely disseminated among human bacterial, plant and animal populations with unpredictable effects."

In some experiments, new types of plasmids resistant to antibiotics might be created, the panel said. A plasmid is a self-replicating DNA element resistant to antibiotics. As an example of an experiment to be avoided, one of the panel members, Dr. Stanley H. Cohen of Stanford University, cited the introduction of a penicillin-resistant gene into the bacteria pneumococci, which was sensitive to penicillin.

The committee was chaired by Dr. Paul Berg of Stanford, and had among its members Dr. James Watson of the Cold Spring Harbor (N.Y.) Laboratory, who along with English geneticist Francis Crick deciphered the structure of DNA.

Research guidelines set. A conference of 139 molecular biologists from 17 nations, held Feb. 24–27, 1975, approved a set of guidelines to reduce the risks of gene-grafting research.

The conference, held at the Asilomar Conference Center in Pacific Grove, Calif., had been called by a committee of U.S. scientists, who feared such experiments might accidently produce drug-resistant or cancer-causing organisms.

As a result of the conference, gene-transplant research was expected to resume. At the urging of the conference's conveners—an ad hoc National Academy of Sciences committee chaired by Stanford University biochemist Paul Berg—U.S. biologists previously had voluntarily agreed to observe a moratorium on some research until safeguards could be drawn up. The ban had become part of the regulations of the Medical Research Council in Great Britain and was generally followed throughout the world.

Essentially, the scientists were concerned with laboratory techniques by which genes of one organism were grafted to the DNA of another organism. Transplanted genes became a permanent part of the recipient organism and its descendants.

The research background of the Asilomar conference was this:

Stanford biologists had discovered a peculiarity of the relatively simple, single-celled bacterium. While most of the DNA in a bacterium was found in their chromosomes, they also had plasmids that often lay outside the chromosomes. The biologists learned to extract a strand of plasmid DNA, cut out a segment and insert in its place a segment of foreign DNA. Moreover, the technique, which also could be used with certain viruses infecting bacteria, was refined so that almost any kind of cell could be grafted to bacteria.

Researchers investigating gene recombination argued that the potential benefits of such grafting were incalculable, but they conceded that there were potential dangers. If it were true that certain bacterial plasmids were resistant to antibiotics, a strain of recombinant streptococcus (the cause of rheumatic fever and other diseases) could be rendered resistant to penicillin, some scientists suggested. Of equal concern were experiments in early 1974 in which DNA's of viruses infecting animals were recombined in test tubes. In one experiment, genes from a virus infecting humans were combined with genes thought to cause cancer in hamsters. The hybrid strand of viral DNA was then inserted into bacterial plasmid DNA. The scientists stopped short of grafting the virus genes to bacteria, however.

Against this background, the National Research Council of the National Academy of Sciences asked Berg to chair a committee to look into the dangers of gene recombination.

As the scientists were basically worried about recombinant organisms that might escape the laboratory, the guidelines drafted at the Asilomar conference concerned "containment." The suggested containment procedures ranged for those in use in hospital-type bacteriology laboratories to high-security measures involving use of protective clothing and air locks. In addition, the guidelines urged scientists to determine necessary containment procedures before beginning experiments.

NIH panel urges use of guidelines—An advisory committee to the National Institutes of Health (NIH), meeting in San Francisco Feb. 28, 1975 recommended that federal grants for research in genetic engineering be conditioned on the recipients' agreeing to follow the guidelines adopted by Asilomar conference.

Dr. A. A. Bayev, the leader of the Soviet Union's delegation to the Asilomar conference, said Feb. 27 that the guidelines were "reasonable and acceptable." (The Soviets attended but did not participate in the conference.)

Genetic research curbed. Guidelines that banned certain forms of genetic experimentation and strongly regulated others were issued June 23, 1976 by the National Institutes of Health.

The new rules barred experiments involving highly poisonous substances, the transfer of drug-resistant properties to dangerous bacteria and the deliberate release of synthetic genetic material into the environment.

Safety precautions included providing ventilation and sewage facilities designed to filter outgoing air and wastes, the transfer of supplies through airlocks and confinement of high-security laboratories to isolated areas.

The guidelines directly applied to the 25,000 NIH grantees and contractors, which included most of the nation's universities. The NIH was the government's main agency for the conduct and support of biomedical research.

The issuance of the guidelines ended the two-year voluntary national moratorium on recombinant DNA research.

Cambridge (Mass.) ban. The Cambridge (Mass.) City Council voted July 7, 1976 for a three-month moratorium on recombinant DNA research at Harvard University, where officials recently had approved plans to construct a genetics research laboratory. The nine-member council also voted to organize a review board of scientists and citizens to investigate further potential hazards.

Scientists urge wider DNA guidelines. Recombinant DNA research guidelines should apply to all federal, academic and industrial groups engaged in such exerimentation, scientists testified Sept. 22, 1976 before the Senate Labor & Public Welfare Committee's subcommittee on health. To date, National Institutes of Health (NIH) guidelines to assure that genetically modified bacteria did not escape from laboratories and create health hazards applied only to recipents of NIH funds.

NIH director Donald S. Frederickson said that nearly all federal agencies, except the Agriculture Department and the Central Intelligence Agency, had agreed to comply voluntarily with the NIH restrictions. Senators Edward M. Kennedy (D, Mass.) and Jacob K. Javits (R, N.Y.) made public a letter they had written July 19 to President Ford urging him to take steps to require adherence to the NIH guidelines "in all sectors of the research community."

Sen. Kennedy, chairman of the subcommittee, said that his concern over industry's compliance with the guidelines was raised when the General Electric Co. refused to send a spokesman to the hearings. General Electric was currently working on developing a bacterial species capable of eating up oil spills.

New York Attorney General Louis J. Lefkowitz convened a public hearing Oct. 21 to discuss whether legal restrictions should be placed on potentially dangerous genetic engineering experiments in the state. The public hearings focused on the questionable stringency of the federal guidelines, which did not apply to the industrial research and were not backed by legal sanctions.

NAS forum on DNA research. The National Academy of Science sponsored a public forum on recombinant DNA research Mar. 7–9 in Washington, D.C., where opposing viewpoints were heard on whether such work ultimately would help cure diseases or unleash new ones. Those who voiced concern about disrupting the natural genetic heritage of life were countered by a majority of biologists who felt the work would lead to the discovery of life-saving drugs.

Hours before the conference opened, a group called the Coalition for Responsible Genetic Research announced its formation and called for "an immediate international moratorium on all research that would produce novel genetic combinations between distant organisms which have not been demonstrated to exchange genes in nature."

The new group, claiming 400 sponsors from the U.S. and abroad, included Harvard University biologist and Nobel Prize winner Dr. George Wald, who described recombinant DNA research as perhaps the biggest issue in the history of science.

NIH builds gene research facility. The National Institutes of Health was preparing the nation's first certified P4 level laboratory, where the most hazardous genetic experiments could be conducted, in Ft. Detrick, Md., the Washington Post reported March 8. The $3-million facility would be housed in a remodeled building previously used to develop the Army's germ warfare projects.

The P4 classification, the most stringent physical containment level outlined in the NIH recombinant DNA guidelines, required airlocks, use of protective clothing and sterilization of all wastes. P4-level experiments involved any work with the DNA of primates (monkeys or man) or with an animal tumor virus.

Administration urges U.S. DNA control. Federal legislation to regulate biological experimentation with recombinant DNA was proposed by the Carter Administration April 6, 1977. The proposals were based on the recommendations made March 16 by a federal interagency panel that had been assigned to study the controversial field of genetic research.

The committee, representing all 16 federal agencies concerned with the research, had advised that the Department of Health, Education and Welfare (HEW) assume primary responsibility for recombinant DNA regulation and that federal law supersede state and local laws on the same subject. Exceptions to the federal supremacy rule would be allowed in cities or states that set standards "as stringent as, or more stringent than," the federal regulations, as in the case of Cambridge, Mass.

HEW Secretary Joseph A. Califano told the health and scientific research subcommittee of the Senate Human Resources Committee that "legislation in this area constitutes unusual government involvement in the workings of basic science." He said, however, that the potential hazards of the revolutionary gene-splicing technique "justify such a measure at this time."

Scientists reproduce insulin gene. Drs. Howard M. Goodman and William J. Rutter of the University of California at San Francisco reported May 23, 1977 that they had mass-produced the gene for insulin. They used the recombinant-DNA technique and spliced the genetic material that produces insulin in rats into colonies of the bacteria Escherichia coli (E. coli). Bacteria normally did not make insulin and had no natural genetic instructions for doing so.

The bacteria duplicated the transplanted genetic material, thus marking a major step toward providing limitless supplies of insulin, a vital hormone needed by diabetics, whose own bodies could not produce it.

The possibility of developing new drug resources had been a major goal of advocates of recombinant DNA technology.

Diabetics currently obtained insulin from the pancreas glands of pigs and cattle.

EPA urges federal controls. The U.S. Environmental Protection Agency (EPA) favored federal regulation of recombinant DNA research, EPA deputy assistant administrator Dale Barth said March 8, 1977. Barth, EPA representative on the interagency committee currently preparing federal legislation to control the so-called "new genetics," said the risks created by science's ability to make new forms of life in the laboratory made protective measures necessary.

A bill to create a regulatory licensing scheme for recombinant DNA research already had been introduced in Congress Feb.

4. Sen. Dale Bumpers (D, Ark.), one sponsor of the bill, had said he would prefer to ban the research entirely, but that that was an impractical suggestion.

Viral gene sequence completed. British scientists reported Feb. 24, 1977, in the journal, Nature, that they had determined the sequence of 5,375 nucleotides that made up the DNA strand of a bacterial virus. DNA (deoxyribonucleic acid), was the core material of genes.

The research, conducted by Fred Sanger at the Medical Research Council in Cambridge, England determined the entire genetic structure of phiX174, a virus consisting of nine genes. The most significant aspect of the work was that it overthrew the genetic theory that each gene carried the information code to reproduce only one type of protein molecule. Sanger's discovery showed that phiX174 could use the same stretch of DNA to code for two different proteins. In phiX174, the nucleotide sequence signaling the stop of one protein shared its final nucleotide with the start sequence of another protein. This economical use of DNA within the gene indicated that there could be a great deal more information compressed into DNA than was previously thought possible, Sanger said.

Scientific curbs scored—News of the British research group's breakthrough arrived at the AAAS conference in the wake of a discussion Feb. 22 on the issue of self-regulation by the scientific community. The symposium topic, "Science, the Key to our Political Future," was raised in response to recent state and municipal actions to restrict recombinant DNA research. George Ball, a former U.S. undersecretary of state and currently an investment banker, described the threat of public participation in scientific regulation as a "new medieval church." Lord Zuckerman, formerly the British Government's chief science advisor, said he saw "danger in democratizing scientific advice or decision." Both men were critical of the action of the Cambridge, Mass. city council to impose its own guidelines on genetic research conducted in laboratories at Harvard University and the Massachusetts Institute of Technology.

DNA research bills stalled. Legislation aimed at federal regulation of recombinant DNA research was stalled in both bodies of Congress, it was reported Oct. 24, 1977. The delay on the House and Senate draft bills, once considered urgent measures, was attributed to intensive lobbying by members of the scientific community opposed to governmental restrictions on their work.

Opponents of such controls contended that the potential risks originally associated with genetic engineering had been overstated. They cited recent experiments that discounted the threat of producing unnatural monstrosities or deadly diseases. The controversial technique was capable of creating new forms of life by manipulating or recombining the basic hereditary material (DNA) of unrelated species.

The legislative slowdown was traced to open letters to Congress expressing scientists' concern that regulatory legislation could deny society the benefits of biomedical research and might jeopardize the future of all such experimentation.

Sen. Edward M. Kennedy, (D, Mass.), chairman of the health subcommittee, Sept. 27 withdrew support for his own bill that would have established an 11-member, presidentially appointed commission with the authority to oversee all recombinant DNA research. Speaking before a group of medical writers in New York City, Kennedy said his decision was based on "fluctuating scientific data and the emotional atmosphere of the debate." (See below)

Kennedy proposed compromise legislation that would extend existing National Institutes of Health guidelines for one year while a non-governmental commission evaluated recent developments to re-establish the need, if any, for federal legislation.

Rep. Paul Rogers (D, Fla.) was quoted Oct. 24, as saying it would be "very difficult" to get his bill, vesting regulatory power in the Department of Health, Education and Welfare rather than creating a new bureaucratic body, through Congress this session. Critics of Rogers' legislation argued that HEW's National Institutes of Health was in charge of promoting research and would therefore be ill-suited to monitoring it.

Scientists debate DNA safety. A personal letter to the National Institutes of Health's director from the chairman of a recombinant DNA risk-assessment meeting in June led Sen. Edward Kennedy to modify his highly restrictive legislation, New Scientist magazine reported Oct. 6.

Following the gathering, Dr. Sherwood Gorbach wrote NIH Director Donald Frederickson that the organism used most often in DNA research—a weakened form of the bacterium Escherichia coli (E. coli), K-12—could not be converted into any type of hazardous substance. Gorbach said laboratory techniques used by genetic engineers were almost foolproof and he offered other reassurances that received wide coverage in the press.

Jonathan King, a Massachusetts Institute of Technology biology professor who represented Science for the People, a group committed to stringent recombinant DNA regulation, claimed Gorbach's letter contained significant cautions that were never publicized, according to New Scientist. King said reports of the meeting, held in Falmouth, Mass., "seriously distorted the consensus" reached there.

In their own letter to Frederickson, King and Harvard biology professor Richard Goldstein expressed their concern "over possibly misleading and incomplete reports" that might give the impression that recombinant DNA experimentation was safe.

Genetic recombination cited in nature—The unpublished work of two Stanford University researchers, Stanley Cohen and Shing Chang, reported in Science News Oct. 8, suggested that genetic manipulation carried out by laboratory researchers occurred as a matter of course in nature. That view was cited by Sen. Kennedy as a challenge to the belief that artificial recombinant DNA techniques could produce novel organisms.

Natural gene engineering of this type was confirmed by the research of Canadian bacteriologists reported in New Scientist Oct. 27. The bacteriologists contended that an unusual outbreak of diarrhea in pigs was caused by a naturally mutated strain of E. coli 86 in which the gene for enterotoxin—the substance that caused diarrhea—had combined with the gene for antibiotic resistance.

The E. coli organism existed in the intestines of nearly all warm-blooded animals, including humans. It caused illness when it carried genes for enterotoxin, but was otherwise harmless. However, experiments showed that plasmids—the cleaved pieces of DNA that joined with foreign DNA fragments to form the so-called recombinant DNA molecule—could spread from one strain of E. coli to another. The bacteriologists believed the continued indiscriminate use of antibiotics could lead to a proliferation of antibiotic-resistant bacteria.

Gene conferees back research—Biologists attending the week-long 1977 Gordon Conference on Nucleic Acids drafted June 17 an open letter to Congress arguing against the need for recombinant-DNA legislation. The statement warned that two pending bills that would place genetic engineering under federal control "might be so unwieldy and unpredictable as to inhibit severely the further development of this field of research."

(The first warning of genetic engineering's potential hazards and all subsequent attempts to establish safeguards for the technique came from participants at the 1973 Gordon Conference.)

The letter to Congress, signed by 110 conference participants, said "the past four years has given no indication of actual hazard." It called the proposed restraints "unwarranted."

New Genentech issue takes off. The public sale for the first time of one million shares of Genentech Inc. on the over-the-counter market in New York Oct. 14, 1980, was one of the hottest new offerings in stock market history.

Originally offered at $35 a share, Genentech's price shot up to $89 twenty minutes after trading started.

Genentech, a genetic-engineering company founded four years ago in San Francisco by Robert A. Swanson (president) and Herbert W. Boyer (vice president), was one of a handful of companies involved in research on gene formations in living organisms. Genentech manufactured, among other things, insulin for humans with diabetes, a human growth hormone involved in the treatment of dwarfism and interferon, a disease-fighting protein hailed by scientists as a possible cure for cancer.

Underwriters, led by Blyth Eastman Paine Webber and Hambrecht & Quist, were so inundated by requests for the stock that they were forced to allocate shares among securities firms for sale to their customers.

Based on the total outstanding shares of Genentech (7,427,102), the company was worth $532 million when the Oct. 14 trading session ended, with Genentech listed at $71.25. Since its founding, the company had actually lost $1 million and had only begun to show a small profit late in 1979. In the first half of 1980, Genentech earned $80,000 on sales of $3.4 million.

One individual involved with Genentech during its early days was a 26-year-old graduate student named Robert Scheller. While working with Genentech in 1976, Scheller had received the standard assistant's fee of $5,000 and was given 30,000 shares of stock, half of which he gave back when he left the company. After the day's trading Oct. 14, Scheller's 15,000 shares of Genentech were worth about $1.1 million, making him an instant millionaire.

Genentech's co-founders, Swanson and Boyer, each held 985,000 shares of the company, valued at $70.2 million Oct. 14.

First vaccine made by gene splicing. An effective vaccine against foot and mouth disease had been developed by the science of genetic engineering, it was announced June 18, 1981 by the U.S. Department of Agriculture. Secretary John R. Block said, 'We believe this to be the first production through gene-splicing of an effective vaccine against any disease in animals or humans.

The virus, also known as hoof and mouth disease, was considered one of the most economically serious livestock infections, afflicting cattle, sheep and swine throughout the world. Although the disease, which caused sores in the mouths and on the feet of cloven-hoofed animals, was seldom fatal, it was highly contagious, and had in rare cases been contracted by humans.

Outbreaks of the disease had often reached epidemic proportions, interfering in animal product trading and reducing the world supply of meat. It was hoped that use of the new vaccine would result in annual savings of billions of dollars.

The vaccine, produced by Genentech Inc. scientists in collaboration with the Agriculture Dept., consisted of a protein known as VP3, one of the four major proteins of which the hoof and mouth virus was comprised. It was effective against only one common strain of the disease, but held a great advantage over previous vaccines, in that it would be incapable of actually producing the disease in a vaccinated animal. Vaccines had in the past occasionally been a causal factor in outbreaks of the disease.

Genentech vice president Robert Byrnes stated that work had begun on the development of vaccines specific for other strains of the disease, of which there were approximately 30. "Ideally, we'll eventually end up with a universal vaccine effective against all strains of the disease to serve all world markets," he added.

NIH votes to keep federal DNA rules. A National Institutes of Health advisory committee recommended, by a 16 to five vote, Feb. 8, 1982, that mandatory federal guidelines on genetic engineering research be retained. The panel's decision represented a change of heart. In September 1981, it had endorsed a proposal to make the rules voluntary.

Genetic engineering, gene-splicing or recombinant DNA research, as it was variously known, was created less than a decade ago. It was a technology that enabled biologists to mix the genes of two or more species, and was now the subject of much university research as well as the basis of a burgeoning industry.

Original fears prompting the formation of federal guidelines had been scientific ones centering around the possibility that a harmless organism could be changed into a pathogenic one. Most such fears had since dissolved in the scientific community, but a significant segment of the public remained concerned that gene-splicing techniques could produce disease-causing or toxic organisms.

Current guidelines allowed more than 90% of gene-splicing experiments to be conducted without special oversight but required review and approval of those experiments that mixed the genes of dangerous organisms. Committee members pointed out that the two kinds of experiments that caused most public concern—giving an organism the genes to produce biological poisons, and those to make it resistant to antibiotic drugs—could be carried out without using gene-splicing techniques.

The vote favoring mandatory guidelines was based on political factors, according to several press accounts. In view of concern on the part of universities, congressmen and other sectors of the public about genetic engineering, the scientists decided that the absence of federal regulations could result in a patchwork of local laws and regulations. These might severely hamper the scientific research and the biotechnology industry that depended upon the new techniques.

The NIH Recombinant DNA Advisory Committee (RAC) relaxed the rules slightly to ease restrictions on the special handling of organisms, particularly nonpathogenic ones. The proposal, however, retained institutional biosafety committees, which the RAC members felt provided a channel for communication between scientists and the community. The guidelines would be binding for all institutions receiving NIH funding.

DNA duplicated in lab—A team of scientists at Stanford University had discovered a laboratory process that successfully initiated DNA reproduction, it was reported Jan. 5, 1982. Although DNA had been synthesized using gene-splicing techniques, the initial process that sparked creation of the genetic material within a cell had remained a mystery.

The Stanford researchers, led by Nobel laureate Arthur Kornberg, discovered a test-tube technique that combined all the components needed to trigger chromosome duplication in a common bacterium. Kornberg, also responsible for the first synthetically created DNA, mixed several proteins, one of which was apparently the catalyst for the reaction, thus achieving DNA duplication in a test tube.

Although not certain which protein or proteins were responsible for beginning the process, Kornberg said the achievement marked a "milestone" in DNA research and was the culmination of four years work.

The advance was significant in part because an understanding of the basic mechanism of cell reproduction could prove crucial in controlling diseases, such as cancer, that were characterized by uninhibited, rapid cell growth.

Patenting Life

Patent order lifted. The Commerce Department Feb. 24, 1977 suspended an order issued Jan. 10 which had accelerated the granting of patents to companies involved in recombinant DNA research. The order had bypassed a major guideline laid down by the National Institutes of Health (NIH), by allowing private industries to withhold data and protect trade secrets which would otherwise have been reviewed by a safety board. The NIH guidelines, which applied only to federally funded research projects required advance disclosure of bacterial or other genetic material to be used in experimentation.

The regulation was rescinded after Health Education and Welfare Secretary Joseph A Califano Jr. and two California State Assembly committees protested the ruling. In a letter Feb. 7 Califano asked that the Commerce Department await the recommendations of a federal interagency committee currently considering how to regulate firms involved in genetic research.

Major U.S. pharmaceutical companies currently conducting recombinant DNA experiments included Hoffman-LaRoche, Upjohn and Eli Lilly. Abbott Laboratories in North Chicago, Ill. issued a statement Mar 9 that although they were preparing staff facilities and techniques for such research they were "not at present actually recombining DNA molecular pieces."

Court grants microbe patent. Upjohn Co. of Kalamazoo, Mich. Oct. 6, 1977, became the first firm to patent a form of life under a new ruling by the U.S. Court of Customs and Patent Appeals. The decision extended existing patent laws, protecting the products of microbes, to include the original organism used in the manufacture of those products.

The first patented microorganism, streptomyces vellosus, was used by Upjohn to produce the antibiotic lincomycin. It was developed from a naturally occurring bacterium using traditional genetic techniques. It had been reported erroneously Oct. 11 that the life form was the result of the controversial method of genetic manipulation known as recombinant DNA.

In the past, inadequate patent and ownership protection reportedly had discouraged many industries from investing in various areas of scientific research.

Patent granted to gene-altered bacteria. The Court of Customs and Patent Appeals March 2, 1978, ruled, 3–2, that General Electric Co. could patent a bacteria its laboratories had developed using genetic recombination techniques.

In 1977 the patent court had approved the award of a patent for a microbe developed by Upjohn Co. that would be used in the manufacture of an antibiotic. The microbe patented in 1977, however, had been obtained through the use of traditional genetic techniques. The GE bacterium, on the other hand, was created using the so-called "gene-splicing" technique.

The court majority said that the basic question of whether a form of life could be patented had been decided in the Upjohn ruling. The issue in the GE case was the same, the majority said, and thus the company should be allowed to obtain a patent.

The majority decision observed that "the nature and commercial uses of biologically pure cultures of microorganisms . . . are much more akin to inanimate chemical compounds such as reactants, reagents and catalysts than they are to horses and honeybees, or raspberries and roses."

The GE bacterium fed on oil and was seen as a possible means of cleaning up oil spills. It had been developed from a bacterium strain called pseudomonas.

Court OKs patents for microorganisms. The U.S. Court for Customs and Patent Appeals March 29, 1978 reaffirmed two earlier decisions that corporations were entitled to patents on microorganisms developed in their own laboratories.

In its earlier rulings, the appeals court had upheld patent claims filed by General Electric Co. and Upjohn Co.

The Supreme Court had vacated the ruling in the Upjohn case and ordered a reconsideration of the issues based on its ruling in another patent suit. In that case, the Supreme Court had ruled that a computer program was not patentable because its only novel feature was a mathematical formula. This amounted to the discovery of a "law of nature," or a "principle," the court ruled.

After reconsidering the issues, the appeals court ruled, 4–1, that the computer-program decision had no bearing on whether to grant a patent for microorganisms. The life forms developed by Upjohn and GE had not been "products of nature," according to the appeals court.

The court saw no "legally significant differences between active chemicals which are classified as 'dead' and organisms used for their chemical reactions which take place because they are 'alive.' "

The court noted that Louis Pasteur had been granted a patent in 1873 for his discovery of yeast—also a living organism.

The Supreme Court on October 29, 1979. Agreed to decide whether patents could be issued on living organisms. The U.S. Court of Customs and Patent Appeals had ruled in *Parker v. Bergy* that two companies, Upjohn and General Electric, had improperly been denied government patents on biological microorganisms generated in the laboratories of the companies.

Test-Tube Babies

'Test-tube baby' born in Britain. The first authenticated birth of a human baby conceived outside the body of a woman occurred July 25, 1978, in Lancashire, England. The 5-pound, 12-ounce infant, an apparently normal girl, was delivered by Caesarian section at Oldham and District General Hospital.

The parents were Lesley Brown, 31, and her husband, John, 38. The child was named Louise.

The slightly premature birth was the culmination of a procedure that had begun Nov. 10, 1977 when an egg cell was removed surgically from one of the mother's ovaries and fertilized with the father's sperm in a petri dish. After two and a half days of "in vitro" development in a laboratory culture, the embryo was placed in the mother's uterus through a tube inserted in the cervix.

The procedure had been developed by Dr. Patrick C. Steptoe, a gynecologist, and Dr. Robert G. Edwards, a Cambridge University specialist in reproductive physiology. They had collaborated for more than a dozen years in research and experimentation.

Steptoe had developed a surgical procedure, known as laparoscopy, to enter a woman's abdomen through a small incision near the navel to withdraw nearly mature egg cells. (He estimated the actual extraction time as 8.5 seconds.)

Edwards had evolved methods to control the hormones that affected production of the eggs and the willingness of the uterus to accept the embryo.

The Steptoe-Edwards efforts had failed a number of times previously for various reasons. Steptoe estimated he had tried the implantation 200 times before the Brown success. It was reported that the women who had become pregnant, approximately 30, had failed to carry the artificially conceived babies to term.

Research with rhesus monkeys by Dr. John H. Marston of the University of Birmingham Medical School suggested that embryo implants could be performed successfully at a very early stage—even after one division of the original egg cell. The experiments were reported at a Cambridge conference in July. Preliminary findings of the study were known before the Brown implant.

Steptoe-Edwards apparently inserted the Brown embryo at an earlier stage of development that in any of their prior attempts. They had previously cultured some embryos four and a half days.

Hope for childless couples—The successful birth of the "test-tube baby" held promise for many sterile couples who desired children. The procedure by-passed the fallopian tubes, the place of origin of approximately 30% of the fertility problems affecting at least 150,000 women in the U.S. Leading gynecologists cautioned, however, that the technique would have to be refined and further research undertaken before too much hope could be placed in the new procedure.

There was the question of possible genetic defects that might not appear until babies born by the method reached maturity. Eggs ripened under hormonal stimulation and sperm that was not screened in competition for fertilization possibly would not be the same as those produced under normal circumstances.

Numerous experiments with animals had gone far beyond the test-tube approach, which was commonplace with cattle. Livestock embryos have been successfully flushed from uteruses and frozen in embryo banks for reimplantation or for transfer to a foster mother.

Reaction—Religious reaction was generally cautious and approval hinged on both husband and wife being the parents of the child. Jewish, Moslem and Protestant figures, with reservations about any possible broader use, generally accepted the procedure as an advance in meeting the problem of childlessness facing some married couples. Roman Catholic leaders continued to oppose any form of artificial insemination.

Edwards, in response to critics, questioned why anyone would object to "giving these couples their own children." He added that to discontinue research because of possible undesirable manipulations would be comparable to foregoing the development of airplanes because they made bombings and hijackings possible.

New York lawsuit—In New York, a similar procedure had been used at Columbia Presbyterian Medical Center in 1973 to enable Doris and John Del Zio to have a child. After the day-old embryo was destroyed while still in the laboratory, the Del Zios filed a $1.5-million damage suit against the hospital and the director of obstetrics and gynecology. The medical center claimed the experiment was clandestine, posed safety hazards for the woman and was contrary to its regulations. A jury trial began July 17 in federal court.

N.Y. 'test-tube baby' damages won. A federal court jury in New York awarded damages Aug. 18, 1978, to Doris and John Del Zio for emotional stress in 1973. An embryo transplant experiment that the Del Zios contended could have produced for them the first laboratory-conceived human baby had been halted in a hospital the day after a fertilization attempt was made in a test-tube culture.

The jury of four women and two men awarded Mrs. Del Zio $12,000 each against Columbia Presbyterian Medical Center and Columbia University, operator of the center. It awarded her $25,000 against Dr. Raymond Vande Wiele, the center's director of obstetrics and gynecology, who had interrupted the procedure by ordering the culture removed from an incubator and placed in a freezer.

Mr. Del Zio was given a token award of $1 against each of the three defendants.

The jury, however, unanimously found Vande Wiele innocent of wrongfully converting property belonging to Mrs. Del Zio—the test tube material that another doctor had planned to implant in her body.

Vande Wiele testified that he had intervened because he feared that the procedure might have proved fatal for Mrs. Del Zio.

The suit had asked $1.55 million in damages.

'Test-tube baby' born in India. The second birth of a human baby conceived outside the body of a woman occurred Oct. 3, 1978, in Calcutta, India. The 7-pound, 6-ounce baby girl was delivered by Caesarian section. She was reported normal and healthy.

The parents were Bela Agarwal, 31, and her husband, Pravat, 35. The child was named Durga, after a Hindu goddess.

A three-doctor team headed by Saroj K. Bhattacharya, associate professor of obstetrics and gynecology at Calcutta Medical College, atttempted the laboratory method because the mother's fallopian tubes were blocked. The other two doctors were Subash Mukherjee and Sunit Mukherjee (who were not related to each other).

The procedure differed from that used in England that resulted in the birth of the first "test-tube baby." Ova were removed through the vaginal canal rather than with an instrument inserted into the abdominal wall. After three and a half days in an incubator, an ovum was fertilized in the laboratory by the husband's sperm. It was then kept deep-frozen for 53 days before being implanted in the mother's uterus. Bhattacharya said the delay was for the purpose of timing the implant to coincide with the mother's ovulation. The English implant had been performed after two and a half days.

The doctors said that although Durga Agarwal was the second "test-tube baby," they preferred to call her the first "deepfreeze baby." They also said a lack of sophisticated equipment had forced them to devise the different technique.

The Agarwals had been childless for more than 15 years.

The world's third "test-tube baby"—the first boy—was born Jan. 14, 1979 at Stobhill Hospital in Glasgow, Scotland. Born a month prematurely, he was reported in "excellent health."

First 'test-tube baby' clinic approved. Virginia health authorities gave final approval Jan. 8, 1980, for the opening of the first "test-tube baby" clinic in the U.S., despite strong opposition from antiabortionists and other groups.

Final governmental approval came from Virginia state Health Commissioner Dr. James B. Kenley, who authorized a "certificate of need" for the laboratory clinic at the Eastern Virginia Medical School in Norfolk, Va.

The clinic would be used to aid women who were unable to conceive children normally.

The procedure to be used for the conception of human embryos outside the mother's body would involve surgical removal of mature human egg cells. The egg would be artificially fertilized in a laboratory and then reimplanted in the mother's uterus in a few days.

The technique was developed by Dr. Patrick C. Steptoe and Dr. Robert G. Edwards, the English physicians, who oversaw the first "test-tube" birth in July 1978.

Lesley Brown, mother of the world's first "test-tube baby" in 1978, had also become the first woman to give birth to a second

125

child conceived outside the body by way of the "in vitro" fertilization technique, her doctor announced June 15, 1982. Brown's second test tube baby, Natalie Jean, was born in Bristol, England. "Both mother and daughter are very well," the doctor said.

Frozen egg produces pregnancy. Doctors in Melbourne, Australia, announced May 2, 1983 that an Australian woman had become pregnant after having been implanted with a fertilized egg that had been frozen. Doctors at Monash University said the woman was in her 14th week and the pregnancy appeared normal.

It was reportedly the first case of a fertilized human egg being frozen and then used successfully to start a pregnancy. (Human sperm had been successfully frozen and stored for decades, and both sperm and fertilized eggs had been frozen and then used in animals.)

In 1982 the woman had had four ova removed for "in vitro" fertilization with her husband's sperm. Three of the eggs, after being fertilized, were implanted fresh in the woman, while the fourth was frozen.

This first implantation resulted in a pregnancy, but after eight weeks the woman miscarried. The couple later requested that the fourth egg be thawed and implanted, and this was done in January.

Other Technology

Artificial heart use riles FDA. The third man ever to receive an artificial heart implant died Aug. 2, 1981, of "overwhelming" complications, including kidney failure, lung problems and bacterial infection. Thirty-six year-old Willebrordus A. Meuffels, a Dutch tour bus driver, had lived for 54 hours sustained by the artificial heart, and then a week longer with a transplanted human heart.

The mechanical heart used in the emergency operation had been developed at the Texas Heart Institute at St. Luke's Epis-

copal Hospital in Houston. The surgeon was pioneer Dr. Denton Cooley, who had performed the first implantation of a mechanical heart, in 1969. (The only other known artificial heart implant in a live human patient was reported by surgeons in Argentina earlier this year.)

Meuffels, who had flown from the Netherlands to undergo open heart surgery for clogged arteries, suffered a massive heart attack July 23 immediately following a triple bypass operation. Rather than lose his patient, Cooley decided to implant an electrically powered, air-driven plastic heart that had been developed at the institute. The device worked, and Meuffels returned to a stable condition.

The mechanical heart was operated through a console outside the body about the size of a television set and had been tested in hundreds of calves but never in a human being. It was a two-chambered pump that performed the function of the human heart's lower chambers, or ventricles, sending blood throughout the body. The device was connected to the patient's own auricles, the two upper chambers that collected blood between contractions of the lower chambers. Eventually, researchers hoped to give its recipients mobility by providing power for the device through batteries worn on a belt.

Two days later, after a nationwide appeal, a suitable heart donor was found and another operation performed, replacing the mechanical heart with a human one. Meuffels died a week later.

Shortly after the implantation July 24, spokesman William Rados of the Food and Drug Administration criticized Cooley's use of the artificial device, which had not been approved by the agency for human use. "Our regulations are designed to protect the patients," he said. "We think it best in the development of an artificial heart to get approval [in advance]."

A hospital spokesman, however, referred to an FDA provision that permitted the use of experimental devices "in emergency situations where there is not sufficient time or that circumstances are such that the physician is confronted by a life-threatening situation and there is no alternative method of approved or generally recognized therapy that may save the patient's life." The FDA was reportedly investigating the case.

A team of researchers at the University of Utah that had developed a similar device, to be implanted by heart surgeon Dr. William C. DeVries, were awaiting approval for its use. The team had announced its own readiness in January, but the FDA decided in March to delay granting permission for human use, requiring the team to answer detailed questions about the device. Although the Utah team had had opportunities to use the device, it had refrained from doing so. Nevertheless, Dr. DeVries applauded the unexpected attempt in Houston, adding that the case could easily become a test of the FDA's recent attempts to regulate experimental medical devices.

Permanent artificial heart implanted by Utah doctors. Doctors at the University of Utah Medical Center in Salt Lake City Dec. 2, 1982, successfully implanted a permanent artificial heart in a 61-year-old retired dentist.

The seven-and-a-half hour operation was the first of its kind. The patient, Barney B. Clark, had been near death from heart failure when the operation began, but after the artificial heart was implanted he appeared on the path to recovery.

Given the experimental nature of the procedure, however, doctors were cautious in assessing Clark's chances. A second operation became necessary Dec. 4 to deal with subcutaneous leaks of air from the patient's lungs. The major leaks were closed and it appeared that they were unconnected with the new device. (Such air leaks were not uncommon after chest surgery.)

Unlike transplants of human hearts, there was no possibility of rejection. However, there was a considerable danger of infection or some other complication.

The medical team that implanted the artificial heart was led by Dr. William DeVries.

The heart itself, made out of polyurethane plastic and aluminum, had been developed by Dr. Robert Jarvik, who also served as a member of the surgical team.

The artificial heart was connected by six-foot-long (1.8-meter-long) hoses to a compressor that provided power. Because the compressor weighed about 375 pounds (179 kilograms), Clark's mobility would be restricted. The compressor was housed in what doctors described as "a grocery cart."

There had been two earlier cases in which artificial hearts were implanted in humans. In both those cases, however, the artificial hearts were intended as short-term expedients designed to keep the patient alive until a natural heart became available.

At 61, Clark was considered too old for a human heart transplant. Other heart operations, such as a bypass, were of no value in treating his condition, which was known as cardiomyopathy. This disease involved a progressive deterioration of the heart muscle to a point at which it could no longer function. Clark, doctors said, was near death when the operation began: in fact, the operation had to be moved up several hours from its initially scheduled time because of a worsening in his condition.

The cost of the mechanical heart was put at $16,450. This figure did not include the cost of Clark's hospital stay or the operation.

Artificial heart recipient recovers. Barney Clark, the first human being to have an artificial heart implanted as a permanent measure, survived several early setbacks and improved to the extent that by Dec. 27 doctors decided to discontinue daily press briefings on his condition.

On Dec. 7, five days after the artificial heart had been implanted, Clark suffered several seizures involving involuntary muscle contractions. The seizures lasted more than two hours, but did not appear to have caused brain damage. It was not clear what had caused the seizures.

A week later, on Dec. 14, Clark had to undergo new surgery to replace the left side of the artificial heart, which had begun to fail. His blood pressure had fallen dramatically as a result of the mechanical failure, a crack in a valve of the polyurethane heart that was permitting the blood to regurgitate.

Clark had also developed a case of mild pneumonia. He was at that time listed as in "extremely critical condition," and one of the doctors noted that he was "a very, very sick man who's gone through multiple surgeries."

However, his condition improved in the following days. On Dec. 19 he stood up, with assistance, for the first time since the artificial heart was implanted Dec. 2. He took a few steps for the first time since his initial operation Dec. 22, and on Dec. 23 he received his first soft food by mouth. A spokesman for the University of Utah Medical Center, where Clark was being treated, said Dec. 22 that "what we have seen in the last two or three days is what we should phrase as a return to normalcy, both on the part of Dr. Clark, his family and the hospital staff."

Artificial heart patient dies. *Barney B. Clark*, the first human to have an artificial heart implanted as a permanent measure, died March 23, 1983, 112 days after the polyurethane heart was placed in his body.

The artificial heart continued working to the end, and in fact was turned off by the attending physicians only when they determined that irreversible changes in the rest of Clark's body had rendered him "essentially dead."

Clark's death occurred at the University of Utah Medical Center, where he had undergone the operation to implant the artificial heart. Dr. Chase Peterson, the university vice president for health sciences, said March 24 that the "cause of death was vascular collapse, resulting from a multitude of causes." Dr. William DeVries, who had carried out the initial operation on Clark, said that "his colon failed. Then his kidneys failed . . . Then his lungs failed. Then his brain failed, and lastly, when the key was turned off, his heart failed."

DeVries said that "bacteria may have affected the circulation around the heart, and the muscle cells of the blood vessels dilated and essentially died. The heart couldn't support the rest of the body."

Clark, who was 61 when the heart was implanted and 62 when he died, was considered too old to qualify for a transplant of a natural heart. At the time he received the artificial heart he had been close to death, suffering from inoperable cardiomyopathy, a degenerative disease of the heart.

Cloning. University of Geneva scientist Karl Illmensee announced that he had succeeded in transferring the nucleus of a mouse embryo cell into the egg cell of another mouse, Science News reported July 28, 1979. The treated egg was then inserted in a mouse foster mother, and eventually a normal mouse was produced.

The experiment was considered a major step toward the cloning of a mammal. Cloning, in turn, was seen as a valuable technique for gaining information on how genes operated, which would help scientists to understand phenomena such as cancer and aging.

Plant gene transplant claimed. Independent groups of scientists in the U.S. and Belgium claimed Jan. 18, 1983, to have succeeded in transferring a bacterium gene into plant cells. The gene was said to have functioned normally in the plant cells.

The U.S. team of researchers was composed of scientists attached to Monsanto Co., the chemical producer, while the European group was led by a scientist attached to Belgium's University of Gent. The research was considered noteworthy, because previous gene transplants had generally involved bacteria and mammals. Plant genetics were sufficiently different to make a gene transplant less straightforward.

The two groups claimed to have transplanted a gene that conferred resistance to certain antibiotics. Several different plants, including petunias, sunflowers and tobacco, had proved receptive to the bacterium gene.

Experimenting on Human Subjects*

Ethical and Legal Problems

Kennedy on benefits vs. responsibility. In a discussion in the Senate Aug. 1, 1972, Sen. Edward M. Kennedy (D, Mass.) sought to place in perspective the responsibility of society in the face of the dangers faced by human subjects of the medical experiments needed by society. This topic was part of a speech on the overall subject of bioethics. Kennedy said:

One of the most significant problems in this entire area is that of human experimentation. Historically the advance of modern medical science has traditionally made use of human experimentation, frequently with the scientists using themselves as experimental guinea pigs. Without some human experimentation it would not have been possible to develop the smallpox vaccine or to begin to cope with malaria. And the development of modern drugs is dependent on a certain amount of experimental drug use among special patient groups. Such drug testing has to be much more closely monitored and regulated than it has been in the past, but under the proper controlled conditions it has to occur; for

human experimentation is an essential requirement for medical progress.

The thrust of my remarks today is not that human experimentation is inherently bad or that it should be banned or prohibited. Human experimentation is essential in a balanced program of medical research. But the problems posed by human experimentation—in medicine, ethics, law, and social policy—are enormous. How we resolve these issues will have a major impact on the lives of millions of Americans over the coming years.

The kind of impact human experimentation can have has been dramatically demonstrated in recent days with revelation of the tragic syphilis project at Tuskegee. The disclosure of a 40-year experiment on hundreds of poor, black men stricken with syphilis in Alabama, raises the spector of an Orwellian nightmare. Because we now have complex devices like kidney machines, and because we can now transplant a man's heart; and because we have now ended the deathly plagues of smallpox and polio—too many Americans have been lulled into a false sense of security about the powers and practices of medical science. But the news that a Federal agency—the Public Health Service—has used taxpayers' dollars to conduct a program to experiment on poor, sick, black people—without their knowing it—is an alarming revelation at best.

Many questions leap to mind with that outrageous news:

Why were not the patients treated with

*Note that the major legal issue, informed consent, is the same as that involved in sterilization of mentally incompetent individuals and denial of medical treatment to terminally ill incompetents (see the chapters on Contraception: Sterilization, Death & Dying, Ethical Issues: Informed Consent, and Drugs).

penicillin after that "wonder" drug had been discovered?

Why did the experiment include only men? And why were only black men included?

How many of those men are now in mental institutions, because the syphilis infection caused irreversible brain damage?

How many of those test patients fathered children who contracted congenital syphilis?

Are Federal agencies conducting any other such experiments?

And, why has the news of the Tuskegee experiment come to light right at this time?

Ethics panels created. The Wall Street Journal reported April 14, 1971 that there had been a large increase in the creation of medical-ethics committees at hospitals involved in research using human subjects. These committees are usually composed of doctors who are involved neither in the research nor in the treatment of the patients involved. The article, by Liz Roman Gallese, said:

Some hospitals have had ethics committees for many years. But the real impetus to establish them came in 1966, when the National Institutes of Health decided not to award research grants to hospitals or other institutions that don't have such panels. In that year there were 371 committees; today there are more than 1,900. The NIH made grants totaling $827 million in 1970, thus financing a major part of U.S. medical research.

Sen. Edward Kennedy, discussing the issues raised by the article, told the Senate July 19:

One of the cardinal principles that medical-ethics committees must be guided by is the necessity to obtain the fully informed consent of every patient involved in a research project. If the patient is a minor, the consent of the parents is also required. But the Wall Street Journal article points out cases where obtaining the necessary consent presents special problems. For example, one study conducted by a Johns Hopkins Uni-

versity researcher involved juvenile delinquents in State institutions. One of the concerns of the American Civil Liberties Union was that proper safeguards were not being used to prevent parents from feeling coerced into giving permission.

Difficult problems arise, in many cases. Sometimes, according to Dr. John E. Plager, a member of the ethics committee at Roswell Park Memorial Institute in Buffalo:

Real, informed consent would send patients into acute anxiety and terrify them.

Investigational drugs & the FDA. The main federal agency charged with regulating the trade in medicines is the Food & Drug Administration (FDA). Sen. Abraham A. Ribicoff (D, Conn.), chairman of the Senate Subcommittee on Executive Reorganization & Government Research, charged in the Senate Sept.19, 1973 that the FDA had been lax in its regulation of "investigational new drugs—drugs approved for testing but not for public sale." These were drugs, he said, that "had been administered in clinical experiments to human subjects." Ribicoff made his charge on the basis of an investigation conducted on his orders by the Government Accounting Office (GAO). Ribicoff said in a statement published in the Congressional Record:

The GAO study discusses only 10 of the more than 6,000 drugs currently classified as investigational new drugs. But the results of the GAO study and the subcommittee staff findings strongly suggest that FDA regulation of investigational new drugs has been lax and has not adequately protected the patients who take these drugs. They also show a failure to adopt safe testing procedures by certain drug companies, as well as resistance to FDA regulation. The FDA and the companies involved have shown a disregard for public safety which is incompatible with their responsibility to protect and promote public health.

Specifically, the report found that in eight cases, FDA failed to halt human tests after receiving indications that the drugs were not safe. As a result, over 2,000 people were exposed to the hazard of unsafe drugs. GAO further found that the drug companies unnecessarily delayed reporting adverse drug effects to FDA and that once this data was received, FDA did not require necessary patient followup in six cases to protect the health of the people who had been given suspect or unsafe drugs.

Since the passage of the Kefauver-Harris amendments of 1962, the law has required the FDA to regulate the use of all drugs shipped in interstate commerce for investigational use on human beings. Under FDA procedures established pursuant to this statute, FDA has required the sponsor— usually a drug company, but in some cases an institution, such as NIH—to submit an investigational new drug application before such shipment could take place. Prior to August 14, 1970, a sponsor could begin clinical experiments on human subjects immediately upon submission of its application— that is, prior to any FDA review of its data. Since August 14, 1970, however, FDA has required sponsors to wait 30 days after submission of an IND application before initiating human testing. No positive FDA approval is required once 30 days have passed, and sponsors may initiate such testing unless FDA has affirmatively directed them not to do so.

FDA's procedures for the testing of investigational new drugs are divided into three phases:

Phase I covers the first trials in human subjects. This trial is normally limited to a group of 20 to 50 healthy people. If the results are satisfactory, testing proceeds to phase II.

Phase II involves testing the drug on 100–200 patients with the disease the drug is expected to treat. If phase II results are satisfactory, testing may proceed to phase III.

Phase III involves expanded trials on a much larger group of patients. It is not uncommon for phase III testing to include several thousand patients.

Before an experimental drug may be administered to human beings, it must first be given to animals. Prior animal testing is required because there is often some correlation between the ability of a drug to produce adverse effects in animals and its ability to produce such effects in human beings. While the precise relationship between animal results and human results is often indeterminate, it is clear that a drug that has been shown to produce cancerous tumors in animals presents a greater potential risk to human beings than a drug that has shown no adverse health effects in animals.

Current FDA regulations require both substantial animal testing and substantial human testing before a drug is approved for general public sale, rather than investigational use. Under current FDA practice, a drug may be administered to human beings in phase I studies for up to 2 weeks after only 2 weeks of animal studies and prior to full evaluation of those animals studies. Human subjects in phase I and phase II experiments may be given the drug for up to 3 months after only 1 month of animal studies, and may be given a drug for an unlimited period after only 3 months of animal studies. Phase III subjects may be given the drug for an unlimited period after only 6 months of animal studies.

The GAO study contains a comprehensive discussion of each of the drugs it reviewed. . . .

The GAO survey showed a consistent pattern for FDA delay in reviewing the data submitted with the IND application. For Practolol, the delay was 3 months. For Triflocin, it was 8 months. In both cases, animals given the drugs developed cancerous conditions. For the other drugs reviewed, the delay ranged from 4 months to a full year. During this time, the drug companies routinely began human testing. . . .

The most dramatic example of FDA's failure to halt human testing after notice of evidence of cancer in animal tests is the drug Practolol, sponsored by Ayerst Labs. When the test data was reviewed, the medical officer concluded that "this study is indefensible and unacceptable." On March 11, 1970, FDA recommended to the sponsor that human testing be discontinued. Testing continued. On April 8, FDA again advised the sponsor to discontinue testing, but the sponsor refused. At that time, the sponsor submitted to FDA the results of a study showing that cancerous tumors had been found in mice. (Ayerst had notice and substantial documentation of the results of this study on August 14, 1969, but had failed to provide it to FDA until nearly 8 months later. By contrast, the Canadian Food and Drug authorities had had possession of the study since August 27, 1969.) Still, FDA took no effective action to terminate testing on human subjects.

In January 1971, FDA tried for a third time to persuade the sponsor to discontinue tests on human beings. Ayerst not only refused to discontinue the tests, but also refused even to make the finding of the mouse study—indicating cancerous tumors—available to the doctors who were conducting the experiments. Those doctors thus had no way of evaluating the risks to which their patients were being subject. Finally, on August 27, 1971, fully 17 months after FDA had first advised the Ayerst to discontinue testing, and after a fourth request from FDA to discontinue, the tests were stopped.

This case is not unique. Another similar case history is that of Oxprenalol Hydrochloride, sponsored by Merrell-National Labs. In this case, it took the FDA 6 months and two requests to stop human testing after tumors had been found in mice. . . .

The GAO found that the time lag between discovery of the effects of human and animal tests and reporting them to FDA ranged from 40 days to 19 months. The case of Triflocin, sponsored by Lederle Labs, was typical. There, the sponsor took 7 months to analyze the results of a study which eventually showed bladder cancer in rats. Meanwhile, human testing was in progress, FDA concluded that the delay was "not unjustified because such delays were apparently stan-

dard operating procedure for this company. FDA stated that it "did not consider the delay unusual." The fact that the delay was not unusual, rather than supporting a finding that it was justified, seems to point to the very opposite conclusion.

With respect to Practolol, sponsored by Ayerst Labs, the sponsor failed for 8 months to supply FDA with the results of a study showing cancerous tumors in mice.

In the case of MK-665, an oral contraceptive sponsored by Merck, Sharp and Dome Research, the sponsor waited over a month before notifying FDA that cancer had been found in dogs treated with the drug. The Justice Department declined to bring a criminal prosecution in this matter. . . .

Ribicoff insisted that the FDA "should more closely monitor all human testing" and require test sponsors to perform follow-up checks on FDA orders. Companies that failed to perform proper follow-up tests should be disqualified as IND (investigational new drug) sponsors, Ribicoff declared. He said:

"Several of the cases reported by GAO illustrate the need for these steps. One of them was MK-665, sponsored by Merck, Sharp and Dome, which was shown to cause breast cancer in dogs. Only about one-third of the patients who received the drug in clinical tests have been examined.

"Another is Hexobendine. When dogs which were given the drug developed cataracts, human testing was halted in September 1971. The sponsor, Merrell-National Labs, resisted an FDA request to do a follow-up on all patients who received the drug. As of December 22, 1972, 48 percent of the patients who had received followup eye examinations showed evidence of cataract development. While it cannot be said with certainty that this cataract development was drug related, as of March 1973, only 48 percent of the persons who had received Hexobendine had received eye examinations. The FDA regarded this followup as inadequate. (One problem the FDA encountered with respect to Hexobendine was that no one—neither FDA nor the sponsor—seemed to know precisely how many people had taken the drug, how long they had taken it, and when it had been administered.)

"One of the most flagrant cases of a drug company's resistance to FDA with respect to followup is that of Cinanserin, sponsored by E. R. Squibb & Sons. Human testing had been discontinued in August 1969, because of the appearance of tumors in the livers of rats. In October 1969, Squibb informed FDA that it was not considering followup. According to a letter of July 30, 1970, from the FDA Commissioner Edwards to Squibb, the question of followup had been raised by FDA with Squibb in a telephone conversation on December 9, 1969, with Dr. Lawrence Marks, a Squibb vice president. According to the letter, "he—Marks—stated that he would investigate and call back in a week. There was no reply."

"Squibb continued to resist FDA's suggested followup procedures. As a result of Squibb's refusal, FDA medical officers recommended a full evaluation of Squibb's qualifications to be a sponsor of any investigational new drugs, because of its failure to fulfill its responsibility to patients placed in jeopardy.

"After several FDA letters had gone unanswered, FDA officers visited the Squibb facility in New Brunswick, N.J., on June 26, 1972. As of November 17, 1972, the FDA still considered Squibb's followup on Cinanserin inadequate. It is noteworthy, however, that throughout this protracted and sometimes heated disagreement, FDA relied exclusively on persuasion in attempting to require a followup. In the absence of regulations requiring followup, FDA apparently felt itself powerless to act more vigorously. FDA could have at any point, however, required followup as a condition of IND approval or required followup by regulation. Thus, the agency's inability to require followup was a direct result of its own inaction.

Realizing that its lack of followup regulation was leaving patients unprotected and

that drug companies would not voluntarily perform adequate followup, FDA contracted with the National Academy of Sciences for a study to be conducted by an NAS committee. The committee was formed in April 1972. Its chairman was Dr. Lawrence Marks, the Squibb vice president who had participated in the controversy over followup on Cinanserin.

"As mentioned previously, after receiving no reply to a series of letters asking Squibb to undertake further followup, on June 26, 1972, FDA officials visited the Squibb plant in New Brunswick, N.J. According to a memorandum dated June 29, 1972, by an FDA inspector, Dr. Marks telephoned the inspector from Squibb headquarters in Princeton while the inspector was at the New Brunswick plant. According to the memorandum, Dr. Marks advised the inspector of his position as chairman of the NAS committee studying the very question of followup. The memorandum continues:

> In view of this, Dr. Marks did not feel that as a representative of Squibb, he should commit the firm to a followup procedure until such a procedure is standard throughout the industry. He further supports this belief in that he feels that the FDA is not completely sure as to what followup should be made as evidenced by the fact that they set up the NAS Committee. Dr. Marks said that he had advised Dr. Marion Finkel (an FDA official) of his position several weeks ago and questioned the need for our assignment.

"Dr. Marks confirmed to the subcommittee his conversation with Dr. Finkel and stated that he does not remember the conversation with the inspector. It was confirmed, however, by the two other FDA employees. At the time of the conversation, June 26, 1972, Dr. Marks was still Chairman of the NAS Committee. He subsequently resigned in August 1972, for reasons unrelated to the Cinanserin followup problem.

"It was poor policy for FDA to tolerate a situation where the chairman of a committee established and financed by FDA for the purpose of recommending followup procedures is at the same time personally attempting, on behalf of his firm, to dissuade FDA from requiring followup examinations in a particular case. It is clear that responsible officials at the FDA were quite aware of Dr. Marks' dual role. . . . ''

New law monitors research. President Richard M. Nixon July 12, 1974 signed into law the recently approved National Research Act, which created a commission to monitor the use of human subjects in biomedical research and established a biomedical research training awards program. The bill had been passed by the Senate 72–14 June 27 and by the House 311–10 June 28.

The first U.S. legislation ever to consider the ethical questions of medical research, the act aimed at developing guidelines for research involving humans. A temporary, two-year commission appointed by the secretary of health, education and welfare (HEW)— to be succeeded July 1, 1976 by a permanent National Advisory Council for the Protection of Subjects of Biomedical and Behavioral Research—would study and make recommendations on controversial research and procedures. The temporary commission would pay close attention to research on children, prisoners, the mentally ill and live human fetuses, as well as psychosurgery, a brain operation designed to control behavior.

The commission would be without any power to enforce its recommendations and could be overruled by the HEW secretary, who would be only required to publish his reasons for rejecting the proposed guidelines. However, the permanent commission would not be obligated to publish its recommendations nor could it be overridden by the HEW secretary.

The act also required appointment of the 11-member temporary commission within 60 days of the bill's signing. Within four months of the members' appointment, the commission would recommend policies for research involving live human fetuses. Until these recommendations were presented, all fetal research using HEW funds would be prohibited, except to save the lives of infants.

HEW lifts fetal research ban. Acting on a recommendation from a national review board that conducted hearings on the subject, Caspar W. Weinberger, secretary of health, education and welfare, July 29, 1975 ended a 13-month ban on federally funded research with human fetuses.

The moratorium had begun in 1973 when the National Institutes of Health said April 17 that it had banned research by NIH-supported scientists on all live, aborted fetuses. The NIH had been studying guidelines, suggested in 1971 by an independent group of doctors, under which research would be permitted if the aborted fetus were not older the 20 weeks, were no larger than 500 grams (1.1 lbs.), and no longer than 25 cm. (9.8 in.). The presumption was that such fetuses were incapable of surviving.

The 1975 rules allowed experimentation with fetuses both inside the mother's womb and, in many cases, on aborted fetuses temporarily alive. Research was still prohibited on live fetuses if it would kill them, or keep them alive artificially.

If the fetus was still in the womb, the research had to be either necessary for keeping it alive, or to seek important facts which could not be learned otherwise. The regulations added that the experimentation must pose only "minimal" risk beyond any the fetus already faced.

The recommendations, which were first made by the National Commission on Protection of Human Subjects of Biomedical and Behavioral Research, were approved by Weinberger without major changes.

The rules required the mother's consent in all cases. They required the father's consent except where his identity could not be learned or if pregnancy resulted from rape.

Because risks to the fetus could be assessed differently in different cases HEW was charged by the commission to establish a set of national ethical review boards to review questionable research. The new rules applied only to HEW projects, but almost all fetal research was federally funded. Also, hospitals' ethical review committees genrally applied the same rules to all research as was applied to federal projects.

Opposition to the renewal of such research came, in large part, from anti-abortion groups, including the U.S. Catholic Conference, which maintained that no fetal research was ethical. The anti-abortion groups argued that a fetus was unable to give consent and that a woman planning an abortion had given up her right to decide what was done to the fetus.

However, an introduction to the new rules said a woman "may not be presumed to lack interest in her fetus" even if she had decided to opt for an abortion. Therefore, she could be "validly asked to consent for research."

The study commission heard a number of research reports on the usefulness of fetal research. One such report, made by the Battelle Institute of Columbus, Ohio, said that certain fetal research had saved the lives of hundreds of thousands of babies.

The report focused on four medical advances that resulted from such research. Included was a treatment of Rh hemolytic disease of the newborn. The disease resulted from an incompatibility of blood types between the mother and the fetus. Advances through fetal research eventually led to a vaccine that saved 450,000 fetuses between 1930 and 1975, the Battelle report said.

Also touched on in the report were the development, through fetal research, of a vaccine to fight rubella, a viral infection, and its resultant birth defects; research on a respiratory distress syndrome of newborns; and the development of amniocentesis, a technique for sampling fetus cells from the fluid surrounding the fetus of the womb. The director of the Battelle project said that none of the research could have been done on animals.

One member of the commission hearing the report said the study, submitted March 14, was the "most striking evidence we've heard yet on the potential future importance of fetal research."

Dr. Maurice J. Mahoney, a Yale scientist who was heading another research project for the commission, said there had been a "quantum jump" in fetal research in recent years. In the report, first submitted to the Commission for the Protection of Human Subjects Feb. 15, Mahoney cited over 1,000 studies worldwide. He attributed the rapid growth to advancing medical science and the legalizing of abortions that made fetuses more available.

"By far the smallest" number of studies, Mahoney said, was in one of the controversial areas of research involving the early fetus outside of the womb. Mahoney said he could only cite three studies in which fetuses were purposely kept artificially alive for a time. They were all part of attempts to develop a new type of fetal incubator for "test-tube births," where the mother could not herself carry the baby.

Another report made by a team of scientists headed by Dr. Richard Behrman, head of pediatrics at Columbia University, and presented to the commission March 15, said more prematurely born fetuses survived than was expected. The survey indicated that annually, several hundred babies might be surviving birth before the end of the first two-thirds of pregnancy in the U.S.

The report also said that research done on fetuses younger than 24 weeks still in the womb, and studies after birth on a fetus younger than 25 weeks, were biologically safe. No fetuses that young had been known to live more than minutes without artificial assistance, and none survived to leave the hospital, the report said.

Opposition to fetal experimentation continued, however. In its platform for 1976, the Republican Party said:

> While we support valid medical and biological research efforts which can produce life-saving results, we oppose any research on live fetuses. We are also opposed to any legislation which sanctions ending the life of any patient.

Massachusetts curbs fetal research—Gov. Francis Sargent of Massachusetts June 26, 1974 signed a bill prohibiting doctors from testing vaccines on developing fetuses.

Rep. William Delahunt, principal sponsor of the bill, said June 27 that the law would not interfere with most fetal research. He added that researchers should be grateful that the law was not as restrictive as a recently enacted Illinois statute barring research on living or dead human fetal tissue.

Dr. Michael N. Oxman, a Boston microbiologist, was critical of the new legislation. Vaccine studies, he contended June 28, "can only be done by administering the vaccine to women already planning abortions and then testing the fetal tissues to see if the vaccine reached the fetus."

HEW Amends Definition of Informed Consent. The Department of Health, Education and Welfare in 1978 proposed a revision of its definition of informed consent to include human subjects of medical and behavioral research which might involve injury. The regulation requires that information about the experiment be given to prospective subjects if they inquire, in order for the research to be eligible to receive HEW grants. In addition, institutions must designate an official from whom information can be obtained on compensation for and treatment of injury.

Controversial Experiments

Hepatitis breakthrough. Researchers at New York University's (NYU) Medical Center in New York reported March 29, 1971 that they had apparently succeeded in immunizing a handful of children against serum hepatitis, a highly infectious and sometimes fatal liver disease.

Serum hepatitis, one of two virus diseases that involved inflammation of the liver, affected more than 150,000 Americans a year, claiming about 3,000 lives. Unlike infectious hepatitis, which was spread through contaminated food and water, serum hepatitis was generally transmitted by blood transfusions from a carrier.

The breakthrough was announced by Dr Saul Krugman, head of the NYU research team.

In the tests described by Krugman, 14 retarded children at the Willowbrook State School were inoculated with a protective serum containing Australia antigen, a virus like particle associated with serum hepatitis Krugman said serum containing the antigen normally would transmit the disease, but tha boiling apparently eliminated the infectious ness factor without affecting its ability to stimulate antibodies in the body of a patien that protect against the disease.

Ten of the 14 were inoculated with a single shot. The single injection protected five of them against a subsequent injection of infecting serum. The other four children were inoculated twice. In each case the two injections gave complete protection when an attempt was made four months later to infect them.

Black men untreated in Tuskegee syphilis experiment. Some of the details of a U.S. syphilis study involving 600 Alabama black men that dated back to 1932 were made public July 25, 1972 in an Associated Press report.

According to AP reporter Jean Heller, the U.S. Public Health Service (PHS) conducted the study in which 400 black men with syphilis went untreated, even after a cure for the disease was known. The other 200 men, who had no syphilis, were monitored as a control group.

The study, Heller said, was organized to determine from autopsies what untreated syphilis did to the human body.

Dr. Merlin K. DuVal, assistant secretary of health, education and welfare for health and scientific affairs, said July 25 he would begin an investigation at once. Other federal health officials said they were giving whatever medical services they could to the project's survivors while they continued to chart the disease's course.

The experiment, known as the Tuskegee Study, was begin by the PHS in 1932 with 600 black men from Tuskegee, Ala. At that time, Tuskegee had the highest syphilis rate in the nation. The men were induced to join the program with promises of free lunches, free transportation, free medicine for any disease other than syphilis and free burial after autopsies were performed. Four hundred of the group had syphilis and never received deliberate treatment for it. The other 200 had no syphilis and received no specific therapy.

The study was begun 10 years before scientists found penicillin to be a cure for syphilis. But even after penicillin's healing qualities were known, the group of 400 with syphilis were not treated with it.

According to the AP report, a 1969 study by the PHS's Center for Disease Control in Atlanta found that seven men of the original syhilitic group of 400 had died of the disease. Another 154 died of heart failure that U.S. health officials said was not specifically related to syphilis.

A Health, Education & Welfare Department (HEW) advisory panel said in a report made public June 13, 1973 that the syphilis study had been "ethically unjustified." The panel recommended that a permanent governmental authority be established to regulate all federally supported research involving human subjects.

CIA subject of LSD experiment committed suicide in 1953. The widow and the children of a Central Intelligence Agency (CIA) employee who killed himself in 1953 after unknowingly taking LSD in a job-related experiment learned the circumstances of his death only after reading the Rockefeller Commission report on CIA activities, published in June 1975, according to July 10 news accounts.

The family of Frank R. Olson—his wife, Alice, his sons Nils and Eric and his married daughter Lisa Hayward—decided after weeks of discussion to contact reporters "to get the story out, so our father's friends and colleagues—and also our friends—could know what the CIA has done," the New York Times July 10 quoted Eric Olson as saying. The Times also said that David W.

Belin, director of the Rockefeller panel, had confirmed Olson's death. Belin added: "The staff didn't feel it was necessary to talk to the family. They didn't know what it would add—once we found out what had happened."

In a statement given to reporters at the family home in Frederick, Md., Mrs. Olson said her husband had been a researcher for the CIA in biological warfare at nearby Fort Detrick, Md., and that two weeks before his death he had attended several days of meetings and had been given LSD "without his knowledge or consent." He returned home and "was very quiet, he was an entirely different person," Mrs. Olson said. 'I didn't know what had happened. I just knew that something was terribly wrong. The entire weekend he was very melancholy and talked about a mistake he had made. He said he was going to leave his job." During the following week, Olson was taken to New York City to consult Dr. Harold A. Abramson, a psychiatrist, and several days later his family was told he had committed suicide by jumping from the 10th floor of the Statler Hotel in Manhattan. Mrs. Olson declared that a CIA employee, her husband's escort, had told of waking up at 1:30 a.m. and seeing Olson run across the room and jump through both a closed window and a drawn shade.

The New York Times July 11 cited a 1953 police report by Detective James W. Ward which gave another version of Olson's visit to New York. It said he had arrived with Col. Vincent Ruwet, also attached to Fort Detrick, and had returned to Washington after two consultations with Dr. Abramson. When Olson came back to New York later that day, according to Ward's report, he was accompanied by a man who called himself Robert Lashbrook. "They again visited the doctor and as a result of this visit Olson was advised to enter a sanitarium as he was suffering from severe psychosis and delusions," Ward said. That night, Lashbrook told Ward, he woke up at about 3:20 a.m. to a "crash of glass," telephoned the hotel operator and, "at this time, learned that Olson had jumped out of the window."

The New York Times July 12 said the Olson family believed Lashbrook and a man they identified as Sidney Gottlieb had given the drug to Frank Olson, but the CIA refused to say whether either Lashbrook or Gottlieb had ever been employed by the agency.

The Washington Post July 13 reported a telephone interview the previous day with James Roethe, the attorney in charge of the Rockefeller Commission's study, who said the document did not contain all the panel had learned about CIA drug experiments. Roethe said: "I really don't feel that I'm going to be in a position to make a comment unless something so outrageous comes out that I feel I have to, and at this point I haven't seen anything." The Post printed a list of names, furnished by the Olson family, of those present at the 1953 meeting in which Frank Olson and others were given the LSD.

Lashbrook says Olson agreed—Robert V. Lashbrook, a former CIA employee who was with Frank Olson at the time of his suicide in 1953, said July 17 that Olson had agreed in principle beforehand to be the subject of an LSD experiment.

In a telephone interview with the New York Times, Lashbrook, now a high school science teacher in Ojai, Cal., declared: "It was my understanding that actually everyone there had agreed in advance that such a test would be conducted, that they were willing to be one of the subjects. The only thing was that the time was not specified." He said it would be misconstruing things quite a lot to say that any individual or group of individuals were the subject of anyone doing them in." In its account of the interview with Lashbrook, the New York Times July 18 quoted a section of the Rockefeller Commission report that said: "Prior to receiving the LSD, the subject [Olson] had participated in discussions where the testing of such substances on unsuspecting subjects was agreed to in principle. However, this individual was not aware that he had been

given LSD until about 20 minutes after it had been administered."

Lashbrook said he himself had been a "guinea pig" several times in LSD tests and "didn't like it." He noted, however, that any "direct relationship" between the drug and Olson's death "would be a little hard to justify" because Olson's body would have been eliminated of all elements of the drug long before his death, which took place more than a week after the experiment. "Possibly LSD had brought up something in his past that was bothering him," Lashbrook ventured.

The Washington Post July 18 reported that when asked who had decided to administer the drug to Olson and when, Lashbrook replied he was "not too sure" and that "in any case, I don't really want to name them."

Gottlieb destroyed LSD data—The New York Times July 18 reported that Dr. Sidney Gottlieb, a biochemist and former head of the CIA's program of testing LSD, had destroyed the program's records in 1973, ten years after the experiments were believed to have been halted.

The Times, alluding to sources on the staff of the Rockefeller Commission, said Gottlieb had thrown out a total of 152 separate files and that Richard Helms, then director of the agency, had also destroyed records.

Olson files released—Alice Olson, Frank Olson's widow, made public Jan. 10, 1976 the CIA documents that dealt with her husband's death. She had received the documents after President Ford ordered the CIA to turn them over to her.

The attorneys for the Olson family said that the documents, although containing "inaccuracies and self-serving statements," nevertheless "make it quite clear that Frank Olson was unknowingly given LSD by CIA officials as a result of which he died on Nov. 28, 1953, and that an intentional cover-up followed his death."

The cover-up charge rested on the decision of the CIA to give police investigating the death as little information as possible, so that it would be taken for a routine sui-ide. Also, a cover identity, as an Army consultant, was provided for the CIA agent with Olson at the time of his death.

The documents did not give firm answers to certain questions relating to Olson's death, or to the policy of the agency regarding the LSD experiments. It was not clear whether the CIA employees responsible for giving LSD to Olson had been reprimanded. A CIA official, Luis de Florez, had argued shortly after the death that "in the interest of maintaining the spirit of initiative and enthusiasm so necessary to our work," no reprimand should be issued. Documents dated Feb. 1954 seemed to indicate that Florez' view was adopted. However, documents apparently prepared in early 1975 stated that two employees had been reprimanded.

The documents also raised doubts whether there had been a review board for experiments "in which human lives could possibly be jeopardized." Allen W. Dulles, then director of the CIA, ordered one established after Olson's death, but there was no record in the documents of its establishment or functioning.

The documents described orders issued six months before Olson's death by two senior CIA officials, Richard Helms and Frank Wisner, requiring their permission for experiments involving LSD. Records showed, however, that neither official was notified before the experiment involving Olson.

The papers furnished to Mrs. Olson were only a small proportion of those which had originally existed on the case.

Army also tested LSD. News sources reported July 18, 1975 that the Department of the Army had conducted LSD experiments with some 1,500 persons in the 1950s and the 1960s, some of them at the Edgewood Arsenal in Maryland, the Army's chemical warfare research counterpart to Ft. Detrick, where Frank Olson was a CIA employee at the time of his death.

A total of 585 persons, most of them soldiers, were said to have participated in experiments at the Edgewood Arsenal, at Fort Bragg in North Carolina, Fort McClellan in Alabama, Dugway Proving Ground in Utah and Fort Benning in Georgia.

An additional 900 civilians were tested in Army-sponsored experiments at the University of Maryland Psychiatric Institute, the New York Psychiatric Institute, the University of Wisconsin, the University of Washington Medical School and the Tulane University Department of Neurology and Psychiatry.

The tests were reported to have been conducted between 1956 and 1967.

Army suspends drug test program—The Army said July 28 it was suspending drug and chemical experiments on human subjects in order to "determine all the facts connected with the test programs." The announcement said that the Army planned to find all those on whom it had tested LSD so that it could give them physical and mental exams to find out whether they had suffered any ill effects.

The New York Times reported July 29, however, that suspension of the testing had occurred partly because of questions raised about the background of the head of the research program, Dr. Van M. Sim, as well as queries from the press, members of Congress and former test subjects.

Sim, at a Pentagon press conference July 23, had defended the test program, which involved 900 civilian and 6,983 military volunteers over a 20-year period. The Army had ended its testing of LSD on humans in 1967, but continued experiments on soldiers with other drugs that produced hallucinations similar to those caused by LSD, said Sim, civilian medical research director at the Army's Edgewood Arsenal in northeastern Maryland.

Sim said none of 585 Army volunteers given LSD was told the name of the drug or that it sometimes produced side effects. To have identified the drug and its possible effects would have prejudiced the experiment, he said. (Sim added that follow-up studies had been done on 10% of the men, but he retracted this statement Aug. 2, saying he had made a mistake and that the Army had done a follow-up on only two test subjects.)

He said he considered the experiments "very important" to national security and did not consider them hazardous because the subjects were carefully supervised. He knew of no deaths or prolonged hospitalizations resulting from the LSD experiments, Sim said. Seven men subsequently showed side effects, but the doctors treating them were sent "full explanations" of the experiments, Sim said.

Sim, who said other test subjects in the Army's program were given drugs ranging from alcohol to barbiturates, claimed he was unfamiliar with the LSD experiments involving 900 civilians. These tests were conducted by universities and private institutions under Army contracts, he said.

Following Sim's news conference, the Army disclosed that 2,940 of the program's military volunteers had been tested with BZ (3-quinuclidinyl benzilate), a hallucinogenic drug more powerful than LSD. BZ, whose effects of disorientation and hallucinations lasted up to 80 hours, was developed for use in situations such as civilian riots, protection of military combat areas and military rescue missions, the Army stated. (No follow-up examinations on volunteers who took BZ were performed, the Army said Aug. 14.)

The Washington Post reported Aug. 3 that the Army had manufactured BZ in 1963–64 and was still stockpiling the drug at its Pine Bluff Arsenal in Arkansas. The Post said that the international protocols banning biological and toxic chemical weapons signed by President Ford Jan. 22 excluded several riot control agents, including BZ.

Nerve gas tests admitted—Dr. Sim Aug. 8 confirmed a report by Rep. Thomas J. Downey (D, N.Y.) that the Army had tested lethal nerve gas on soldiers at the Edgewood Arsenal without telling them exactly what the substance was. Downey said more than 1,000 human subjects had been exposed.

Sim described the nerve gas as similar to agricultural pesticides and claimed it was administered in small doses, with no resulting serious illness. The purpose of the tests, he said, was to develop antidotes for nerve gas. He added that information from the experiments, conducted between 1955 and 1967, had been widely utilized in the treatment of farmers and crop dusters exposed to lethal pesticides.

1953 fatality linked to drug test—The Army disclosed Aug. 12 that a patient in a New York City mental hospital had died in 1953 during an Army-sponsored experiment with a hallucinogenic drug. The patient, Harold Blauer, 42, died shortly after being injected with a derivative of mescaline, said the Army, which had not previously admitted sponsoring the experiment.

According to the Army, Blauer had been given the drug in a series of five tests at the New York State Psychiatric Institute by civilian physicians working under an Army contract with the institute. The first four tests, the Army said, produced mild or no effects. However, Blauer apparently suffered an allergic reaction on the fifth test and his cardiovascular system collapsed.

Army officials indicated they could not say whether Blauer, a tennis pro, had consented to the experiment. One of his daughters, Elizabeth Barrett, 35, said she remembered being told that the drugs were administered on his doctor's orders.

Blauer's widow, who was never told of the Army's involvement, sued the New York State Department of Mental Hygiene and the institute but later settled out of court for $13,000.

The daughter, who said she was only 13 years old at the time of her father's death, recalled being told by her mother (who died in 1974) that her father had received LSD. In addition, she said her mother had said that her father had been given experimental drugs twice before his death and had reacted badly both times. She said her father "absolutely" had not volunteered for the experiment.

Project Sanguine report. Sen. Gaylord Nelson (D, Wis.) Dec. 10, 1975 made public the results of a 1973 scientific inquiry into the effects of the Navy's Project Sanguine on the human body. Project Sanguine, also known as Project Seafarer, was a proposed system by which the Navy would use low-frequency radio waves to communicate with its submarines. The proposal had come under strong attack from environmentalists.

The Navy had commissioned a seven-member panel of scientists in 1973 to assess the biological consequences of the project at its Wisconsin test site. The panel found that low-frequency radiation raised the level of triglycerides in the blood of six of eight people working near the site. Triglycerides, a blood fat related to cholesterol, had been linked to heart disease.

Nelson charged the Navy with suppressing the panel's findings. "For at least the last two years," he said, "I have asked admirals who have visited my office about Sanguine, whether there was anything to indicate that the system had adverse environmental impact and was told there was nothing."

The Sanguine project head, Navy Capt. W. C. Cobb, denied any coverup. He added that "we do not think that harmful, adverse effects" from Sanguine-type emissions "have ever been validated."

Plutonium tested in humans in 1940s. The Energy Research and Development Administration (ERDA) had confirmed that the government injected plutonium into human subjects from 1945 to 1947 to determine what the poisonous, radioactive substance would do to workers manufacturing the atom bomb, The Washington Post reported Feb. 22, 1976.

The injections were administered in varying quantities to eighteen persons (13 males and 5 females) ranging in age from four to 68. All were believed suffering from terminal illnesses.

Officials of the ERDA said records on the experiment were so unclear that it was not known how the subjects were selected or who ordered the tests. The ERDA could

only be certain that one person had consented to the injection.

According to a fact sheet prepared by the ERDA, the purpose of the experiment was to gather information that would permit scientists to determine the amount of plutonium to which humans could safely be exposed.

The fact sheet said that seven persons who received injections lived less than one year afterward; three lived between one and three years; two between 14 and 20 years; and one 28 years. The fate of two was unknown, and three were still living.

A-tests on prisoners—ERDA confirmed Feb. 28 that its predecessor, the Atomic Energy Commission, had used 131 prisoners in radiation experiments in the 1960s.

According to the ERDA, the AEC beamed x-rays into the testicles of 131 prisoners in Oregon and Washington to see if heavy radiation could cause sterility. A spokesman for the ERDA said that the prisoners had given written consent to the experiment and later undergone vasectomies to avoid fathering deformed children due to the damage caused by the test on their reproductive systems.

It is unknown whether the radiation produced cancer in any of the subjects because no comprehensive follow-up studies had been made.

Unethical Radiation Tests Charged. Government scientists who from 1957 to 1974 exposed up to 194 cancer patients to high-dose radiation, did so at least part of that time in order to provide the National Aeronautics and Space Administration with information about the limits of human tolerance to radiation, according to a magazine article published Aug. 20.

NASA began providing funds for the Oak Ridge, Tenn. federal cancer center in 1964. The center, which had opened in 1957, gradually shifted its focus under NASA influence from providing last-resort treatment for terminally ill leukemia patients to providing radiation test results for the space program, the Mother Jones article charged. The article cited an internal Oak Ridge report that referred to an "urgent need" by NASA for human clinical data on radiation exposure.

Between 1964 and 1974 NASA paid the center $2.3 million. Previously, the center had been funded entirely by the Atomic Energy Commission, predecessor of the Nuclear Regulatory Commission.

The Oak Ridge facility was closed in 1974, reportedly for economic reasons. An AEC inspection report in March of that year labeled the program "dismal" and cited "ethical questions" raised by its use of experimental techniques.

The treatments given to the unwitting cancer patients included total-body radiation doses of up to 500 rads over a period of hours, according to the article by Howard Rosenberg. A dose of 450 rads in a single exposure was estimated to be fatal to approximately half the people exposed.

Another experimental treatment involved an unproven procedure for transplanting irradiated bone marrow.

Some of those patients, Rosenberg wrote, might have been given extreme radiation treatments before it was determined whether they would have responded to standard treatments such as chemotherapy. The patients were in effect being used as guinea pigs, he charged, to protect astronauts from suffering ill effects from radiation exposure while in space.

Documents he had obtained under the Freedom of Information Act showed that the Oak Ridge scientists had little expectation of beneficial results to the patients from the mass radiation, Rosenberg argued. One document quoted in the article was a report to the AEC written by scientists at the center in 1957, before NASA became involved in the program. Stating that the exposures to high doses of radiation were not expected "to produce better clinical results," the report said: "At present we feel that some pattern of fractionated exposure . . . probably offers a preferable approach."

Drugs

Introduction:

The sale of medicines has almost always been a lucrative business. In many cases, it is charged that alleged medicines actually do harm rather than good—sometimes because the potion itself is harmful, other times because a useless medicine, even if basically harmless, might keep the user from seeking effective treatment.

These two situations give rise to the two major legal issues raised by drugs of purported or questionable medical value: whether patients should have access at all to drugs whose medical effectiveness has not been proved, and product liability—whether a manufacturer knew or should have known of the risks posed by a drug, yet sold the drug anyhow.

The issue of product liability is illustrated here by the controversy that has erupted over diethylstilbesterol (DES), a synthetic estrogen that was given to pregnant women in the 1950s and 1960s, sometimes without their knowledge, because it was believed to prevent miscarriages. DES has been linked to cancer in the daughters of women who took the drug.

Laetrile is the most prominent example of the legal controversy over access to drugs of unproven medical value. Claims that laetrile is useful in treatment of cancer are as yet unsubstantiated by FDA testing. Currently, the sale of laetrile is banned in most states, forcing patients who want to use it to travel to Mexico for expensive treatments. The issue confronted by courts, and by state legislatures deciding whether to legalize laetrile is whether the privacy rights of terminally ill patients allows them to choose their method of treatment, or whether reliance on an unproven drug would prevent patients from seeking other treatment currently recognized more valuable by physicians.

The issues of product liability and access are represented primarily by cases and news items about DES and laetrile, respectively, as well as a few items on medical uses of marijuana. The last section of this chapter, Cost-Benefit Standards, illustrates trends in the making of regulatory decisions.

Product Liability

DES

Courts split on liability issue in DES actions. The widespread use of drugs in the United States over the past few years, coupled with the growing numbers of drug manufacturing companies, has presented the courts with new problems arising out of products liability suits brought against the drug companies. Typical of these problems have been the issues raised by lawsuits concerning DES.

During the 1950s and 1960s, diethylstilbestrol (DES) and related drugs were widely given to expectant mothers to prevent spontaneous abortions. Studies in the late 1960s began to connect the use of DES with a rare and malignant form of cancer and other abnormalities of the reproductive organs of the female offspring of DES users. In 1971, the federal Food and Drug Administration (FDA) ordered the drug companies to cease promoting DES for preventing miscarriages and to warn physicians and the public of the danger posed by its use by pregnant women. In the past few years numerous suits have been brought by women whose mothers used DES, resulting in a statistically high probability of abnormality or cancer in the plaintiffs. Common to all of these suits has been the inability of the plaintiffs to identify the particular manufacturer of the drug taken by their mothers. Frequently, however, the plaintiffs have been able to identify the possible manufacturers of the drug, and have sued them together under theories of shared liability. The cases below demonstrate how some courts have dealt with this problem.

In *Sindell v. Abbott Laboratories* (Cal. 1980), the California Supreme Court reversed a lower court dismissal of a class action brought by daughters of DES users against the drug's manufacturers. The plaintiffs brought two claims against eleven drug companies. First, the plaintiffs alleged that each of the drug companies was individually negligent in its sale of DES without adequate testing or warning. Second, the plaintiffs claimed that all of the defendant companies were liable regardless of which particular brand of DES the plaintiffs' mothers had taken, because the defendants had "collaborated in marketing, promoting and testing the drug, relied upon each other's tests, and adhered to an industry-wide safety standard." The plaintiffs also claimed that DES was "produced from a common and mutually agreed upon formula," and that the defendants "knew or should have known that it was customary for doctors to prescribe the drug by its generic name rather than its brand name and that pharmacists filled prescriptions with whatever brand of the drug happened to be in stock."

The California high court held that although the plaintiffs could not trace their injury to a particular manufacturer of DES, all of the manufacturers could be held jointly liable in proportion to their share of the DES market. The court placed on defendants the burden of disproving their liability by showing that they could not possibly have produced the drug that caused the plaintiffs' injury. The court stated three major policy reasons for this allocation of the burden of proof. First, California precedent held that "as between an innocent plaintiff and negligent defendants, the latter should bear the cost of injury." Second, the court found that the "defendants are better able to bear the cost of injury resulting from the manufacture of a defective product." Third, the court noted that, in situations involving fungible, mass-produced medications, "the consumer is virtually helpless to protect himself. . . ." Thus, the California court chose to place the legal and financial burden on the party it saw as most able to bear it. Later in 1980, the United States Supreme Court declined to review the California Surpeme Court's decision.

Also in 1980, the Michigan Court of Appeals reversed a lower court's dismissal of a DES suit in *Abel v. Eli Lilly Co.* (Mich. Ct. App. 1980). That case also involved a class action by daughters of DES users against all of the known manufacturers of DES who sold that drug in Michigan during the relevant time period. The plaintiffs stated two claims. First, they put forward the "alternative liability" theory relied upon in *Sindell*, alleging that each individual manufacturer had acted wrongfully, and therefore all should be liable where their individual harms could not be distinguished. Second, the plaintiffs claimed that the defendant companies "acted in concert to produce and market ineffective and dangerous products without adequate testing and without adequate warnings.

The Michigan court held that these claims stated a proper cause of action, and therefore the case should not have been dismissed by the trial court. As the California court did, the Michigan court held that the alternative liability theory would shift the burden of proof to the defendants to disprove their involvement with the plaintiffs' injuries. The court noted that, in order to prevail, the plaintiffs must show "that each manufacturer breached its duty of care in producing the product, that the harm to each woman was the result of the ingestion of DES by her mother, and that one or more of the named manufacturers made the DES so ingested."

The New Jersey courts have been divided in their treatment of DES cases. In 1980, the New Jersey Court, in *Ferriguo v. Eli Lilly & Co.* (N.J. Sup'r. 1980), followed the *Sindell* court's lead and refused to dismiss a case against several drug companies arising out of DES-related injuries. The plaintiffs alleged that the defendant drug companies had been negligent in producing, testing, marketing, and labeling their drugs. Although acknowledging their inability to identify the particular manufacturer of the drug causing their injuries, the plaintiffs relied on the market-share theory of liability adopted by the California court in *Sindell*.

Citing New Jersey's "strong policy which favors recovery by innocently injured plaintiffs who could not otherwise recover because they cannot identify the source of their injuries," the Superior Court held for the plaintiffs. Consistent with other New Jersey precedent, the court held that the burden of proof would shift to the defendants to exculpate themselves if the plaintiffs could prove certain necessary facts. Those facts were the same ones cited by the Michigan court in *Abel*. In addition, the plaintiffs would have to show that each defendant manufactured or marketed DES sold in New Jersey during the relevant time period, and that the drug was sold as a miscarriage preventative. The court also held that FDA approval of the marketing of the drug, though relevant, would not conclusively exonerate the defendants from claims of negligence.

Seven months after the *Ferriguo* decision, the New Jersey Superior Court's Appellate Division decided the case of *Nambe v. Charles E. Frosst & Co.* (N.J. Sup'r. A.D. 1981). There the plaintiffs relied on the "alternative liability" theory applied in the cases above. They also put forth the theory of "enterprise liability" based on the claim that the acceptance of DES by the medical profession and the unsuspecting public was the consequence of a cumulative effort by all who entered the market as manufacturers. . . ." Thus, in most respects, these plaintiffs' claims closely resembled those in *Sindell*. The New Jersey court, however, rejected those theories and held for the defendants by affirming the dismissal of the case.

The Appellate Division pointed out that although over 300 companies had been engaged in the manufacture of DES, the plaintiffs had brought suit against only 74 companies. The court stated that alternative liability was not appropriate since plaintiffs had not joined all the parties who might possibly have been responsible for their injuries. Thus, it was "pure and undistinguished speculation" to assume that one of the named defendants was necessarily responsible for the injuries. The court also rejected the enterprise liability theory as contrary to all legal precedent and principle. Such a theory, the court objected, would "result in the total abandonment of the well settled principle that manufacturers are only responsible for damages caused by a defective product upon proof that the product was defective and that the defect arose while the product was in the control of the defendant."

Women sue over DES experiment. Three women April 25, 1977 filed a $77 million class action lawsuit against the University of Chicago and Eli Lilly & Co. The plaintiffs charged that during pregnancy they and 1,078 other women had been given DES without their knowledge.

The women had been given the drug while receiving prenatal care at the school's Lying-In Hospital in Chicago in 1951 and 1952. The suit charged that none of the women had been advised that she was participating in a 20-month experiment to test the ability of DES to prevent miscarriages. In the experiment, an equal number of women had been given placebos.

The suit was filed in U.S. District Court in Chicago by attorneys for the Health Research Groups, a unit of Ralph Nader's Public Citizen Inc. One of the three plaintiffs was Patsy Mink, a former Democratic congresswoman from Hawaii and currently an assistant secretary of state.

Ironically, the university had concluded as a result of its 1951-52 study that DES was ineffective in preventing miscarriages and discontinued hospital use of the drug.

The university April 26 said a National Institutes of Health-sponsored follow-up survey of 1,250 offspring of the DES mothers had found no evidence of vaginal or cervical cancer in their daughters nor any indication of genital deformity or sterility in their sons.

The university said it had begun contacting the women involved in the DES experiment in 1971 after the Food and Drug Administration banned its prescription for pregnant women.

Mink received a form letter of notification, dated Jan. 29, 1976, in Honolulu March 5, 1976. The letter urged her to have her daughter examined by a physician. It was later found that the 23-year-old woman was afflicted with adenosis, an often pre-cancerous condition also linked to DES offspring.

Lilly, the drug manufacturer, April 27 said its "only involvement" in the university study "was in furnishing the DES and placebos that were used."

Suit dismissed. Wayne County (Mich.) Circuit Court Judge Thomas Roumell May 16, 1977 rejected a $625 million damage suit filed by 144 women and 40 of their husbands. The suit charged that the women had contracted cancer because their mothers had taken DES during pregnancy.

Roumell dismissed the lawsuit because of each woman's inability to identify either a specific DES brand name or manufacturer responsible for her particular illness. The judge ruled in Detroit that the women could not jointly sue the 16 pharmaceutical firms named solely because they all had produced the carcinogenic hormone.

Since DES had not been patented by those who first had manufactured it, the product had been sold under its generic (chemical) name, not under brand names. As a result, lawyers for the women could not pin responsibility for a specific case of DES-related illness on a specific source of the drug. The lawsuit, filed in 1974, had contended that the drug manufacturers were jointly liable for any cancer or other medical problems the women had developed as a result of their mothers having taken DES.

Attorneys for the women had argued for industry-wide liability. They maintained that the drug firms had promoted and sold DES in a negligent manner aware that it contained a cancer-causing agent called stilbene.

Michigan, with some 85,000 DES daughters, had been a test market for the drug, which had been prescribed to prevent miscarriages. All the female plaintiffs had undergone surgery for removal of cancerous or precancerous lesions.

In the 1981 New York case of *Bichler v. Eli Lilly & Co.* (N.Y. Sup. Ct. A.D. 1981) a New York appellate court applied an expansion of the concerted action theory recognized in *Abel*, and affirmed a verdict for a DES plaintiff brought against a single drug company. As in the previous cases, the plaintiff was unable to identify the particular manufacturer of the DES taken by her mother. The plaintiff was able to show, however, that the defendant company had engaged in concerted action with twelve other drug companies by pooling information, agreeing on the basic formula for the drug, and the other companies' adoption of Lilly's package inserts for joint submission to the FDA for approval.

The New York court held that this evidence established that "these manufacturers were acting on behalf of all later manufacturers." Furthermore, evidence of later "conscious parallel activity" by other manufacturers who entered the DES market established the defendant's involvement in concerted action. Therefore, the court held, the defendant "is jointly and severally liable as but one of a number of wrongdoers. Despite the fact that Lilly may not be the direct cause of the woman's injury, imposition of liability is not unfair. It is a plaintiff's option to proceed against any joint tortfeasor."

In 1982, the Massachusetts Supreme Judicial Court was faced with four state law questions posed by the Federal District Court for the District of Massachusetts, which was hearing a DES suit. *Payton v. Abbott Laboratory* (Mass. 1982) involved a class action by women who had been exposed to DES *in utero,* thus creating a statistically high probability that those women would develop abnormalities or cancers of the reproductive organs. The women sought to recover against six drug companies which manufactured and distributed DES in Massachusetts. The plaintiffs claimed that they suffered emotional distress due to their anxieties regarding the increased likelihood of developing abnormalities or cancers. The Massachusetts Supreme Judicial Court found that the drug companies would not be liable for such emotional distress under Massachusetts law.

The Massachusetts high court held, with three justices dissenting to this part of the decision, that negligently caused emotional distress without any physical harm is not compensible. This determination was based on policy grounds that emotional disturbances alone is too easily feigned, and that mere negligence was not a sufficient basis for exposing the defendants to liability when there was no physical harm. The court also held that the plaintiffs could not recover if the trier of the fact found that the plaintiffs would not have been born but for their mothers' use of DES to avoid miscarriage.

"The provider of the probable means of a plaintiff's very existence should not be liable for unavoidable, collateral consequences of the use of that means."

The Supreme Judicial Court found that Massachusetts law allows for recovery for prenatal injuries to plaintiffs. The court, however, rejected the plaintiffs' "market share" theory of liability, approved by the courts in *Sindell* and *Ferriguo.* The Massachusetts court objected that the plaintiffs' theory failed to distinguish between guilty and innocent manufacturers, and could lead to the eight named defendants being liable for more injury than they caused. The court further noted that such liability might threaten the development and marketing of other generic drugs.

DES Threat Called Less Serious. The cancer threat to daughters of women who took synthetic DES (diethylstilbestrol) in pregnancy was less than earlier believed, a Boston pathologist said March 6, 1979.

Dr. Stanley J. Robboy of Massachusetts General Hospital, reporting on a two-year study conducted at four medical centers, said that only four cancers of the genital tract were found among a total of 3,339 daughters of women who took DES. In one group of 1,275 daughters who were studied thoroughly, no cancers were found.

Dr. Robboy said, "The results are very encouraging." His study was financed by the Department of Health, Education and Welfare and published in the March issue of Obstetrics and Gynecology.

Other Products Liability Issues

Tampon Manufacturer Held Liable. A federal jury April 21, 1982, found Procter & Gamble Co., the manufacturer of Rely tampons, liable for the toxic shock syndrome death of a 25-year old woman. The jury awarded $300,000 in actual damages to the victim's family.

The case, in a Cedar Rapids, Iowa federal district court, was the second of more than

400 similar suits against Procter & Gamble to come to court.

The plaintiff, Michael Kehm, was awarded no punitive damages. He had originally sought $30 million in punitive and compensatory damages.

Kehm's wife, Patricia, had died in September 1980, four days after using Rely tampons.

Kehm's attorneys had claimed that Rely had not been adequately tested for safety. They argued that Procter & Gamble had known as early as July 1980 that Rely was linked with toxic shock syndrome deaths, and said it had been negligent in not withdrawing the product or warning the public of the possible danger.

Attorneys for Procter & Gamble had questioned the reliability of scientific evidence linking Rely to toxic shock syndrome. They also had denied that Patricia Kehm died of toxic shock syndrome, saying her death was the result of an infection caused by the use of an intrauterine contraceptive device.

Retrial Ordered in 1st Rely Case—A federal judge June 4 ordered that the first toxic shock syndrome suit against Procter & Gamble Co. be retried after the jury reached a contradictory verdict.

The jury in a Denver federal court March 19 had found Procter & Gamble negligent and had ruled that Rely tampons were defective. But, in an unusual move, the jury had awarded no damages to the plaintiff, who said she had suffered from toxic shock syndrome as a result of using Rely tampons.

Judge Sherman G. Finesilver threw out the jury's verdict and ordered a new trial.

Deletha Lampshire, an 18-year old University of Denver student, had sued Procter & Gamble for $25 million in damages. She had claimed that her physical and emotional health had been permanently damaged by contracting the disease after using Rely tampons.

Procter & Gamble had argued that Lampshire's illness resulted from influenza complications and that she had never suffered

from toxic shock syndrome. It also held that no clear link had been proven between toxic shock syndrome and Rely tampons.

Playtex Settles Toxic Shock Suit—The International Playtex unit of Esmark Inc. had agreed to pay an estimated $500,000 to the family of a woman who died of toxic shock syndrome, the Wall Street Journal reported Jan. 11.

The agreement settled a $2.5 million wrongful death suit brought against the company by the family of Janice Ritter. The suit claimed that Ritter's death in November 1980 had been caused by the use of Playtex deodorant tampons.

The settlement had been reached less than one month before the case had been scheduled to go to court in Muskogee, Okla.

Record Toxic Shock Award. A California jury awarded $10.5 million in damages to a woman who had suffered from toxic shock syndrome after using tampons made by a unit of Johnson & Johnson, the Wall Street Journal reported Dec. 24.

Lynette West had been hospitalized for a week in 1980 with kidney problems, nausea, a sharp drop in blood pressure and various other symptoms associated with toxic shock. She had since recovered, but her lawyers claimed that the syndrome recurred in three out of 10 cases and its long-term effects were unknown.

Half a million dollars of the award was compensatory damages, the $10 million was punitive damages. The size of the award was a surprise, since the largest previous award in a toxic shock case, $500,000, went to the family of a woman who had died as a result of toxic shock.

The jury foreman said the award was intended to serve as "a reminder to other companies to please test their products before marketing them."

Arthritis Drug Withdrawn. Eli Lilly & Co. Aug. 4, 1982, voluntarily agreed to suspend the sale of its controversial anti-arthritis drug Oraflex.

The action followed by only a few hours a decision by British health authorities to ban the sale of the drug for 90 days in Great Britain, pending review of its possible adverse health effects.

Pressure on Eli Lilly & Co. had escalated as the number of deaths linked to use of the drug reached nine in the U.S. and 61 in Great Britain.

Three groups had filed suit in federal district court in Washington, D.C. Aug. 2, seeking to force Health and Human Services Secretary Richard S. Schweiker to ban the sale of Oraflex immediately. The groups were the Health Research Group, the American Public Health Association and the 13.5-million-member National Council of Senior Citizens.

Dr. Sidney Wolfe of the Health Research Group Aug. 4 said, "It is about time they did something. It is too bad that so many people had to die or be injured."

Wolfe asserted that Eli Lilly and the Food and Drug Administration had ignored reports of at least 27 deaths from the use of the drug in Great Britain when the FDA approved it for marketing in the U.S.

Eli Lilly had denied knowing about the British reports, and the FDA said it did not have the resources to solicit medical information from countries where a drug had been in use.

Despite the suspension of Oraflex sales, a spokesman for Eli Lilly said "The company continues to believe the drug is safe and effective when used as prescribed."

Eli Lilly Prosecution Recommended—A government investigator had recommended in September 1981 that Eli Lilly & Co. be prosecuted for failure to report adverse reactions to four of its new drugs, including Oraflex. That recommendation was disclosed at a House subcommittee hearing Aug. 3.

Rep. L.H. Fountain (D, N.C.), chairman of the government operations subcommittee, disclosed the 1981 memo written by Dr. Michael Hensley, a former investigator for the Food and Drug Administration. Hensley had conducted a two-year investigation of Eli Lilly and had suggested that his findings be

turned over to the Justice Department for possible criminal prosecution of the company and its employees.

Hensley's memo stated that Eli Lilly had "repeatedly failed to make required reports of important adverse findings," on drugs it was testing for possible marketing.

Specifically, Hensley found that the company had failed to alert the FDA to 65 reports of adverse reactions to the anti-arthritis drug Oraflex. He said data had been "deliberately withheld" in order to improve chances that the drug would be approved for marketing.

In addition, Hensley's memo stated that the company had similarly withheld data on three other drugs. These included Aprindine and Drobuline, both experimental drugs regulating heartbeat, and Monensin, a cattle feed that was already on the market.

The FDA was still considering Hensley's recommendations, and a spokesman said the agency needed more time to examine the ramifications of the memo.

Eli Lilly Vice President Edgar G. Davis told reporters Aug. 3 that the company "takes vigorous exception to any implication that it has withheld data, maintained inadequate records or failed to comply with the scientific reporting requirements of the FDA."

Fountain released the memo at a hearing on FDA procedures and on the administration's proposal to streamline the approval process for new drugs.

He condemned the FDA for delaying action on Hensley's recommendations.

Tamper-Proof Package Rules Set. New packaging regulations designed to protect consumers from product tampering were approved Nov. 4, 1982, by Secretary of Health and Human Services Richard S. Schweiker. The rules, requiring over-the-counter medicines to be sold in tamper-resistant packages, were to be implemented in several steps.

The new standards were a response to the deaths of seven Chicago-area residents who had died after taking Extra-Strength Tylenol capsules. The capsules had been laced with cyanide. Hundreds of reports of "copycat" poisonings had further aroused consumers' fears.

The rules were drawn up by the Food and Drug Administration with the cooperation of drug manufacturers. The FDA was an agency of the Health and Human Services Department.

The first regulations would take effect 90 days after their Nov. 5 entry into the Federal Register. These rules would require tamper-resistant packaging on all newly manufactured proprietary capsules and liquid drugs. Eyedrops and mouthwashes were to be included in this category, which comprised products most susceptible to tampering.

(Tamper-resistant packages were those that made tampering more difficult and that easily showed if a product had indeed been altered. Bottles with vacuum seals placed over their mouths and boxes encased in heat-sealed plastic were two examples.)

Within 180 days, tamper-resistant packaging would be required for over-the-counter tablets and suppositories. Also, products covered by the regulations would have to have distinctive packaging designs that would enable consumers to see clearly if a product had been tampered with. Further, packaging would have to bear a prominent warning telling consumers not to buy the product if they saw evidence of tampering.

Secretary Schweiker estimated that the regulations would cost the drug industry up to $40 million, or about two cents per package. The industry had retail sales of $6 billion per year, according to the Wall Street Journal.

Reaction from the industry to the regulations was generally favorable. A spokesman for an industry trade group, the Proprietary Association, said, however, that he objected to a rule that would ban the sale after 15 months of products without tamper-resistant packaging. The spokesman, John T. Walden, said Nov. 4 that many products now on store shelves would still be effective after that time.

Reagan backs product liability bill. The Reagan administration July 15, 1982, signaled its support in principle for legislation that would establish uniform national standards for product liability lawsuits. Such a bill had been introduced in the Senate June 16 by Robert W. Kasten Jr. (R, Wis.).

The administration took its stand during a cabinet meeting July 15. According to an unidentified White House source, the cabinet had been deeply divided over the bill. The dispute was said to have been settled when President Reagan sided with Commerce Secretary Malcolm Baldridge and Transportation Secretary Drew Lewis, both adamant proponents of product liability law reform.

The chief opposition to supporting the Kasten bill was said to have come from Attorney General William French Smith and Labor Secretary Raymond J. Donovan. Both were said to have argued that the administration should carefully study the legislation before endorsing its passage.

The administration backed only the concept of the Kasten bill, not its particulars, which were being worked out by the Senate Energy and Commerce Committee.

The regulation of product liability standards was largely under the jurisdiction of the states. The result was a mass of conflicting laws and state court rulings across the nation.

The major thrust of the Kasten bill would be to preempt all state laws on the subject, while setting a uniform standard for product liability torts (injury claims). Similar legislation had failed in Congress in 1981 because it was unable to balance the often competing interests of business, labor, insurers and consumers.

The Kasten bill had been introduced in two alternative versions. One would bar an injury claim on any consumer good at any point 10 years after that product had entered the stream of commerce. The second version would exempt from injury claims any machine or piece of industrial equipment from any point 25 years after its initial sale.

As introduced, the bill established a product as "unreasonably dangerous" if its manufacturer knew, or should have known, that it would pose a health or safety hazard through its prescribed usage, and if the manufacturer failed to take practical steps to correct the hazard.

A product would not be unreasonably dangerous if consumers knew there was an unavoidable risk in using the product, if the product was altered in some unanticipated way by a user, or if it lacked warnings or instructions regarding an "obvious" danger.

Both manufacturers and sellers could be held liable for selling an unreasonably dangerous product. Their liability would depend on the extent of "harm" caused a claimant. The bill defined harm as physical injury, illness or death, or mental anguish caused by injury or illness.

In torts against manufacturers, the claimant would have to prove that the product was manufactured by the particular defendant in the suit. In cases dealing with a product made by a group of manufacturers, the claimant would have to prove he had made a reasonable effort to identify all the makers of the product before targeting one for a claim.

The bill was the subject of intense lobbying, with consumer groups on one side and business groups on the other.

Organizations such as the Consumer Federation of America and Congress Watch opposed the bill as introduced. They argued that if it became law, it would make it more difficult to file and win injury suits.

The legislation drew strong support from such organizations as the Product Liability Alliance, a coalition of business and trade associations that included the U.S. Chamber of Commerce, the Business Roundtable and the National Association of Manufacturers.

Laetrile's background—It was in the days of Prohibition that a California doctor first used an apricot extract to improve the taste of moonshine whiskey. Later, the doctor experimented with the extract to treat tumors in animals. When the supposed anti-cancer agent did not prove effective, its use died out. But the San Francisco physician's son, Ernst Krebs Jr., isolated an alleged cancer-fighting substance from the apricot pit in 1949. He called the extract "laetrile." Since then laetrile has been a source of conflict in the field of medicine. Here is a chronology of the Laetrile controversy:

1920—The forerunner of laetrile was first used by Dr. Ernst T. Krebs Sr. in treatment of cancer.

1949—Dr. Krebs' son, biochemist Ernst T. Krebs Jr., isolated an extract from apricot pits and called it "laetrile."

1952—Biochemist Krebs claimed to have made laetrile safe for injection into humans.

1953—The California Medical Association's Cancer Commission investigated laetrile as a cancer treatment. The commission found it "completely ineffective" when used in large doses on cancer in laboratory animals.

Oct. 10, 1962—President John F. Kennedy signed into law the Drug Amendments of 1962. The law provided that the FDA has to certify new drugs to be effective as well as safe, thereby laying the legal basis for the ban on laetrile and other questionable cancer cures.

1962—Ernst T. Krebs Jr. and the John Beard Memorial Foundation pleaded guilty to violating the new drug provisions of Federal Food, Drug & Cosmetic act. Krebs was placed on probation provided he did not ship any new drugs interstate (specifically including laetrile) without an effective new drug application from the FDA.

1963—The California State Department of Public Health issued a regulation prohibiting the use of laetrile in the state.

March 1963—The FDA reported no evidence that laetrile is effective in cancer treatment.

May 15, 1965—The Canadian Medical Association Journal reported negative findings on laetrile in cancer treatment.

Aug. 2, 1965—Dr. Ernst T. Krebs Sr. agreed to a permanent court injunction against further distribution of laetrile.

Sept. 1965—Dr. Krebs pleaded guilty to criminal contempt of court for disobeying a restraining order prohibiting the shipment of laetrile.

Jan. 21, 1966—Dr. Krebs pleaded guilty to contempt of court for shipping Laetrile.

Feb. 3, 1966—Dr. Krebs was given a one-year suspended sentence by a U.S. District Court in California for failing to register as a producer of drugs.

April 20, 1970—FDA assigned an Investigative New Drug application number to the McNaughton Foundation in California for testing amygdalin-laetrile.

May 12, 1970—The application was terminated when the FDA found "serious preclinical and clinical deficiencies."

Sept. 1, 1971—FDA found "no acceptable evidence of therapeutic effect to justify clinical trials" of laetrile.

1976—Alaska became the first state to permit doctors to prescribe and administer laetrile. (Alaska law, however, prohibits the sale of the drug.)

Jan. 21, 1977—U.S. District Judge Gordon Thompson Jr. ruled in San Diego that terminally ill patients may import laetrile.

April 8, 1977—U.S. District Judge Luther Bohanon in Oklahoma City specified conditions under which patients may have access to laetrile.

Ban on laetrile continued. The importation and sale of laetrile, an alleged cure for cancer, would continue to be banned by the federal government, U.S. Food and Drug Administraton chief Donald Kennedy said May 6, 1977. The controversial substance, also known as vitamin B-17 and the chemical amygdalin, occurred naturally in the pits of apricots and peaches, in bitter almonds and other plants. It was available in 26 countries and was currently being smuggled into the U.S. from Canada and Mexico. Amygdalin contained small amounts of the poison cyanide.

Promoters of laetrile use claimed that it could prevent and cure cancer. They contended that since there was no evidence of the chemical being harmful, the ban on it should be lifted. However, the FDA noted that laetrile was the most tested of all potential cancer cures and that five studies by the National Cancer Institute alone had indicated that it was therapeutically worthless. (According to the 1962 Kefauver-Harris amendments to the Food, Drug and Cosmetic Act of 1958, drug manufacturers were required to prove not only that a product was safe, but that it was also effective.) Some laetrile advocates maintained that it was a vitamin, not a drug, and should therefore be exempt from the legislation.

An FDA bulletin issued April 14 to physicians and other health professionals nationwide said supporters of laetrile use were "more vocal and better organized than in the past." The agency warned that early cancer patients who believed in laetrile's efficacy might be putting "their lives on the line" by failing to receive orthodox medical treatment.

Courts grant access to laetrile. Under a ruling by federal District Court Judge Luther Bohanon of Oklahoma City, some cancer patients had been importing laetrile from Mexico legally, it was reported April 17, 1977. Bohanon initially had ruled in favor of one cancer patient who sought the alleged cancer remedy. He later expanded the ruling to include about 20 other terminally ill persons.

Judge Bohanon April 8 issued a list of conditions under which patients could have access to laetrile, stressing that he had made no attempt to determine the drug's ability to fight cancer. Bohanon's order stipulated that laetrile be made available to terminal cancer patients who had sworn statements from a doctor on their condition. The physician's statement had to include "evidence of a rapidly progressive malignancy" and specify that recognized forms of cancer treatment would be administered in conjunction with laetrile.

Federal district court judges in New York and California also had ordered that terminally ill cancer patients be allowed to import laetrile. In San Diego, Calif., U.S. District

Court Judge Gordon Thompson Jr. had said Jan. 21 that to deny a patient freedom of choice in the absence of a known remedy for his illness "would be grossly paternalistic of this court." Three doctors who had certified that no cure was available for the patient in question also had approved his use of laetrile.

FDA holds laetrile hearings—The Food and Drug Administration May 2 opened hearings on laetrile on behalf of a cancer patient seeking to obtain the substance. The hearings, in Kansas City, Mo. had been ordered by the 10th U.S. Circuit Court of Appeals in October 1976. The court had ruled in Denver that the FDA's laetrile records were "grossly inadequate."

The hearings were intended "to compile a record of the available evidence about the substance" rather than formulate a final policy on its use, according to Dr. John Jennings, associate FDA commissioner for medical affairs.

Supporters of laetrile use were represented by the Committee for Freedom of Choice in Cancer Therapy, whose spokesman called the hearings a "kangaroo court." An opponent of laetrile, Dr. Samuel C. Klagsbrun, a psychiatrist at St. Luke's Hospital in New York City, testified that the drug was a "hoax" and alluded to its use as "suicide."

States challenge FDA ban. The Indiana state legislature May 1, 1977 overrode a veto by Gov. Otis Bowen and made Indiana the first state to authorize the manufacture, sale and use of laetrile, which was banned from interstate commerce by the Food and Drug Administration. The bill, effective June 1, also legalized the use of the artificial sweetener saccharin.

The Florida state legislature approved a bill May 2 to allow doctors to administer laetrile when requested by a patient.

By June 23, with action by Louisiana, ten states had authorized the manufacture and sale of laetrile. Arizona, Nevada, Texas, Washington, Delaware and Oklahoma had taken such action by June 21.

At least one bill had been introduced in Congress to amend current federal law restricting the use of laetrile.

While the federal government and the scientific and medical communities contended that laetrile was worthless as an anticancer treatment, the National Cancer Institute (NCI) announced June 23 that it had agreed to conduct clinical tests of the substance on humans. The agency's acting director, Dr. Guy Newell, said that growing public interest and pressure had led the institute to reconsider its previous decision against human trials. The NCI assumed that definitive proof of the substance's ineffectiveness would discourage its use. Previous laetrile experiments had been conducted exclusively on animals.

The NCI also planned to assess claims that laetrile, which contained the poison cyanide, was harmless. A 10-month-old girl died June 11 at the Buffalo Children's Hospital of cyanide poisoning after accidentally swallowing an unknown number of laetrile pills her father was taking for cancer. The infant's death was believed to be the first linked to a laetrile overdose.

In 1976 Alaska had become the first state to allow doctors to prescribe and administer laetrile. The sale of the substance was still prohibited there, however. An estimated 300 Alaskans were using laetrile, it was reported April 17, but there was no information available on the success or failure of the treatments.

Sloan-Kettering finds laetrile useless—Researchers at Memorial Sloan-Kettering Cancer Center in New York City said at a press conference June 15 that laetrile did not possess preventative, tumor-regressing or curative anticancer powers. Their findings were based upon a four-year study of the chemical's effects upon cancerous tumors in animals. The scientists conceded that laetrile's alleged pain-relieving properties could not be evaluated by their study.

The Sloan-Kettering report stated that scientists had been unable to confirm experiments conducted by Dr. Kanematsu

Sugiura in 1972–73 that had shown laetrile to be effective against lung cancer in mice. The authors of the report noted Sugiura's current contention that "laetrile is not a curative, but is a palliative agent."

Dr. Lewis Thomas, president of Sloan-Kettering, recommended human testing of laetrile and surveys of long-term laetrile users to determine if it had pain-killing, mood-altering or other effects on cancer patients.

AMA rejects laetrile proposal—A proposal by a special committee of the American Medical Association suggesting that laetrile be made available without a prescription was rejected June 21 by the AMA's policy-making body. The committee, which had not found any beneficial properties in laetrile, had recommended its over-the-counter sale in order to curtail the black market trade of the substance. It was estimated that laetrile smuggling had grown into a $20-million industry. Approximately 50,000 Americans were using laetrile as a cancer treatment.

Laetrile smugglers sentenced—Robert W. Bradford, 46, president of the Committee for Freedom of Choice in Cancer Therapy Inc., was fined $40,000 and put on three years' probation May 16 for smuggling laetrile into the U.S. from Mexico. Three co-defendants, Frank Salaman, Dr. John A. Richardson and Ralph S. Bowman, were also placed on probation and fined a total of $40,000.

All four defendants were sentenced by federal district court Judge William B. Enright in San Diego. Salaman, 52, was vice president of the Freedom of Choice committee, which claimed a membership of 35,000. Richardson, 54, was a physician whose medical license had been revoked in 1976 for treating cancer patients with laetrile, in violation of a 1969 California statute. Bowman, 52, was Richardson's business manager. Bradford and Richardson, like many of those in the laetrile movement, were members of the John Birch Society.

The convicted laetrile conspirators were the first of 19 defendants indicted on smuggling charges to stand trial. Andrew R. L.

McNaughton, 60, a Canadian citizen living in Mexico, was described by investigators as the "kingpin" of the operation. McNaughton, who had been involved in several stock fraud cases in the U.S., admitted that his McNaughton Foundation in Tijuana had once received $130,000 from Joseph Zicarelli, the alleged head of organized crime in Hudson County, N.J.

States approve laetrile. Louisiana June 23, 1977, became the tenth state in the country to legalize the manufacture and sale of the controversial cancer treatment laetrile. Delaware and Oklahoma had approved similar measures June 21, joining Alaska, Indiana, Florida, Arizona, Nevada, Texas and Washington. The drug was banned from interstate commerce by the Food and Drug Administration.

Laetrile Legalized in New Jersey. Laetrile, the controversial anticancer substance, was legalized in New Jersey Jan. 10, 1978, when Gov. Brendan Byrne signed a bill authorizing its intrastate sale and use. The state legislature had approved the measure Jan. 5. New Jersey became the 13th state to take such action despite the apricot-pit derivative's reputation within the medical community as a worthless, possibly harmful treatment for cancer patients.

The U.S. Food and Drug Administration had banned laetrile—also known as amygdalin or vitamin B-17—from interstate commerce. In 1977, legislation to legalize laetrile had been vetoed by Govs. James R. Thompson (R, Ill.) and Hugh Carey (D, N.Y.).

New Jersey senators who supported the bill cited cancer victims' civil rights and freedom of choice as the major factor in casting their votes. Detractors of laetrile, such as Democratic State Senator Joseph L. McGahn, a physician, had told the 1976–77 legislature that should someone die because they chose to use laetrile over a more conventional cancer treatment, "that death will be on your head."

Laetrile Deaths Reported. An 11-month infant died from cyanide poisoning in Buffalo, N.Y. after accidentally swallowing one to five Laetrile tablets, according to a report published Feb. 1, 1979, in the New England Journal of Medicine. It was the first documented case of a death caused by an accidental overdose of the substance derived from the pits of apricots, peaches, or bitter almonds.

Other deaths had been reported from overuse of Laetrile, but those victims were said to have been taking the pills to treat cancer. The pills taken by the infant had belonged to her father.

Laetrile (amygdalin) was said to release cyanide when metabolized by the body and had never been approved as a drug in the U.S. There was a federal ban on its shipment. The doctors who reported the infant's death wrote that the lay and medical public should be alerted to the potential toxicity of Laetrile, the need to store it in child-proof containers and the immediate need for therapy for cyanide poisoning if accidentally ingested.

In other Laetrile-related developments: The parents of Chad Green, a three-year-old boy suffering from leukemia, were ordered by the Massachusetts Appeals Court Jan. 30 to stop treating him with Laetrile after court-ordered laboratory tests found evidence of cyanide poison in the boy's blood. The order upheld a Jan. 23 ruling by the Massachusetts Superior Court. The parents, in defiance of the order, fled Massachusetts Jan. 25 and checked the boy into a Laetrile clinic in Tijuana, Mexico Jan. 26.

Japanese doctors said an element contained in Laetrile, benzaldehyde—but not Laetrile itself—had been found effective against two lung cancers, according to a statement Jan. 28 by Andrew A. Benson, a biologist at Scripps Clinic & Research Foundation in La Jolla, Calif. Benson quoted the Japanese researchers as saying that although Laetrile contained benzaldehyde, bacteria in the human intestine were unable to break down Laetrile to benzaldehyde which had to be given independent of Laetrile.

Laetrile Testing Delayed. The National Cancer Institute announced March 13, 1979, that it was delaying Laetrile experimentation on humans with untreatable tumors because the Food and Drug Administration had not responded to its request for permission submitted in December 1978.

The institute had announced plans in September 1978 for a six-month test, but FDA approval was a prerequisite for testing any experimental drug on humans. The institute was continuing negotiations, the spokesman said, to resolve the FDA's questions, which principally involved chemistry and the concern that Laetrile, which contained cyanide, could poison patients.

In other Laetrile-related events:

A South Burlington, Vt. firm sent recall letters to purchasers of Laetrile March 8 after a shipment of the drug was determined to contain fever-causing chemicals called pyrogens. It had been sold to cancer patients in Vermont, Florida, California, Massachusetts, Michigan, Missouri, Wisconsin and the Philippines.

The recall fell into a category covering products which might "cause temporary or medically reversible adverse health consequences." The FDA, which ordered the recall, said the chances of serious consequences were "remote."

Chad Green, a leukemia victim whose parents took him to Mexico for Laetrile treatments, was reported March 7 by his parents' attorney to have three times the normal level of poisonous cyanide in his blood. But the amount was still "well below" toxic levels, the lawyer said.

FDA Laetrile Ban Upheld. The Supreme Court ruled unanimously June 18, 1979, that the Food and Drug Administration had the power to ban the interstate sale and distribution of Laetrile, the controversial drug purported to cure cancer.

Laetrile, a substance derived mainly from the pits of apricots and peaches, contained levels of cyanide. Seventeen states had adopted laws approving the manufacture and sale of the drug within their borders. The

MEDICAL SCIENCE AND THE LAW

FDA, contending that Laetrile had not been proven either safe or effective, had prohibited the importation and interstate transportation of the drug in 1963. Most U.S. supplies of the substance were smuggled into the country from Mexico and Europe.

In the case in question, a group of cancer patients had sued the FDA on behalf of all terminally ill cancer patients. Two lower federal courts ruled in favor of the plaintiffs. The case was *U.S. v. Rutherford.*

The Supreme Court reversed a ruling by the U.S. 10th Circuit Court of Appeals that the FDA's "safe and effective" standard could not be applied to drugs administered to the terminally ill.

Justice Thurgood Marshall, writing for the court, rejected that argument. He maintained that the Food, Drug and Cosmetic Act of 1938—the basis of FDA authority—contained no hint that "Congress intended protection only for persons suffering from curable diseases. . . . To the contrary, in deliberations preceding the 1938 act, Congress expressed concern that individuals with fatal illnesses, such as cancer, should be shielded from fraudulent cures."

Marshall stressed that the high court was not ruling on the merits of Laetrile as an anticancer drug. However, he said that to deny the FDA's authority over Laetrile for the terminally sick would be to deny its authority "over all drugs, however toxic or ineffectual, for such individuals."

The case was sent back to the appeals court with instructions to consider arguments used by the plaintiffs to win their case in federal district court. These arguments, which had not been addressed by the appeals court, included the contention that the ban violated the constitutional right to privacy of cancer patients.

The Supreme Court, on Nov. 13, 1979, declined to hear a constitutional challenge to a California law prohibiting the sale of the purported cancer cure Laetrile. The case, *Privitera v. California,* involved a physician convicted of conspiring to sell the drug. The defendant maintained that the law violated

the privacy rights of cancer patients and their doctors.

Laetrile Found to Enlarge Rat Tumors. Two researchers found that when they gave Laetrile to rats with cancerous tumors, the tumors grew larger and the rats died from cyanide poisoning, it was reported July 13, 1979.

Laetrile was found lethal to rats in studies by Dr. Janardan D. Khandekar and Harlan Edelman of the Evanston, Ill. Hospital and Northwestern University's medical school.

Khandekar's report in the Journal of the American Medical Association described the progressive increases in the size of tumors in rats given Laetrile as "realistic in terms of human ingestion." He also said that the study's findings raised serious questions about the use of Laetrile in clinical medicine "under any circumstances."

Laetrile had been widely promoted as a cancer treatment until the Food and Drug Administration banned it as ineffective and potentially harmful. In support of the FDA was a June 18 ruling by the U.S. Supreme Court that allowed the government to continue its ban of Laetrile in interstate commerce.

Chad Green, 3, Dies in Mexico. Chad Green, 3, the center of a Laetrile controversy, died Oct. 12, 1979 of leukemia in Tijuana, Mexico.

The child's illness had sparked a legal and medical dispute between his parents and the medical profession over the merits of Laetrile in the treatment of cancer.

The parents had fled with the child to Mexico Jan. 25 in defiance of a Plymouth, Mass. court order that had directed the discontinuance of Laetrile after laboratory tests had found evidence of cyanide poisoning attributed to the substance in the boy's system.

The parents had entered the boy in a Laetrile clinic in Tijuana, where they continued him on combined treatments of chemotherapy and Laetrile until some time in mid-August. At that time, the child's leukemia was thought to be in complete remission and his parents apparently believed that his illness had been cured.

The parents stopped the chemotherapy against the advice of Mexican physicians at the clinic in favor of a strict Laetrile treatment combined with a vegetarian diet. The parents also hoped to stop what they said were the painful side effects of the chemotherapy cancer treatment.

The child's personal physician reportedly warned at that time: "I don't think the boy can make it without chemotherapy. It would be terribly difficult for him to make it."

In September 1979, the child showed signs of anemia and low blood-platelet count, indicating that a recurrence of the disease was near. But the parents, according to Mexican physicians, refused to submit the child to bone marrow tests to determine the status of the leukemia or to resume chemotherapy.

An autopsy, reported Oct. 21, was said to have indicated that the child "had a relapse in his leukemia and he died of it."

The autopsy report came in the wake of questions as to whether the child had died from leukemia or from the Laetrile treatment.

The parents still faced legal charges in Massachusetts of contempt of court for flouting the court's authority in their fight to treat the child with Laetrile.

FDA Approves Laetrile Tests. The Food and Drug Administration gave tentative approval Jan. 3, 1980, to the National Cancer Institute to conduct the first clinical study of the effects of Laetrile on humans.

The FDA, however, set forth two conditions before clinical trials on humans could begin.

The institute, the federal government's main cancer-fighting agency, would first have to repeat a Laetrile test on rabbits. Then it would have to conduct a three-month toxicity study on six patients to make sure that they did not ingest excessive cyanide from Laetrile, while on a "metabolic" diet during the treatment.

The institute trial was expected to take a year and would involve 200 to 300 advanced cancer patients who had volunteered for the Laetrile treatment.

Four cancer research centers were to participate in the study: Mayo Clinic in Rochester, Minn., the University of California at Los Angeles, the University of Arizona at Tucson and the Memorial Sloan-Kettering Cancer Center in New York.

FDA approval of the cancer institute study had reportedly been stalled for more than a year over the debate on testing an allegedly ineffective drug.

Challenge to Laetrile Ban Declined. The Supreme Court Oct. 20, 1980, declined to review a challenge to the Food and Drug Administration's ban on the interstate sale and shipment of Laetrile, a purported cancer-curing drug.

The case, *U.S. v. Rutherford,* had come before the Supreme Court in 1979. At that time, the court ruled that the FDA could legally inhibit the distribution of the drug based on the agency's "safe and effective" standard. The case was remanded to the U.S. 10th Circuit Court of Appeals for consideration of other arguments used by the plaintiffs.

The appeals court held in February 1980 that the FDA ban did not violate the privacy of cancer patients, and that Laetrile did not come under a "grandfather" exemption to federal drug regulation. Under the exemption, some drugs in wide use before 1962 did not have to undergo FDA testing or have the agency's approval for marketing. However, Laetrile had not been widely used before 1962.

Laetrile Fails Test as Cancer Cure. A $500,000 study sponsored by the National Cancer Institute found Laetrile, or amygdalin, ineffective as a treatment for cancer, it was announced April 30, 1981. The controversial drug, derived from apricot pits, had been defended by many, despite opposition by the Food and Drug Administration, as the last hope for patients with terminal cancers.

Dr. Charles G. Moertel, who announced the results of the study at a meeting of the American Society for Clinical Oncology, said the findings were both "decisive" and "disappointing," and roughly what would have been expected had the 156 patients involved been given placebos or no treatment at all. Nine months after the beginning of the study, 102 of those patients had died, and the remaining 54, with seriously "progressive cancer," had not responded to the Laetrile treatment.

In addition to Laetrile injections and pills, the treatment included "metabolic therapy" touted by Laetrile proponents—a diet stressing fresh fruits, vegetables and whole grains and restricting animal products, salt, alcohol and refined sugar and flour. In a continuation of the study, 14 of the surviving patients were recently started on very high doses of the drug.

Four medical centers took part in the test program: Mayo Clinic in Rochester, Minn.; Memorial Sloan-Kettering Cancer Center in New York; Jonsson Cancer Center in the University of California, and University of Arizona Health Sciences Center.

Dr. Moertel, director of cancer treatment at Mayo, added that he hoped the study's results would end "the exploitation of desperate cancer patients" by doctors who prescribed the drug. Twenty-three state legislatures had declared its use legal, although the FDA had placed a ban on its interstate sale and shipment.

Advocates of Laetrile discounted the test results and accused the centers of having used a less than optimum form of Laetrile. They said the tests had been rigged to discredit Laetrile treatment.

Other Access Issues

Krebiozen ban upheld. The Supreme Court Oct. 15, 1973 let stand a ruling that the drug Krebiozen was not recognized as a safe and effective cure for cancer and therefore could be banned from the market.

Nevada authorizes Gerovital. The Nevada legislature May 20, 1977 authorized the manufacture of the controversial drug Gerovital (GH3). Gerovital was hailed by its proponents as a powerful antidepressant and rejuvenator. The measure was passed as part of the bill legalizing the manufacture and sale of the purported anticancer drug laetrile. The chemical Gerovital, discovered and popularized in Europe, had never been licensed by the U.S. Food and Drug Administration.

The so-called "fountain of youth" drug consisted mainly of procaine hydrochloride, which was used by dentists as a local anesthetic under the trade name Novocain. It allegedly relieved depression, tension and reversed physical degeneration. Its developer, Dr. Ana Aslan, director of the Institute of Geriatrics in Bucharest, Rumania, claimed it could extend the human life span.

American researchers who had tested Gerovital's efficacy had found it to be an effective antidepressant with fewer side effects than expected from drugs currently available. Marvin Kratter, 61, controlling stockholder of Rom-Amer Pharmaceuticals Ltd., which had the U.S. rights to market Gerovital, had withdrawn the company's application for FDA approval, the Wall Street Journal reported June 2.

Marijuana OK'd for Glaucoma Victim. The therapeutic use of marijuana to relieve the symptoms of the eye disease glaucoma was approved in the case of Robert Randall, it was reported May 19, 1978, in the Washington Post.

Randall had sued when his drug supply provided under a federal government research program was cut off after his ophthalmologist, who participated in the program, left the Washington, D.C. area. Randall contended that the laws and policies regulating marijuana distribution denied him his constitutional right to his health.

The settlement of the suit provided for his present doctor to supply him with marijuana for at least two years through a Public Health Service pharmacy.

More States Approve Medical Use—Four more states passed laws that would allow controlled access to marijuana for medical purposes, the National Organization for the Reform of Marijuana Laws said June 1. The organization said that legislation passed in Iowa, Minnesota, Texas and Oregon brought to 11 the number of states that permitted patients with diseases such as glaucoma and cancer, to use the drug.

In Oregon, Gov. Vic Atiyeh June 18 signed a law legalizing the use of up to one ounce of marijuana for medicinal purposes. The new law would allow persons who underwent treatment for glaucoma or received chemotherapy treatment for cancer to possess the drug in small quantities.

Supporters of the Oregon law said marijuana was one of the most effective drugs for reducing ocular pressure from the glaucoma and for relieving nausea often experienced by chemotherapy patients.

Although the state legislature voted unanimously to pass the law, the Oregon Health Division said June 12 that implementation of the measure could be delayed by federal rules.

FDA Drug Approvals Set High in '81. The Food and Drug Administration had approved more new medical drugs in 1981 than in any year since 1962, it was reported Jan. 22. The total of 27 new drug chemicals was more than twice the number approved in 1980, and included important heart drugs known as calcium blockers.

Health and Human Services Secretary Richard Schweiker, making the announcement, said of the FDA: "We promised the American people we would reform the drug approval process and last year marked a long step toward that goal. Speeding the review of life-saving new drugs will allow the public to benefit from medical advance without needless delay."

The FDA had been criticized in a September 1981 report by the General Accounting Office, which stated that although its performance had improved, it should take further steps to accelerate its drug-clearance procedure.

According to the FDA's own figures, the average time for clearance of a drug application had dropped to 21.3 months in 1980 from 33.6 months in 1979, reversing a previous trend of longer and longer clearance times since 1975.

New Drug Approval Rules Proposed. Health and Human Services Secretary Richard S. Schweiker June 23, 1982, proposed a series of changes in the Food and Drug Administration's procedure for approving new drugs.

Schweiker's proposals were designed to put into effect the Reagan administration's goal of reducing the so-called "drug lag," or the amount of time between the discovery of a new pharmaceutical drug and the appearance of that drug on the market.

Schweiker announced the plan at a meeting of drug company officials in Washington, D.C. He proposed to:

Reduce by up to 70% the amount of paperwork required in approving a new drug; toward that end, full case reports on individuals participating in tests of new drugs would be elminated in favor of summarized reports.

Cut the period of reviewing a new drug by up to 20%, particularly for drugs that were similar to those already on the market.

Allow drug approval to be based entirely on studies conducted in foreign countries.

Introduce a new system of appeals for disputes between scientists and drug companies.

Expand the requirements for reporting on adverse effects of new drugs once they had been marketed.

"What we must seek is a proper balance— a process that fully ensures the safety of drugs but without unnecessary delays or overregulation," Schweiker said. Schweiker called the plan "the most significant revision" of the drug approval process in the last 20 years.

But Fay Peterson, a spokesman for the FDA, June 23 said the proposals would have a minimal effect on new drugs that represented important therapeutical advances. She said the FDA already put such drugs on a "fast track" approval system, and that the Schweiker proposals would mainly affect the marketing of new combinations or dosages of drugs that already had been approved.

Dr. Eve Bargmann, a researcher for the Health Research Group, founded by consumer advocate Ralph Nader, blasted the proposals.

"What they're doing is risking safety and forcing thousands of Americans to be unwitting subjects for human experimentation," she said.

The proposed changes had to be approved by the Office of Budget and Management, and then submitted for a period of public comment before going into effect.

Saccharin Ban Barred for 2 Years. Congress April 13 cleared a bill prohibiting the Food and Drug Administration from banning saccharin, an artificial sweetener linked to cancer in laboratory animals, for two years.

The action was a simple extension of an earlier congressional prohibition against an FDA ban. The bill left in force requirements that saccharin products carry warnings of health dangers.

The bill would also permit the FDA to take action against the sweetener if new scientific findings demonstrated a public health danger from saccharin. The agency was barred only from reinstating regulations against saccharin based on old data collected before 1978.

Sen. Orrin Hatch (R, Utah), the sponsor of the bill, was quoted in the April 16 issue of Congressional Quarterly as saying that two large-scale new studies were expected to produce findings later in the year. "These studies were intended to address numerous questions raised in previous studies, particularly the relevance of past research findings on animals," Hatch said.

The bill was approved by the Senate April 5 by voice vote, and by the House April 13, also by voice vote. President Reagan signed it April 22.

Formaldehyde ban reversed. The Consumer Product Safety Commission May 5 asked a federal appeals court in New Orleans to reconsider a decision voiding the CPSC's ban on urea formaldehyde foam insulation.

A three-judge panel of the U.S. 5th Circuit Court of Appeals April 7 had overturned the agency's 1982 ban on the product's use.

The court had issued a stay of its order, however, pending the outcome of the expected government request for a rehearing.

The panel had ruled that the CPSC had not sufficiently demonstrated that use of the insulation posed an unreasonable risk of cancer.

THe CPSC petition suggested that the panel had seriously misunderstood "the scientific data and technological methodology" that had led to its ban. It also stated that the decision represented an "improper intrusion on the authority granted by Congress to the commission both to resolve conflicting scientific evidence and to make health policy judgments."

The panel had ruled in response to a suit filed by Formaldehyde Institute, a trade group of major manufacturers, the day CPSC had issued the ban.

Uncertified drugs barred. The FDA told two drug companies Feb. 1, 1971 to stop selling a pair of medicines that had been marketed in violation of a law governing "new" drugs. At issue was a law that no drug legally classified as "new" could be sold without FDA approval of a new-drug application.

The two companies—Smith Kline & French Laboratories, maker of a non-prescription decongestant and painkiller called Ornex, and Ayerst Laboratories, producer of a glaucoma treatment called Epitrate—had claimed their products were legally "old drugs" whose active ingredients had been medically accepted for years. The FDA acted on the basis of a letter Jan. 28 from Rep. L. H. Fountain (D, N.C.) who complained that the agency had taken no action although he had brought the matter to its attention two months before.

(The FDA also told Cord Laboratories and Linden Laboratories to recall their versions of chlorpromazine, a tranquilizer, because the products lacked approved new-drug applications.)

In another case involving the "new drug"

provisions of the federal Food, Drug and Cosmetics Act, the Justice Department announced Jan. 19 that Dow Corning Corp. (Midland, Mich.) had entered pleas of nolo contendere in a 1967 indictment charging violations involving a silicone fluid, best known for its use to augment women's figures. The government charged that the drug was shipped illegally and misbranded for its use as an injection into human beings. In not contesting the charges, the company and officials indicted were liable to a maximum fine of $1,000 on each of two counts, or imprisonment for a year, or both.

FDA scientific work criticized. An advisory panel criticized the FDA May 27, 1971 for "poorly managed laboratories" and other inadequacies in the agency's scientific effort. The panel of five professors from leading medical schools, in a report based on a one-year survey requested by FDA Commissioner Dr. Charles C. Edwards, said, however, that the agency "does an extraordinary job in many ways" to protect the public, given budget and manpower limitations.

The report said some of the agency's laboratories were excellent, but it said facilities in Chicago and Philadelphia were antiquated, crowded and unsafe and labs in Denver were only barely adequate. The panel said, "one can also find laboratories so poorly managed that scientists seem to be unable to describe their work coherently or to produce interpretable data books containing their findings." The commission also complained of lack of sound data, "a curious aura of secrecy" and an "unhurried atmosphere."

The panel said the responsibilities of FDA laboratories "are literally overwhelming" and that the agency had "limited resources." Edwards, in a news conference announcing the report, said much had been done to implement many of the panel's 50 recommendations but that the FDA's $85 million budget would have to be dramatically increased to allow complete reform.

Specifically, the panel urged "overall surveillance at the source" of food and drug products to insure quality and safety. The report said the panel members were "dismayed to learn" that the FDA had no continuously up-to-date data on the identity and amount manufactured of all drugs on the U.S. market. The report pointed to one area of "possible danger to the public" in the wide use of antibiotics in livestock and poultry feed despite "the fact that the public health significance of drug residues in meat and poultry is not well understood."

The panel asked that sound science be the basis of the agency's decisions rather than "economic or political factors."

FDA defends tough rules. Commissioner of the Food and Drug Administration (FDA) Dr. Charles C. Edwards, and FDA drug bureau director Dr. Henry E. Simmons told the Senate Monopoly Subcommittee Feb. 5, 1973 that their cautious policy on licensing new drugs had probably prevented thousands of deaths and deformities among Americans. They cited some 25 harmful drugs that had been marketed abroad but never reached the U.S. public because of the policy.

The agency was responding to criticism that amendments to the Pure Food and Drug Act in 1962 had decreased the number of beneficial new drugs appearing on the market. Subcommittee Chairman Sen. Gaylord Nelson (D, Wis.) cited a Jan. 8 Newsweek magazine column by economist Milton Friedman charging that the amendments "condemn innocent people to death." Nelson expressed his "dismay" at attacks on the FDA by "certain elements of the medical profession."

Simmons cited the well-known case of thalidomide, in which over 10,000 babies were born deformed in European countries to mothers who had used the drug during pregnancy in the early 1960s.

"Of even more concern," he said, was a report that an aerosol spray for bronchial asthma had probably led to the death of 3,500 children in England and Wales alone in the mid 1960s. The drug, Simmons claimed, could not have been licensed in the U.S. without extensive animal and human testing. In another case, an appetite suppressant called aminorex, which the FDA had barred from further human tests in 1968 because of safety problems, might have caused an "epidemic" of a type of fatal high blood pressure of the lungs among German, Austrian and Swiss citizens in the late 1960s.

The amendments required evidence of effectiveness before a drug could be marketed, informed consent from participants in new drug tests and generally stronger safety measures.

FDA power upheld. In a series of rulings, the Supreme Court June 18, 1973 unanimously upheld the FDA's power to remove ineffective drugs from the market.

The court upheld 1962 Congressional legislation authorizing the FDA to require prescription drug manufacturers to prove their products' effectiveness as well as their safety. The decision was also extended to uphold a part of the 1962 law that gave the FDA power to regulate drugs that previously had been cleared for safety but not for effectiveness.

Reversing an appellate court ruling, the Supreme Court said the FDA could, without going to court, remove "me too" drugs from the market. "Me too" drugs were never approved by the FDA on the grounds they contained the same ingredients as other prescription preparations already being marketed.

The FDA was also held to have the jurisdiction to decide administratively, subject to judicial review, whether a product had to be cleared as a "new drug" before marketing.

The court ruled the FDA could deny a hearing to a drug manufacturer when it failed to provide evidence its product met requirements.

Justice Douglas wrote: "If the FDA were required automatically to hold a hearing for each product whose efficacy was questioned . . . even though many hearings would be an exercise in futility, we have no doubt that it could not fulfill its statutory mandate to remove from the market all those drugs which do not meet effectiveness requirements."

Non-prescription drugs sold over the counter were not affected by the rulings.

FDA to control medical devices. Congress May 13, 1976 voted to expand the FDA's regulatory powers over medical devices of almost all varieties. Both houses approved the bill by voice votes, and the President signed it May 28. The new legislation would allow the FDA to promulgate certain controls applicable to all devices and to require pre-market testing for certain classes of devices.

Pre-market testing for safety and effectiveness would in general be required for life-support devices and for all those implanted in the body. Devices in those categories which had been on the market before the legislation was cleared would have to be approved before they could continue to be sold.

Without the powers contained in the new legislation, the FDA had to wait until a device had been marketed, then seek a court order against it. The agency's statutory authority was restricted to seeing that devices were neither adulterated nor incorrectly labeled.

The legislation required that medical devices be classified into one of three categories, subject to different degrees of FDA oversight. Devices in the first category would be subject only to general controls, allowing the government to set manufacturing and distribution standards and to order manufacturers to repair, replace, or give refunds for items that were risky because of faulty manufacturing.

Devices in the second category would be subject to construction, testing and performance standards and would also come under the first category's general controls.

The third category would be for those devices that required premarket approval. Manufacturers would have to file test reports and other information with the FDA, and generally would have to provide sample devices. The devices also would be subject to the general controls of the first category.

Devices subject only to general controls

would essentially be those which, by virtue of their simplicity and long-standing record of safe use, were not considered to pose hazards to health (e.g., tongue depressors, thermometers). The category of devices subject to performance standards as well as to general controls was described as a "gray" area; it comprised devices that were more vital to a person's health, and less time-tested, than the devices subject only to general controls, but still not so critical to health as those requiring premarket testing. Prosthetic limbs could fall into the category of devices required to meet performance standards.

Cost-Benefit Standards

Introduction:

The factors to be weighed in deciding to ban or approve drugs and other substances to which the public is exposed have been much debated. Sometimes the issue is simply whether the proper procedure was followed in making the decision to approve or ban. Other problems include the substantive weighing of the costs of regulation against the benefits to individuals and society as a whole.

OSHA Rebuffed on Benzene Standard. The Supreme Court voted 5–4, July 2, 1980, to uphold a lower court decision that voided the federal government's work safety standard on exposure to the chemical benzene. The case was *Industrial Union Department v. American Petroleum Institute*.

Benzene, which was suspected of causing leukemia, was widely used as a gasoline additive in paints, solvents and other products. In 1978, the Occupational Safety and Health Administration had issued rules reducing the allowable airborne exposure at a work place to one part benzene per million parts of air, from 10 parts benzene per million parts of air, over an eight-hour period.

The U.S. 5th Circuit Court of Appeals struck down the new standard, primarily because OSHA had failed to weigh the cost to businesses of complying with the standard against expected benefits.

The Supreme Court backed the appeals court, but virtually avoided the much-disputed cost-benefit issue. Instead the majority concluded that OSHA had arbitrarily adopted the new standard.

Justice John Paul Stevens, who wrote the majority's key opinion, observed that OSHA hadn't obtained any "empirical evidence" or "opinion testimony" that "exposure to benzene at or below 10 ppm level had ever in fact caused leukemia." He implicitly rejected OSHA's general policy that the only "safe level" of exposure to a cancer-causing chemical was the lowest "feasible" level.

Such a policy, Stevens said, gave OSHA the power "to impose enormous costs [on industry] that might produce little, if any, discernible benefit."

Justice Lewis F. Powell Jr. was the only member of the majority to directly address the cost-benefit issue. He contended that even if testing could prove a cancer link, "a standard-setting process that ignored economic considerations would result in a serious misallocation of resources. . . ."

Justice Thurgood Marshall, in a dissent joined by Justices Byron R. White, William J. Brennan Jr. and Harry A. Blackmun, called the majority "extraordinarily arrogant and extraordinarily unfair" for claiming that OSHA had not gathered enough evidence of the danger posed by benzene exposure.

CPSC Sued Over Ban on Tris. Thirty-one sleepware manufacturers brought a $27 million damage suit against the Consumer Product Safety Commission in U.S. District Court in Washington March 24, 1980. The suit sought to overturn a ban imposed by the CPSC on the sale garments treated with Tris.

Tris, a chemical flame retardant, was suspected of being a cancer-causing agent. The CPSC had ordered Tris-treated clothing off store shelves in 1977.

The plaintiffs claimed that the commission had failed to follow necessary procedures when it stopped the sale of Tris-treated garments. They further argued that they had suffered large financial losses for complying with the government ban.

Supreme Court Backs OSHA On Textile Worker Safety; 'Cost-Benefit' Standard Rebuffed. The Supreme Court ruled, 5–3, June 17 that the textile industry had to protect the health of its workers, regardless of the cost of complying with federal job-safety regulations. The decision was viewed as a significant setback of the Reagan administration's anti-regulation policies.

The case, *American Textile Manufacturers Institute, et al v. Donovan*, stemmed from regulations drawn up in 1978 by the Occupational Safety and Health Administration (OSHA) aimed at reducing the exposure of textile workers to cotton dust. Prolonged exposure to the dust could cause a debilitating respiratory condition known as byssinosis, or "brown lung" disease.

The 1978 regulations required textile manufacturers to buy and install expensive equipment to lower the amount of cotton dust in factories to no more than 200 micrograms per cubic meter of air.

The industry resisted the regulations, arguing that the cost of the equipment far outweighed the benefit to workers. The industry maintained that the rules were invalid because OSHA had failed to properly consider the costs.

(The so-called "cost-benefit" standard had wide support in business circles and had been adopted by the Reagan administration as a way of curtailing federal regulation.

The OSHA regulations had been upheld by the U.S. Court of Appeals for the District of Columbia. The administration had petitioned the high court to vacate the judgment.

The Supreme Court also upheld the regulations. Writing for the majority, Justice William J. Brennan Jr. found that Congress, in enacting the Occupational Safety and Health Act of 1970, had chosen "to place preeminent value on assuring employees a safe and healthful working environment."

Brennan contended that the legislative branch was aware that job-safety regulations

could be costly to industry. "Congress itself defined the basic relationship between costs and benefits," he wrote, "by placing the 'benefit' of worker health above all other considerations. . . . Any standard based on a balancing of costs and benefits by the secretary [of the Labor Department] that strikes a different balance than that struck by Congress would be inconsistent with the command set forth" in OSHA's enabling legislation.

Brennan noted that the law required industries to comply with job-safety rules "to the extent feasible." He said that the dictionary meaning of the word "feasible" supported OSHA's position: " 'feasible' means 'capable of being done, executed or effected.' "

The high court overturned only one part of the appeals court's ruling—a provision of the regulations that any worker transferred to another section of a textile plant for health reasons be insulated from loss of benefits.

Brennan said that OSHA had not proven the need for the provision. This aspect of the case was sent back to the appeals court for reconsideration.

Justices Potter Stewart, William H. Rehnquist and Chief Justice Warren E. Burger dissented overall. Justice Lewis F. Powell Jr. did not participate.

Stewart found that OSHA's estimates of the costs of implementing its 1978 regulations were based on "unsupported speculation."

Rehnquist and Burger, in a separate dissent, asserted that the 1970 occupational safety law was vague on the question of cost-benefit analysis.

George H. Cohen, a lawyer for the AFL-CIO, praised the decision and said that it affirmed the organization's view that "under the language, history and purpose of the act there is no room for cost-benefit analysis."

Robert E. Coleman, president of the American Textile Manufacturers Institute, expressed disappointment over the ruling and maintained that regulations went "beyond what is necessary to protect the health" of textile workers.

Ethical Issues and Health Care

Informed Consent

Ethics & behavior modification. Ethical problems posed in behavior modification were explored by Associate Prof. James G. Holland of the University of Pittsburgh at a workshop held at an annual meeting of the American Orthopsychiatric Association in San Francisco in March 1970. Among Holland's remarks:

"Behavior modification shares with other therapies all of the usual ethical problems of informed consent, privileged communication, etc. But behavior modification procedures add new problems. The new ethical considerations arise from the very strength of the technique. . . .

"The basic research in the experimental analysis of behavior has provided the means for the development of effective procedures for changing behavior in a variety of settings. . . . [T]here has been extensive use of programed instruction and contingency management in classrooms, manipulation of behavior of mental patients on the ward as well as in individual therapy, and a host of other applications. When a behavior modification procedure is developed, all aspects are empirically defined and hence replicable. . . . With a little training anyone able to arrange the necessary reinforcers or aversive stimuli can carry out the procedures, and training workshops are common for teachers, parents, psychiatric nurses, prison personnel, and others to prepare them to use behavior modification. . . .

" . . . The science is at the service of those who command the means to use it.

" . . . For example, when it was discovered that in past wars less than 25% of the men in combat actually fired their weapons, [a Human Resources Research Organization psychologist] . . . prepared training procedures to increase the soldier's willingness to fire more frequently and effectively. . . .

" . . . A survey among experts in weapons systems conducted by Rand Corp. projects the behavioral control of mass population as a major weapons system. Most of the experts expect it to be reality by 1980—American know-how beating by four years the English masters of *1984*. . . .

" . . . Philip Sperling, in his address as president of the APA Division of Military Psychology, promotes 'political psychology' as the newest and most critical aspect of military psychology. 'Political psychology,' Sperling (1968) says, '. . . deals with problems of control of the behavior of groups'. . . .

" . . . The behavioral psychologist is preparing procedures which . . . facts indicate will be used by those in positions of power for their ends rather than for the objectives of the individual whose behavior is being manipulated. . . ."

Cancer diagnosis seldom secret. Most physicians, 97%, no longer kept the diagnosis of cancer secret from their patients, according to a report Feb. 26, 1979, in the Journal of the American Medical Association.

The study, conducted by the University of Rochester Medical Center, used a questionnaire that was identical to one used in 1961. At that time, 90% of the responding physicians indicated a preference for not telling cancer patients the diagnosis.

Those responding to the new survey said they rarely made exceptions to the practice, saying "perhaps more patients are being told because more need to know."

It was also noted that many hospitals were clinical research centers where patients must be told their diagnosis to satisfy legal requirements of informed consent.

Pediatricians were the only specialized doctors who more often made exceptions about giving such information. Age, intelligence, emotional stability and relatives' wishes were most frequently cited as factors in deciding whether to inform the patient.

Virginia court upholds rule that surgery is battery if the patient does not consent. The Virginia Supreme Court followed the traditional rule of law that surgery is battery unless the patient or an authorized representative consents to it. The court's 1980 ruling came as it affirmed a jury's finding that a patient about to undergo surgery had revoked her consent to the surgery. The case was *Pugsley v. Privette*.

Maine court upholds "reasonable practitioner" standard. In the case of *Woolley v. Henderson* (Me. 1980), the Maine Supreme Judicial Court adopted the standard of the reasonable medical practitioner as the measure of a physician's duty to disclose the risks of surgery to a patient. Upholding the trial court's decision, the Maine high court declined to follow the current legal trend toward measuring the adequacy of a physician's disclosure by the patient's individual need for information.

The defendant physician had recommended surgery to cure the plaintiff's chronic back ailment. During surgery, the plaintiff's spinal cord was accidentally damaged, leaving her partially paralyzed. Apparently, the physician had not informed the plaintiff of the possibility of that result.

The Maine Supreme Judicial Court held that, since a physician's failure to obtain a patient's informed consent is a type of malpractice, the standard applied to disclosing medical risks should be the same objective standard applied to other forms of malpractice. The court rejected the more subjective modern view as creating a danger that plaintiffs would rely on self-serving hindsight in bringing such actions. The Maine court's rejection of the modern legal trend toward focusing on patient's personal autonomy made it the second New England jurisdiction to do so in two years.

In October, 1981, the President's Commission for the Study of Ethical Problems in Medicine and Biomedical and Behavioral Research, chaired by Morris B. Abrams, finished its report on medical decision-making. Its report was titled "The Ethical and Legal Implications of Informed Consent in the Patient-Practitioner Relationship." The commission's summary of conclusions and recommendations follows.

Summary of Conclusions and Recommendations

Before the Commission could consider means of improvement, it had to address the underlying theoretical issues. The ethical foundation of informed consent can be traced to the promotion of two values: personal well-being and self-determination. To ensure that these values are respected and enhanced, the Commission finds that patients who have the capacity to make decisions about their care must be permitted to do so voluntarily and must have all relevant information regarding their condition and alternative treatments, including possible benefits, risks, costs, other consequences, and significant uncertainties surrounding any of this information. This conclusion has several specific implications:

(1) Although the informed consent doctrine has substantial foundations in law, it is essentially an ethical imperative.

(2) Ethically valid consent is a process of shared decision-making based upon mutual respect and participation, not a ritual

to be equated with reciting the contents of a form that details the risks of particular treatments.

(3) Much of the scholarly literature and legal commentary about informed consent portrays it as a highly rational means of decisionmaking about health care matters, thereby suggesting that it may only be suitable for and applicable to well-educated, articulate, self-aware individuals. Whether this is what the legal doctrine was intended to be or what it has inadvertently become, it is a view the Commission unequivocally rejects. Although subcultures within American society differ in their views about autonomy and individual choice and about the etiology of illness and the roles of healers and patients, a survey conducted for the Commission found a universal desire for information, choice, and respectful communication about decisions. Informed consent must remain flexible, yet the process, as the Commission envisions it throughout this Report, is ethically required of health care practitioners in their relationships with all patients, not a luxury for a few.

(4) Informed consent is rooted in the fundamental recognition—reflected in the legal presumption of competency—that adults are entitled to accept or reject health care interventions on the basis of their own personal values and in furtherance of their own personal goals. Nonetheless, patient choice is not absolute.

- Patients are not entitled to insist that health care practitioners furnish them services when to do so would violate either the bounds of acceptable practice or a professional's own deeply held moral beliefs or would draw on a limited resource on which the patient has no binding claim.
- The fundamental values that informed consent is intended to promote—self-determination and patient well-being—both demand that alternative arrangements for health care decisionmaking be made for individuals who lack substantial capacity to make their own decisions. Respect for self-determination requires, however, that in the first instance individuals be deemed to have decisional capacity, which should not

be treated as a hurdle to be surmounted in the vast majority of cases, and that incapacity be treated as a disqualifying factor in the small minority of cases.

- Decisionmaking capacity is specific to each particular decision. Although some people lack this capacity for all decisions, many are incapacitated in more limited ways and are capable of making some decisions but not others. The concept of capacity is best understood and applied in a functional manner. That is, the presence or absence of capacity does not depend on a person's status or on the decision reached, but on that individual's actual functioning in situations in which a decision about health care is to be made.
- Decisionmaking incapacity should be found to exist only when people lack the ability to make decisions that promote their well-being in conformity with their own previously expressed values and preferences.
- To the extent feasible people with no decisionmaking capacity should still be consulted about their own preferences out of respect for them as individuals.

(5) Health care providers should not ordinarily withhold unpleasant information simply because it is unpleasant. The ethical foundations of informed consent allow the withholding of information from patients only when they request that it be withheld or when its disclosure per se would cause substantial detriment to their well-being. Furthermore, the Commision found that most members of the public do not wish to have "bad news" withheld from them.

(6) Achieving the Commission's vision of shared decisionmaking based on mutual respect is ultimately the responsibility of individual health care professionals. However, health care institutions such as hospitals and professional schools have important roles to play in assisting health care professionals in this obligation. The manner in which health care is provided in institutional settings often results in a fragmentation of responsibility that may neglect the human side of health care. To assist in guarding against this, institutional health care providers should ensure that ultimately there is one readily identifiable practitioner

responsible for providing information to a particular patient. Although pieces of information may be provided by various people, there should be one individual officially charged with responsibility for ensuring that all the necessary information is communicated and that the patient's wishes are known to the treatment team.

(7) Patients should have access to the information they need to help them understand their conditions and make treatment decisions. To this end the Commission recommends that health care professionals and institutions not only provide information but also assist patients who request additional information to obtain it from relevant sources, including hospital and public libraries.

(8) As cases arise and new legislation is contemplated, courts and legislatures should reflect this view of ethically valid consent. Nevertheless, the Commission does not look to legal reforms as the primary means of bringing about changes in the relationship between health care professionals and patients.

(9) The Commission finds that a number of relatively simple changes in practice could facilitate patient participation in health care decisionmaking. Several specific techniques—such as having patients express, orally or in writing, their understanding of the treatment consented to—deserve further study. Furthermore, additional societal resources need to be committed to improving the human side of health care, which has apparently deteriorated at the same time there have been substantial gains in health care technology. The Department of Health and Human Services, and especially the National Institutes of Health, is an appropriate agency for the development of initiatives and the evaluation of their efficacy in this area.

(10) Because health care professionals are responsible for ensuring that patients can participate effectively in decisionmaking regarding their care, educators have a responsibility to prepare physicians and nurses to carry out this obligation. The Commission therefore concludes that:

• Curricular innovations aimed at preparing health professionals for a process of mutual decisionmaking with

patients should be continued and strengthened, with careful attention being paid to the development of methods for evaluating the effectiveness of such innovations.

• Examinations and evaluations at the professional school and national levels should reflect the importance of these issues.

• Serious attention should be paid to preparing health professionals for team practice in order to enhance patient participation and well-being.

(11) Family members are often of great assistance to patients in helping to understand information about their condition and in making decisions about treatment. The Commision recommends that health care institutions and professionals recognize this and judiciously attempt to involve family members in decisionmaking for patients, with due regard for the privacy of patients and for the possibilities for coercion that such a practice may entail.

(12) The Commission recognizes that its vision of health care decisionmaking may involve greater commitments of time on the part of health professionals. Because of the importance of shared decisionmaking based on mutual trust, not only for the promotion of patient well-being and self-determination but also for the therapeutic gains that can be realized, the Commission recommends that all medical and surgical interventions be thought of as including appropriate discussion with patients. Reimbursement to the professional should therefore take account of time spent in discussion rather than regarding it as a separate item for which additional payment is made.

(13) To protect the interests of patients who lack decisionmaking capacity and to ensure their well-being and self-determination, the Commission concludes that:

• Decisions made by others on patients' behalf should, when possible, attempt to replicate the ones patients would make if they were capable of doing so. When this is not feasible, decisions by surrogates on behalf of patients must protect the patients' best interests. Because such decisions are not instances of personal self-choice, limits may be placed on the range of acceptable decisions that surrogates make beyond those that apply when a person makes his or her own decisions.

- Health care institutions should adopt clear and explicit policies regarding how and by whom decisions are to be made for patients who cannot decide.
- Families, health care institutions, and professionals should work together to make health care decisions for patients who lack decisionmaking capacity. Recourse to courts should be reserved for the occasions when concerned parties are unable to resolve their disagreements over matters of substantial import, or when adjudication is clearly required by state law. Courts and legislatures should be cautious about requiring judicial review of routine health care decisions for patients who lack capacity.
- Health care institutions should explore and evaluate various informal administrative arrangements, such as "ethics committees," for review and consultation in nonroutine matters involving health care decisionmaking for those who cannot decide.
- As a means of preserving some self-determination for patients who no longer possess decisionmaking capacity, state courts and legislatures should consider making provision for advance directives through which people designate others to make health care decisions on their behalf and/or give instructions about their care.

The Commission acknowledges that the conclusions contained in this Report will not be simple to achieve. Even when patients and practitioners alike are sensitive to the goal of shared decisionmaking based on mutual respect, substantial barriers will still exist. Some of these obstacles, such as longstanding professional attitudes or difficulties in conveying medical information in ordinary language, are formidable but can be overcome if there is a will to do so. Others, such as the dependent condition of very sick patients or the ever-growing complexity and subspecialization of medicine, will have to be accommodated because they probably cannot be eliminated. Nonetheless, the Commission's vision of informed consent still has value as a meas-

uring stick against which actual performance may be judged and as a goal toward which all participants in health care decisionmaking can strive.

Massachusetts court rules on informed consent. In a 1982 case, entitled *Harnish v. Children's Hospital Medical Center* (Mass. 1982), the Massachusetts Supreme Court established a two-tier test for determining what disclosure by a physician to a patient is sufficient to enable the latter to give informed consent to treatment.

In this case, the plaintiff underwent surgery to remove a tumor from her neck. During surgery, a nerve was severed, permanently paralyzing the patient's tongue. She brought an action against her physician and the hospital alleging that they had failed to inform her of the risk of paralysis, that it was a material and foreseeable risk, and that she would not have consented had she known. The Supreme Judicial Court reversed a medical malpractice tribunal's dismissal of the action, and remanded the case for trial.

In its decision, the Massachusetts high court held that "a physician's failure to divulge in a reasonable manner to a competent adult patient sufficient information to enable the patient to make an informed judgment whether to give or withhold consent to a medical or surgical procedure constitutes professional misconduct. . . ." Balancing the patient's right to know against the difficulty in communicating scientific information to a lay person, the court concluded that it would be unreasonably burdensome to require physicians in every case to discuss every remotely possible risk with the patient. Therefore, the court held that "a physician owes to his patient the duty to disclose in a reasonable manner all significant medical information that the physician possesses or reasonably should possess that is material to an intelligent decision by the patient whether to undergo the proposed procedure." The standard of information which a physician should possess is that possessed by the average practitioner within the particular specialty. The court further noted that the physician need only disclose those risks which the physician knows or should know are material to a decision by a reasonable person in that patient's position. Materiality should be determined by the trier of fact, considering such factors as the nature of the risk and its probability of maturing, the possible benefits from the proposed procedure, and the alternatives to that treatment and their risks.

Rights of retarded expanded. The Supreme Court ruled unanimously June 18, 1982, that mentally retarded persons in state institutions were entitled to constitutionally protected rights under the 14th Amendment's due process clause. The decision, in *Youngberg v. Romero,* marked the first time that the high court had supported the concept of constitutional protections for the institutionalized retarded.

The case involved a suit against the Pennhurst State School and Hospital in Pennsylvania. The action had been filed by the mother of a Pennhurst resident, Nicholas Romero. Romero's mother accused the institution of violating his constitutional rights, even though he was legally incompetent and had been involuntarily committed to the care of Pennhurst.

A trial court jury had found in favor of the institution. That decision was upset by the U.S. 3rd Circuit Court of Appeals, which ordered a new trial. The appeals court held that the state had to prove it had an "overriding" public interest in limiting the freedoms of the retarded in its care.

The Supreme Court held that the 14th Amendment guarded certain "liberty interests" of the institutionalized retarded under the due process clause. The clause prohibited states from depriving anyone of "life, liberty or property without due process of law."

Led by Justice Lewis F. Powell Jr., the court determined that those interests included the right to live in reasonably safe conditions, the right to be free from unreasonable physical restraints, and the right to "minimally adequate" training in caring for themselves.

On the second point, physical restraints, Powell called for deference to doctors and mental health professionals in determining the need for the extent to which the retarded could be bodily confined.

Powell noted that the high court had recognized the rights of prison inmates concerning safety and restraints, and he said that involuntarily committed retarded persons were entitled to equivalent protections.

Powell described the training issue as a "more difficult question." While backing a "minimally adequate" standard, the court left it up to the states to define the scope of the standard.

Chief Justice Warren E. Burger issued a separate opinion concurring with the result but quarreling with the training standard. "I agree with the court that some amount of self-care instruction may be necessary to avoid unreasonable infringement of a mentally retarded person's interests," he wrote. "But it seems clear to me that the Constitution does not otherwise place an affirmative duty on the state to provide any particular kind of training or habilitation."

The case was remanded to the appeals court to determine if the newly defined protections were applicable to the Romero suit.

The ruling was the second one in two years involving the Pennhurst School. In 1981, the high court had held that a 1975 federal law did not require states to maintain any particular level of care for the institutionalized mentally retarded.

On June 21, 1982, the Supreme Court agreed to review a challenge to the appointment of federal court special master to monitor Pennhurst's compliance with various court orders. The case was *Pennhurst State School v. Halderman.*

Medical Ethics

New AMA Ethics Code

Following are the principles of ethics endorsed July 22, 1980 by the American Medical Association's House of Delegates:

170

Preamble

The medical profession has long sub-scribed to a body of ethical statements de-veloped primarily for the benefit of the pa-tient. As a member of this profession, a physician must recognize responsibility not only to patients, but also to society, to other health professionals, and to self. The fol-lowing principles adopted by the American Medical Association are not laws, but standards of conduct which define the es-sentials of honorable behavior for the phy-sician.

[I]

A physician shall be dedicated to pro-viding competent medical service with compassion and respect for human digni-ty.

[II]

A physician shall deal honestly with pa-tients and colleagues, and strive to expose those physicians deficient in character or competence, or who engage in fraud or de-ception.

[III]

A physician shall respect the law and also recognize a responsibility to seek changes in those requirements which are contrary to the best interests of the patient.

[IV]

A physician shall respect the rights of pa-tients, of colleagues, and of other health professionals, and shall safeguard patient confidences within the constraints of the law.

[V]

A physician shall continue to study, ap-ply and advance scientific knowledge, make relevant information available to patients, colleagues, and the public, ob-tain consultation, and use the talents of other health professionals when indi-cated.

[VI]

A physician shall, in the provision of appropriate patient care, except in emer-gencies, be free to choose whom to serve, with whom to associate, and the environ-ment in which to provide medical serv-ices.

[VII]

A physician shall recognize bility to participate in activities to an improved community.

Ethics of health care studied. In a report made public March 27, 1983 a presidential commission concluded that society had "an ethical obligation to insure equitable access to health care for all" and that the "ultimate responsibility" for ensuring that this obli-gation was met lay with the federal govern-ment.

The study, called "Securing Access to Health Care," was prepared by the 11-member President's Commission for the Study of Ethical Problems in Medicine and Biomedical and Behavioral Research. Shortly before the panel had issued a report endorsing the so-called "right to die" of ter-minally ill patients.

The report on access to health care did not specifically criticize President Reagan, but a number of its conclusions ran counter to policies put forward by the Reagan administration. Recent cutbacks in the Medicaid program and limitations on eligi-bility had diminished access to health care for many poor people, the report said. Plans to charge small fees to Medicaid recipients could impose a "substantial burden" on some and "appear undersirable from an ethical standpoint," the report concluded.

The report was also critical of government efforts to tighten up on Social Security dis-ability payments. "The process of 'weeding out' ineligible enrollees appears to have be-come one of terminating a substantial num-ber of beneficiaries for the purpose of budg-etary savings," the report said.

On the other hand, an administration plan to levy taxes on health insurance premiums paid by employers was seen as acceptable. Such a tax, if implemented properly, would pri-marily affect middle- and upper-income fam-ilies, the commission said, and so would not "compromise access to adequate health care."

After stating that an ethical obligation to afford health care to all existed, the report said that "Equitable access to health care

171

requires that all citizens be able to secure an adequate level of care without excessive burdens. The cost of achieving equitable access to health care ought to be shared fairly."

But, the commission noted, equity did "not require equal access." Equal health status could not be considered a reasonable goal, the panel said, because individuals would always vary in their level of health. The commission also noted that it had declined to judge "whether the term 'obligation' should be read as entailing a moral right" to health care.

The panel did not offer recommendations as to what actions, if any, the government should take in order to see that society met its obligation of ensuring access to health care. Morris Abram, the chairman of the panel, said the report was intended to provide criteria by which the fairness of health care proposals could be judged.

Of the 11 persons on the commission, eight had been appointed by President Reagan and three by former President Carter. One member of the panel, H. Thomas Ballantine Jr., a neurosurgeon at the Massachusetts General Hospital, issued a dissenting view.

Ballantine said that the report had been "politicized to an unacceptable degree." He said he accepted the idea that there was a "moral imperative" for society to insure access to health care, but added, "I do not agree that the failures of the market, of charity and of activities at the local and state levels have been so severe as to warrant at this time increased intrusion of the federal government into the health care sector."

Unnecessary Surgery

In 1975 the Oversight & Investigations Subcommittee of the House Interstate & Foreign Commerce Committee conducted an investigation that, Subcommittee Chairman John E. Moss reported, focused "upon an indepth examination of unnecessary surgery, particularly to the extent to which the Med-

icare and Medicaid Programs contribute to overutilization and support unnecessary surgical procedures." The report, as issued under the date of Jan. 19, 1976, is excerpted on the following pages. Portions of Rep. Moss' letter of transmittal follow on this page:

The report concludes that second consultations before surgery can cut down on unncessary surgical procedures. This report recommends that the Department of Health, Education, and Welfare (HEW) should promptly institute a program of independent second professional opinions to confirm the need for elective surgery underwritten by Medicare and Medicaid. The Subcommittee found that surgical payments by the fee-for-service mechanism encourages surgery in questionable situations. It recommends that a comprehensive study be undertaken to examine this situation in depth. The report determines that HEW has a totally inadequate data and information system and recommends that HEW remedy this situation promptly.

The report spells out concern that Professional Standards Review Organizations (PSRO's) are being developed too slowly and do not encourage a review of the entire gamut of health care. It recommends that this situation be corrected.

The report finds that the Secretary of HEW is not fulfilling his obligations under the mandatory provisions of the Social Security Act that call for establishing appropriate utilization control standards to protect consumers of health care. The report recommends that this situation be corrected forthwith.

Finally, the report indicates that unnecessary surgery has deleterious effects upon the American public. It estimates there were approximately 2.4 million unnecessary surgeries performed in 1974 at a cost to the American public of almost $4 billion, and it futher estimates that these unnecessary surgeries led to 11,900 deaths last year.

III. Summary of Findings
A. SECOND CONSULTATIONS

Testimony by experts studying elective surgery indicates that second consultations can lower surgical abuse as well as concomitant costs. This applies to both voluntary and mandatory consultative programs.

B. SURGICAL PAYMENTS BY FEE-FOR-SERVICE VERSUS SALARIED ARRANGEMENTS

The fee-for-service payment mechanism absent adequate professional controls may encourage and provide financial incentives for surgeons to perfrom surgery in equivocal situations and may encourage the performance of more extensive procedures in questionable situations.

C. DATA NEEDS AND INFORMATION SYSTEMS

The Medical Services Administration (MSA) of HEW has failed to collect the most rudimentary information necessary to monitor significant portions of the Medicaid program and still does not require the states to furnish data on the volume or type of surgery performed.

D. SURGERY ON AN OUTPATIENT BASIS

The evidence suggests that up to one-fourth of surgical procedures now performed in hospitals might be performed without hospitalization. If up to 25 percent of surgical procedures can be performed with equal safety on an ambulatory basis, this would mean substantial savings for both consumers and taxpayers.

At least three factors contributing to this excess hospitalization include—

(1) Consumers receive little, if any, insurance reimbursement if the surgery is not done on an inpatient basis.

(2) Hospitals receive no compensation for unfilled beds and unused operating rooms, and

(3) Physician fee-for-service reimbursement discourages use of the ambulatory mode for minor surgical procedures.

E. SURGICAL MANPOWER

There appears to be a correlation between the volume of unnecessary surgery performed and the number of physicians performing surgery. In some geographic areas, the number of surgeons is excessive.

Many of the surgical procedures are being performed by non-certified specialists who have failed the certification examination and by general practitioners.

F. PROFESSIONAL STANDARDS REVIEW ORGANIZATIONS

Professional Standards Review Organizations (PSRO's) should be considered as an adjunct to but not as a replacement for second consultations before elective surgery. The PSRO machinery as currently constituted will not (1) routinely provide consumers with protection against unnecessary surgery, (2) encourage procedures to be done on an ambulatory basis, or (3) be established at a rapid enough pace to insure high-quality care to consumers in the near future.

G. MANDATORY NATURE OF THE LAW

Section 1903 (g) of the Social Security Act requires the Secretary of Health, Education, and Welfare to monitor state methods and procedures to review utilization of care and services under Medicaid. It is unambiguous, mandatory, and self-executing, and the Secretary of HEW is legally bound to implement that section of the law. Proper implementation would save millions of taxpayer dollars through curtailment of unnecessary procedures.

H. HEW POLICY OF SLIPPAGE AND DELAYS

HEW has been obligated since September 30, 1973 to undertake validation surveys in order to establish that cost controls and quality procedures for Medicaid are in effect. The Secretary has been obligated since that time to make findings in order for states to receive incentive payments. The Secretary has failed to comply with these obligations.

I. MALADMINISTRATION

HEW, since July 1, 1973—

(1) designed and undertook a sample validation survey, commencing October 1973, which the Department later claimed to be invalid;

(2) undertook a second validation survey in the same fiscal year (commencing June 1974), although the HEW General Counsel claimed this was unnecessary;

(3) asked for a "plan of correction" from states but has not indicated the

purpose of this "plan," nor has HEW undertaken adequate followup of the "plan" implementation; and

(4) has not yet undertaken fiscal year 1975 or 1976 validation surveys which are required to be conducted by HEW for states to receive full Medicaid funding.

J. METHODOLOGY

The methodology employed by HEW for the validation survey was developed without appropriate coordination between the Medicaid officers and the HEW General Counsel, a fact which has led to delays of two years and doubt about the validity of the surveys. The surveys emphasized patient records and gave inadequate attention to other aspects of the utilization control review that are required for compliance, such as single-state agency requirements and committee utilization review activities.

HEW procedures on reducing state payments unless quality provisions are met require clearance by the Office of the General Counsel. The workload in that office leads to inordinate delays in mandated requirements.

K. EXAMINATION OF REDUCTION PROVISIONS

A review of penalties, sanctions, and incentives by HEW, such as that announced in September 1975 by Secretary Matthews, is appropriate and important. However, failure to carry out the law during this period of review cannot be excused or justified.

L. COST ISSUES

There are significant costs associated with unnecessary surgery. The Subcommittee estimates that 2.38 million surgical procedures were unnecessarily performed in 1974 at a cost to the American public of $3.92 billion. . . .

Medicare support of unnecessary procedures is estimated to be $816 million, while Medicaid support is estimated to be $272 million. Medicaid also spent approximately $150 million for hospital procedures that could have been performed on an outpatient basis. . . .

M. QUALITY ISSUES

It is estimated that unnecessary surgeries led to 11,900 deaths last year. Medicaid support was involved in an estimated 1700 deaths. . . .

There were striking variations in surgical length of stay by region and wide variations in the rates of surgical removal by organs within small geographic areas studied.

At this time, PSRO's are not a viable substitute for mandated utilization review programs. The effect the present functioning PSRO's have had upon unnecessary surgery needs to be examined fully before they are accepted as a substitute for the mandatory requirements under utilization control.

Specific deficiencies in public accountability are widespread within HEW and include—

(1) a complete lack of information on the incidence, prevalence, and costs of surgery financed under Medicaid;

(2) a lack of coordination in the information requested of the states on financial and statistical matters; and

(3) a lack of timely requirements for state reporting. For example, at the beginning of fiscal year 1976, the most recent statistical report available by HEW was for fiscal year 1972.

Public accountability must be improved by HEW to avoid squandering taxpayer dollars.

IV. RECOMMENDATIONS

On the basis of the above findings, the Subcommittee makes the following recommendations:

A. With respect to second consultations—

(1) The Subcommittee recommends that HEW promptly mandate second professional opinions to confirm the need for elective or non-emergency surgery under Medicare and Medicaid.

(2) The Subcommittee recommends that such a program be carefully evaluated to determine the (a) impact upon quality of care, (b) containment of health care costs, (c) percentage of surgical procedures deemed to be unnecessary, and (d) cost of administering

such a program compared with the cost of paying for unnecessary procedures.

B. With respect to salaried arrangements—

(1) The Subcommittee is impressed with the evidence presented that prepayment plans for consumers and salaried surgeons help reduce surgery in equivocal situations. More evidence is needed, however, to determine the extent to which this result can be achieved nationally. The Subcommittee is also interested in determining what factors other than the payment and salary mechanisms help account for the differences in surgery in different areas, e.g., scarcity of beds, population mix of the pre-paid plans, ratio of surgeons to population, etc.

The Subcommittee, therefore, recommends that HEW immediately undertake a comprehensive study to determine the differences in health indices, costs and the surgical procedure rates between salaried surgeons and fee-for-service surgeons.

(2) Further, the Subcommittee recommends that HEW utilize Section 402 (a) of the Social Security Amendments of 1967 to provide for demonstration projects concerning innovative arrangements for reimbursement to providers utilizing experimental arrangements to provide surgical services in a more cost-effective manner. These arrangements should be monitored carefully for cost containment and quality control.

(3) An annual report should be required of HEW concerning the comprehensive study cited above and the demonstration projects under Section 402 (a) to the following congressional committees:

Senate: Labor and Public Welfare, Finance, Government Operations, Appropriations, and Budget.

House of Representatives: Interstate and Foreign Commerce, Ways and Means, Government Operations, Appropriations, and Budget.

C. With respect to outpatient surgery—
The Subcommittee is impressed with evidence presented that up to 20 or 25 percent of surgical procedures can be performed without the need for hospitalization. More evidence is needed to determine what factors—such as types of surgical procedures or reimbursement mechanisms—retard outpatient surgery.

The Subcommittee will request that the Office of Technology Assessment (OTA) undertake a study projecting the available data on outpatient surgery to the population as a whole, project the savings, and evaluate the impact this increase in outpatient surgery would have on quality of care.

D. With respect to data and information needs—

The Subcommittee is convinced that the Medical Services Administration (MSA) needs to improve its data collection systems immediately. At a minimum, major topical categories, such as the extent of surgery and dollars spent for surgery, must be enumerated.

The Subcommittee recommends and will request promptly from the Secretary of HEW a suggested protocol for data collection that will include the above-listed items.

E. With respect to Surgical Manpower—
The Subcommittee recommends that Congress consider legislation that will require states to adopt uniform minimum standards, to be prescribed by HEW, for certification and recertification for physicians performing surgery.

F. With respect to Professional Standards Review Organizations—

(1) The Subcommittee believes that PSRO's have been implemented by HEW at a pace far slower than Congress intended. The Subcommittee recommends that HEW submit a revised timetable providng for implementation of PSRO's not later than January 1, 1977 to the Congressional committees listed in paragraph B. (3) above.

(2) The Subcommittee recommends that the lack of emphasis by HEW in requiring PSRO's to develop quality control programs for non-hospital care

175

be corrected immediately. HEW should require all designated PSRO's to submit a plan indicating their procedures for determining that care be provided in the most cost-effective manner—especially in cases when hospitalization is unnecessary.

G. With respect to administrative and legal issues—

(1) The Subcommittee recommends that the Secretary of HEW implement the utilization control requirements under Section 1903 of the Social Security Act *immediately*. Further delay shall be considered by the Subcommittee as an intentional failure to carry out the law by the Secretary.

(2) The Secretary of HEW has failed to make compliance findings under Section 1903 (g) of the Social Security Act on a quarterly basis as required by law.

If this willful inaction of the Secretary continues uncorrected, the Subcommittee recommends that Congress review its own powers of enforcement to compel compliance with its statutory mandates and request that the GAO invoke sanctions available against the Department of Health, Education, and Welfare and the appropriate HEW officers under the Budget and Accounting Act of 1921 and the Accounting and Auditing Act of 1950.

(3) The Subcommittee recommends that Congress consider legislation that will provide effective remedies to prevent departmental and agency heads from acting in contravention of specific statutory provisions.

(4) The Subcommittee notes the lack of coordination among health services within HEW. It considers the current system of separate statistical units, different standards, multiple inspections, and overlapping auditing procedures an unnecessary, bureaucratic burden upon providers and a substantial waste of taxpayer dollars.

The Subcommittee, therefore, recommends the need for new legislation to coordinate the health service programs now scattered under the control of the Assistant Secretary for Health, the Administrator of the Social and Rehabilitation Service, and the Commissioner of the Social Security Administration.

(5) The Subcommittee recommends that HEW, wherever possible, take steps promptly to streamline portions of the overlapping bureaucratic process that can be remedied administratively.

(6) The Subcommittee further recommends the need for new legislation that will coordinate Public Health Service (PHS), Medicaid and Medicare health service programs under a new administrative framework.

H. With respect to cost and quality issues—

(1) The Subcommittee recommends that HEW take immediate steps to rectify the appalling lack of information on the incidence, prevalence, per capita utilization, resource supply rates, and costs of surgery financed under Medicaid. It further recommends that the lack of coordination in information-gathering be rectified and that data collection be accelerated.

(2) The Subcommittee recommends that the excessively burdensome procedures for states be streamlined and made more relevant to program planning and operative needs. The Subcommittee recommends that new procedures be implemented by June 30, 1976 and that a draft of the new procedures be submitted to those Congressional committees cited in paragraph B(3) above.

(1) *Mortality due to unnecessary surgery*

On July 15, 1975, Dr. Wolfe testified:

Bunker has estimated that the mortality rate for elective surgery is 0.5 percent (it is higher for emergency surgery). If this rate is applied to unnecessary operations, the U.S. mortality due to unnecessary surgery may be 16,000 deaths per year.[152]

This estimate of 16,000 deaths was based upon the 3.2 million surgical procedures deemed to be unnecessary by Dr. Wolfe.[153]

The Bunker estimate was contained in a study published in the *New England Jour-*

[152]Note 38 *supra* at 67.
[153]*Id.*

176

nal of Medicine, December 6, 1973. Bunker and Wennberg stated:

Discretionary operations all carry a discrete and measurable risk of death. The operative and postoperative mortality for all operations in the United States is approximately 1.4 percent (National Center for Health Statistics, unpublished data). For discretionary operations one might conservatively assume a mortality of 0.5 percent. [154]

HEW's Office of Research and Statistics published in 1975 an extensive study of Medicare recipients demonstrating a much higher mortality rate. This study, using 1967 data on hospital discharges, found that of 1,609,539 discharges *with surgery*, 85,222 patients were discharged dead representing a mortality rate of 5.2 percent.[155]

The study done in 1967 utilized an elderly population, a mixture of discretionary and non-discretionary procedures, including procedures that were necessary as well as unnecessary. All these factors tend to make the 5.2 percent figure an underestimate of the total population. The fact that 85,000 patients died out of 1.6 million procedures performed makes it probable that at least 100,000 patients were discharged dead as a result of the 12,000,000 surgical procedures performed in 1967—a mortality rate exceeding 0.8 percent.

The Commission on Professional and Hospital Activities (CPHA) of Ann Arbor, Michigan gathers data jointly with IMS, America, Ltd., on hospital stays. Dr. Virgil Slee, President of CPHA, estimated that of the 7,600,000 patients operated upon during the first six months of 1975, 105,000 patients were discharged dead. That estimate represents a mortality rate for all surgery of 1.4 percent.

Three operations: hysterectomy, tonsilectomy, and cholecystectomy were examined for the relationship between unnecessary procedures and mortality rates. Dr. Slee provided the following estimates:

1ST 6 MONTHS (1975)

	Operations	Discharged dead	Mortality rate (percent)
Hysterectomy, abdominal	276,000	[1]500	[1]0.2
Tonsilectomy:			
(a) Tonsilectomies	115,000	([2])	. . . .
(b) Tonsilectomies and adenoidectomy	257,000	([2])	. . . .
Cholecystectomy	226,000	2,000	1.0

[1]Approximately.
[2]Virtually none.

These data serve to confirm the reasonableness of the Bunker mortality rate estimate of 0.5 percent, the estimate used by the Subcommittee.

CPHA and IMS, America Ltd., collect data for 30 percent of all hospitals in the United States. They obtained their estimates of mortality rates by projecting data from their 30 percent sample to the population as a whole.

The Subcommittee used a conservative estimate for the volume of unnecessary surgical procedures—2.38 million. Utilizing this figure and the estimated surgical mortality rate developed by Bunker and Wennberg, 0.5 percent, *the number of deaths from unnecessary surgeries approximates 11,900 for* last year.

Needless X-ray use charged. Dr. Karl Z. Morgan, professor of health physics at the Georgia Institute of Technology in Atlanta,

[154]Note 1 *supra.*
[155]U.S. Social Security Administration, Office of Research and Statistics, *Medicare: Health Insurance for the Aged, 1967, Section 4.1: Short-Stay Hospital Utilization,* Washington, D.C. (1975), at 4.1–9.

told the American Cancer Society's seminar for science writers in St. Augustine, Fla. March 27, 1974 that Americans received harmful overdoses of radiation from diagnostic X-rays. Asserting that most U.S. doctors and dentists "didn't have the remotest concept of the risks associated with exposure to diagnostic X-rays," Morgan charged that 3,000 Americans died each year from cancer resulting from unnecessary exposure to diagnostic X-rays.

Morgan, director of health physics at the Atomic Energy Commission's Oak Ridge (Tenn.) National Laboratory 1943-72, urged that outmoded, high-dose X-ray equipment be replaced with new low-dose apparatus; that radiation technologists be appropriately educated, trained and certified; and that dentists reserve use of X-rays for special needs only.

Unneeded hysterectomies charged. Hysterectomies—many of them unnecessary—were performed more frequently than tonsillectomies, two leading medical professors told a House Commerce subcommittee May 9, 1977.

Operations to remove the womb rose by what Dr. Kenneth Ryan of Harvard University called "a staggering" 25% between 1970 and 1975. Some 725,000 hysterectomies were performed in 1975. That figure surpassed the 685,000 tonsillectomies and 319,000 appendectomies performed in the same year. Among all surgery, hysterectomies were outnumbered only by 1,700,000 dilations and currettages (D&C).

The Commerce oversight subcommittee had been investigating unneeded surgery for two years to determine whether federal laws should required a doctor to obtain another doctor's opinion before performing an operation paid for by federal funds.

Ryan and Dr. John Morris, gynecology chief at Yale University, testified that hysterectomies were "excessive treatment" for the purpose of contraception or for the prevention of womb cancer by removing the womb.

An American Medical Association spokesman replied in testimony that only a "tiny percentage" had been unnecessary and that there was not "100% unanimity" among doctors on the extent of unnecessary surgery.

Dr. James Sammons, executive president of the AMA, denied the assertion that more than a few doctors had "a pecuniary motive" in performing hysterectomies. (The rate of hysterectomies had been found higher among patients of surgeons who collected individual fees than among patients of salaried surgeons who were members of prepaid medical plans.)

Sammons said the medical profession had begun to crack down on doctors who ought not to be in practice because of incompetence or unworthiness by tightening the powers of state licensing boards and initiating more disciplinary actions.

Second opinions on surgery urged. The federal government would finance second medical opinions before elective surgery for elderly patients in the Medicare program, Undersecretary of Health, Education and Welfare Hale Champion announced Nov. 1, 1977. In conjunction with the agency's new "major effort" to eliminate unnecessary surgery, Champion urged all Americans to get a second medical opinion on operative conditions except in the case of emergencies.

The undersecretary singled out tonsillectomies, hysterectomies and gall bladder operations as the three commonly abused procedures, for which patients should consult a second doctor. He did not specify how much surgery was unnecessarily performed, but said that the nation's overall surgery rate had increased by 25% between 1970 and 1975.

Few seek second opinion on surgery. A unique program that provided free second surgeon's opinions in Portland, Maine had resulted in less than 2% of the surgical patients availing themselves of the service, according to the Washington Post Jan. 29, 1979.

The cost of the program was borne by Portland's doctors themselves and was organized by them to preempt what they said was a less effective plan proposed by Blue Cross-Blue Shield of Maine. It also was aimed at saving what they considered the unnecessary cost of a new bureaucracy to administer the second opinions.

Doctors attributed the small response to patient's desires to trust their surgeons, to the probability that the patients knew something about surgeons in a small city before they consulted them and to the belief that not much unnecessary surgery was being performed.

In Hartford, Conn., a city about eight times as large as Portland, a similarly small number of patients asking for second opinions was also reported. Insurance plans provided for the cost there.

In New York City, where the size of the population made it even less likely that a patient knew much about his surgeon, requests for second opinions under Blue Cross and Blue Shield had more than doubled in the program's second year which was attributed to advertising. However, participation was said to still be relatively low.

'Unneeded' surgery debated. A study by Blue Cross and Blue Shield of Greater New York that showed 30% of surgical cases since 1976 had not been confirmed by a second opinion was cited March 19, 1979, by officials from the Department of Health, Education and Welfare as they sought to crack down on unnecessary surgery.

Studies sponsored by HEW suggested that about one-third of the estimated 20 million surgical procedures performed in the country were not needed. HEW attributed unnecessary surgery to too many surgeons, too many empty hospital beds and public health-care reimbursement that paid only when a person was hospitalized and surgery performed.

At the same press conference, it was announced that the New York Life Insurance Company had become the first major private health insurer to expand its coverage to pay up to $100 for the cost of second opinions on the need for the surgery.

The American Medical Association responded March 19, 1979 that the estimate of unnecessary surgery by HEW was "grossly exaggerated." The spokesman said that the AMA had no patience with "bad actors who perform unnecessary surgery" and said that its disciplinary procedures had multiplied six times since peer-review procedures were established in hospitals. He added that unnecessary surgery represented only a "very, very tiny percentage" of the surgical procedures performed each year.

One dissenter to the second-surgical opinion campaign was Dr. W. Jack Stelmach, head of the American Academy of Family Physicians. "People definitely should take into consideration that the business of surgeons is to do surgery," Stelmach was reported as saying in the Feb. 5 issue of Forbes magazine. "Cutting is cutting and always traumatic. A nonsurgical alternative should always be given a fair hearing."

Hospital mishap studies reported. A one-year study described in the New England Journal of Medicine had found that the deaths of 11 patients admitted for surgery to Boston's Peter Bent Brigham Hospital were "directly attributable to error," it was reported March 12, 1981. A second study, cited in the same issue, found that of 815 nonsurgical patients in another Boston hospital, over a third had developed complications resulting from their treatment.

The 11 patients who died were part of a group of 36 found to have suffered complications caused by surgeons' mistakes. Twenty-three of those 36 had been admitted to Brigham Hosptial after a mishap occured at another institution. According to the study, "ninety percent of the errors were those of unnecessary, contra-indicated or technically defective surgical activity." Other problems included wrong diagnoses and delays of needed surgery.

The second study, conducted at an unidentified teaching hospital, found that in 9% of the cases reviewed, a complication had threatened the patient's life or produced a serious disability. In 2% of the cases, it was said to have contributed to the patient's death.

Many medical authorities believed the studies findings accurately reflected conditions in hospitals throughout the country.

Health Costs and Scarce Resources

Proposals to cut health-care costs. Guidelines to stem the proliferation of unnecessary medical facilities, procedures and machinery were proposed Sept. 26, 1977, by Secretary of Health, Education and Welfare Joseph A. Califano Jr. The measures were intended to supplement the Carter Administration's hospital cost containment bill that was stalled in Congress.

The cost of health care in the U.S. was rising at twice the national inflation rate, or at the rate of $1 million an hour, according to Califano Sept. 9. "If Americans receive exactly the same amount of care today that they received yesterday, they will pay $24 million more for it today," Califano told the House health subcommittee (of the Interstate & Foreign Commerce Committee). That figure referred to the overall cost of hospital care.

The health care industry, the third largest after construction and agriculture, had $139 billion in revenues in 1976—more than triple the amount in 1966. Those figures reflected the costs of 375,000 doctors, 7,000 hospitals, 16,000 nursing homes and thousands of related medical laboratories and health-product suppliers.

Streamlining measures to boost the efficiency of existing facilities would: eliminate an estimated 100,000 of the nation's 970,000 acute-care hospital beds, set minimum levels for the number of specialized operations performed at individual hospitals and reduce the number, distribution and use of costly, high-technology devices.

The standards would limit the number of hospital beds in any particular area to no more than four per 1,000 persons and would require an overall hospital occupancy rate of at least 80%. In an effort to force consolidation of costly equipment and hospital services, procedures such as open-heart surgery and machines such as CAT scanners would be concentrated in designated hospitals.

The measures would not apply to federal hospitals or facilities devoted to long-term care of the chronically ill.

Experts urge curb on X-ray device. Measures should be taken to limit the acquisition, use and cost of the new X-ray machine known as the CAT scanner, according to a report published May 2, 1977, by the National Academy of Science's Institute of Medicine.

The computerized axial tomographic (CAT) scanner, which cost between $300,000 and $700,000, used a thin beam of X-rays in combination with a computer to produce clear cross-sectional pictures of the body's soft tissue. Currently, 760 such devices were in use or on order, less than four years after the first two units were installed in the U.S.

Critics charged that the CAT scanner was being obtained and used indiscriminately, boosting medical costs and possibly resulting in medical profiteering. Patients were charged between $150 and $700 for a series of scans, according to the study.

The NAS panel, which reviewed the CAT scanner at the request of the Blue Cross Association, advised insurers to pay only for approved use of CAT scanners at institutions where they had been acquired with the sanction of an appropriate health planning agency. This would ensure that scanners would be installed under a certificate of need program and that full use (at least 2,500 diagnostic tests a year) would be made of them.

Medical aid increases. The cost of federal aid to kidney patients increased from $200 million in fiscal 1974 to $1.3 billion projected for fiscal 1980, and the number of patients rose to 47,000 from 15,400 over the same period. The report from Washington appeared in the April 27, 1979, New York Times. Approximately 90% of Americans undergoing dialysis (cleansing the blood of impurities by machine) did so at an institution where yearly costs per patient ranged from $15,000 to $30,000. When the procedure was performed at home, the average yearly cost was $8,000 to $12,000.

In Canada, only 40% of dialysis was done at an institution; in Great Britain, it was 35%.

Kidney dialysis bill signed. President Carter June 13, 1978 signed legislation revising the program providing Medicare coverage for renal diseases. The changes were aimed at encouraging persons with end stage renal disease (kidney failure) to perform dialysis at home or at self-care centers, rather than in hospitals. Kidney transplants were also encouraged as an alternative to hospital care.

Hospital dialysis was much more expensive than dialysis at home or in self-care centers. Since 1972, when Congress legislated the Medicare renal disease program, the percentage of patients performing dialysis at home had dropped to 10% from 40%. Supporters of the bill just signed said the 1972 legislation had caused the decline in self-care by providing financial incentives for patients to go to hospitals.

Annual spending on the renal disease program had reached $1 billion and was projected to climb to $6 billion by 1992 if no changes were made. The patient population was not large: it was expected to reach 75,000 by 1992.

The bill provided that regional councils should set goals to increase the percentage of new patients performing self-care, or having kidney transplants. Other provisions made it easier for patients to obtain Medicare reimbursement for costs associated with self-care or transplants.

The House gave final approval to the bill, by voice vote, May 1. The Senate cleared it, also by voice vote, May 24.

Michigan hospital may charge non-residents more. The Michigan Supreme Court ruled in 1978 that a hospital may charge non-residents its regular fee plus a twenty percent surcharge. The court held that differential fees do not violate equal protection when based on the distinction between residents and non-residents. The case was *Zrenchik v. Peoples' Community Hospital Authority.*

Fewer cancer tests advocated. The American Cancer Society announced March 20, 1981 that it was recommending the elimination of some cancer detection tests and a sharp reduction in the frequency of others.

The society in a major change of policy said that it was dropping its recommendation that certain cancer tests be given every year. Among these were an annual chest X-ray and sputum test for cigarette smokers and others who risked incurring lung cancer.

The society also changed its recommendation of an annual Pap smear to "at least once every three years" for all women 20 to 65 years old and for younger women who were sexually active.

The new guidelines, according to Dr. Saul B. Gusberg, president of the cancer society, were intended only for persons who displayed no symptoms of cancer. They were designed to "deliver essentially the same health benefit as previous recommendations to the public at greatly reduced cost, risk and inconvenience to the patient," he said.

The new guidelines were prompted by growing medical research indicating that some tests failed either to detect a significant number of cancer cases or to appreciably increase a patient's chances of surviving.

The changes in the society's test guidelines were based on evaluations by medical consultants of the benefits, risks and costs of the various tests in cancer detection. Considered in the evaluation were such factors as the ability of the tests to decrease mortality rates, the costs and risks of the tests and their diagnostic accuracy.

Dr. Gusberg emphasized that the new recommendations were intended as guidelines for the public, not rules for specific individuals. He said that "personal histories, risk factors, objectives and budgets are different for each of us and no single recommendation can therefore be fitted for all."

1981 health care costs up 15%. The Department of Health and Human Services July 26, 1982 announced that spending for health care in the U.S. had risen to $287 billion in 1981. That figure amounted to a record high of 9.8% of the gross national product.

The total spending for health care, including payments from insurance companies and the government, had risen 15.1% over the 1980 figure. It was the second largest increase in the last 15 years, following a 15.8% increase in 1980.

Health care spending averaged $1,225 per person in 1981. Nearly 43% of the total costs were carried by federal, state and local governments, including funding for Medicare and Medicaid.

Health and Human Services Secretary Richard S. Schweiker said the fact that health costs were rising "well above the rate of inflation" was "the strongest argument for reforming the existing system of health care cost reimbursement."

Schweiker had proposed changes in the U.S. health care system aimed at controlling prices by increasing competition in the health care field. He also proposed changing federal tax code provisions that he said encouraged excessive use of doctors and hospitals.

Schweiker estimated that about three-quarters of the cost increase had resulted from inflation; almost one-fifth from increased "intensity of care," and 7% from increases in the size and the average age of the population.

The costs of Medicare payments had risen 21.5% since 1980, the department reported. Hospital costs were up 17.5% to $118 billion, nearly a quadruple increase in the last ten years. Payments to doctors amounted to $54.8 billion, and the cost of nursing home care was up to $24.2 billion.

The combined cost of Medicare and Medicaid payments amounted to $76.1 billion.

The department's report stated that patients were isolated from the real costs of health care because two-thirds of the costs were paid either by government programs or by private insurers. In 1965, by contrast, patients had paid directly for slightly more than half of all health care expenses in the U.S.

HHS Secretary Richard Schweiker, according to reports Sept. 10 and 13, 1982, had ordered his department to prepare legislation under which hospitals would be paid in advance for certain types of Medicare treatment. The reimbursement levels would be calculated on the basis of average costs for certain types of treatment. Hospitals would then be paid in advance a slightly smaller amount than the calculated average.

Schweiker and other proponents of the plan contended that the flat payment in advance would give hospitals an incentive to control costs, since the hospitals would be permitted to retain any savings they achieved.

Since different types of treatment would, under the plan, still be reimbursed at different rates (based on the calculated averages), hospitals would presumably not seek to refuse patients whose care would be particularly expensive. Such a possibility had been advanced as an argument against an earlier form of the prepayment plan, in which hospitals would simply have been paid an average amount calculated for all different types of illnesses.

State of the Union: President Proposes Major Transfer of Welfare Programs to States as Part of 'New Federalism'

President Ronald Reagan predicted that the budget deficit for fiscal 1982, which began Oct. 1, 1981, would be less than $100 billion, and he expected that the deficit for fiscal 1983, in the budget he would present Feb. 8, would fall below that.

In the meantime, he was asking Congress to get to work on his "new federalism." It would be a "financially equal swap," he said, in which the states and cities would take over the food-stamp program and Aid to Families with Dependent Children, the basic federal welfare system.

In return, the federal government would assume the total responsibility and cost of the Medicaid program of health care for the poor. Currently, Medicaid was a joint federal-state program.

The President also proposed to turn over to the states responsibility for more than 40 other federal programs in education, community development, transportation and social services.

During the transition period, under the President's program, a temporary trust fund, supplied with $28 billion annually from excise taxes and the "windfall" profits tax on crude oil, would be available to the states for financing the newly transferred programs.

The states would have the option of taking their allotments out of the trust fund and using the money as they saw fit on other programs.

By 1988, under the Reagan plan, the fate of the transferred programs would be up to the states. They could continue them or abolish them, whichever they chose to do. The trust fund also would be phased out, and the right to collect the excise taxes involved would be passed on to the states.

The President's plan was designed to deal with what he considered "the over-powering growth of federal grants-in-aid" programs. There were about 500 of these when he took office, costing nearly $100 billion, Reagan said.

"A maze of interlocking jurisdictions and levels of government confronts average citizens in trying to solve even the simplest of problems," he said. "They do not know where to turn for answers, who to hold accountable, who to praise, who to blame, who to vote for or against."

Neither the president nor Congress could adequately administer "this jungle," the President said.

"Let us solve this problem with a single bold stroke," he said, "the return of some $47 billion in federal programs to state and local government, together with the means to finance them and a transition period of nearly 10 years to avoid unncessary disruption."

The White House was figuring the cost to the states of the welfare and food-stamp programs at $16.5 billion. Together with the cost of the other 40 programs to be transferred under state and local jurisdiction, the total cost amounted to $46.7 billion.

The swap cost to the federal government in the trade-off, by assuming Medicaid costs and the "federalism trust fund," was estimated at $47.1 billion.

The exchange of Medicaid costs for the expense of food stamps and welfare would begin in 1984, under the Reagan plan. Administration officials expected the states to make out better financially in the long run than the federal government, given the normal volatility of medical costs.

Currently, Medicaid was costing $19.1 billion compared with $16.5 billion for welfare and food-stamp expenses. By 1987, the Medicaid cost to the states was estimated to become $25.4 billion, compared with $17.6 billion for the welfare and food-stamp programs.

'Federalism'—a Counterproposal. President Reagan met separately at the White House Feb. 22, 1982, with state and local officals on his "new federalism" plan. There was reportedly general support for the President's plan but disagreement over specifics.

Both groups— leaders of the National Governors Association and the National Association of Counties—preferred changes in the "swap" portion of the Reagan plan under which the federal government would assume all costs of Medicaid care for the poor while states and localities would assume costs and handling of the food-stamp program and Aid to Families with Dependent Children, the major welfare programs.

The governors favored the federal take-over of Medicaid but said transfer of welfare and food-stamp programs would not mesh with their current policies. They suggested further negotiations on that part of the swap.

The county group took a similar position—it endorsed the Medicaid shift but it contended that income-maintenance and welfare programs were federal responsibilities.

There was a general consensus, reportedly, for continuing the discussion and bargaining on the federalism plan.

The governors, according to Gov. Richard A. Snelling (R, Vt.), also voiced opposition at the meeting to the President's new budget, which they felt increased spending pressures on the states because of the federal cutbacks.

Snelling, head of the governors' groups, said "the President did not respond" to the criticism.

Federalism plan on hold. The New York Times reported April 6 that the Reagan administration had suspended its effort to write legislation implementing its "new federalism" plan for turning federal programs back to the states.

Officials of both the administration and the National Governor's Association were quoted as saying that they had reached an impasse on the issue of transferring welfare and food stamp programs to the states in exchange for a federal assumption of Medicaid costs.

An admininstration spokesman was quoted as saying, "We are finished thinking about draft legislation for the swap this year."

The Insanity Defense

Under current law in most states, defendants may be acquitted of murder and other criminal charges if they can prove lack of mental capacity when the crime was committed. In many states, mental incapacity means either inability to appreciate the wrongfulness of the act committed or inability to control one's conduct. The consequence of acquittal by reason of insanity is usually treatment in hospitals for the mentally ill, which define "recovery" by necessarily imprecise standards of whether a patient is likely to be dangerous in the future. Thus the confinement of potentially dangerous people who have already committed crimes may be of uncertain duration.

The validity of the insanity defense has been questioned since a jury acquitted John W. Hinckley, Jr., of the attempted assassination of President Reagan. Legislation has been proposed in Congress and state legislatures which would limit the scope and availability of the defense and would allow consideration of a defendant's mental capacity only at sentencing, rather than determination of criminal liability.

Suspect arrested immediately. John W. Hinckley, Jr., the accused attacker of President Reagan, was tackled immediately by Secret Service agents and police at the scene of the shooting. He was rushed away in a police car and booked on federal charges of attempting to assassinate the President and assaulting a federal employee.

Shortly after midnight March 30–31, 1981, Hinckley was brought before U.S. magistrate Arthur L. Burnett in Washington and the charges were formally filed. The attempted assassination charge carried a maximum sentence of life imprisonment, while the charge of assaulting a federal employee—which referred to the Secret Service agent he had allegedly shot—had a maximum sentence of 10 years. Hinckley was represented at the hearing by two court-appointed lawyers. After it was over he was driven to the Marine base at Quantico, Va. where he was confined in a cell in a correctional facility there.

Hinckley's legal representation was taken over by Vincent J. Fuller, who April 1 asked Burnett to cancel a routine psychiatric examination of Hinckley and to waive a preliminary hearing. Burnett denied both requests.

James Evans, a part-time forensic psychiatrist for the District of Columbia, interviewed Hinckley April 1 to try to determine whether he was mentally competent to stand trial.

Evans' report, released April 2, found Hinckley "mentally competent to stand trial." He had "a rational and factual understanding of the charges and is able to participate with counsel in the preparation of his defense," Evans said.

Federal District Judge William Bryant April 2 ordered Hinckley committed to a

185

psychiatric facility for sanity tests to determine whether he was responsible for his conduct at the time of the shooting.

The ruling upheld a decision earlier April 2 by U.S. magistrate Lawrence Margolis, who also sent the case to a grand jury.

Defense attorneys had objected to the Margolis ruling, demanding "immediate access" to Hinckley by defense psychiatrists before a comprehensive examination by government psychiatrists.

The case was taken to Judge Bryant, who assured the defense it would have "equal access" to Hinckley.

Later April 2, Hinckley was taken to Butner Federal Prison near Raleigh, N.C., where the psychiatric evaluations were to be made.

At the Margolis hearing, defense attorneys had waived Hinckley's right to a preliminary hearing, which would have focused on whether there was "probable cause" to believe that Hinckley shot at the President and the Secret Service agent.

Testing of Hinckley begun—Psychiatric testing of the accused assailant, John Hinckley Jr., began in federal prison at Butner, N.C. April 3, 1981. Comprehensive testing by the prosecution and defense could take up to three months, it was estimated.

Hinckley found sane——Since April, the accused assassin had been undergoing a series of mental examinations to determine whether he was competent to stand trial and whether he was responsible for his actions at the time of the shootings. Those tests were carried out in anticipation of Hinckley's possibly pleading innocent by reason of insanity.

Doctors and lawyers familiar with the case said that a medical report on Hinckley's mental condition, received July 31, had reportedly concluded that he was competent to stand trial and that he was probably sane at the time of the assassination attempt. That report had not yet been released, having been placed under a court seal.

Hinckley Found Not Guilty by Reason of Insanity; Presidential Attacker Committed to Mental Hospital

Effort to change law urged. A federal jury June 21, 1982, found John W. Hinckley Jr. not guilty by reason of insanity on all charges of shooting President Reagan and three others in March 1981.

The verdict, after four days of deliberation, surprised and shocked many observers, in and out of government. There were calls, including one from Attorney General William French Smith, for a change in the law permitting acquittal in such cases.

Hinckley was committed to St. Elizabeth's Hospital in the District of Columbia for an indefinite period. Under the district's law, he was entitled to a hearing within 60 days on whether he was capable of being released from custody.

In his instructions to the jury June 18, federal district Judge Barrington D. Parker had said, in the event of an acquittal based on insanity, the defendant could be released from the hospital "only if the court finds by a preponderance of the evidence that he is not likely to injure himself or other persons due to mental disease."

Judge Parker's instruction to the jury was seen as a key part of the eight-week trial, which produced a confusing welter of conflicting testimony from 41 witnesses, 18 of whom were psychiatrists or other doctors.

Parker told the jury it should find Hinckley not guilty unless the government had proved "beyond a reasonable doubt either that the defendent was not suffering from a mental disease or defect, or else that he nevertheless had substantial capacity on that date both to conform his conduct to the requirements of the law and to appreciate the wrongfulness of his conduct."

Hinckley, 27, had been apprehended with the gun in his hand immediately after the shootings, which hit President Reagan near the heart, White House Press Secretary James S. Brady, in the head, police officer

Thomas K. Delahanty in the back and Secret Service agent Timothy J. McCarthy in the chest.

The President and McCarthy had fully recovered. Delahanty retired on medical disability. Brady remained crippled and disabled with brain damage.

Hinckley has never expressed remorse, in all the hundreds of hours of medical interviews, for the suffering he caused.

The prosecution pointed to this "indifference to the feelings of others" as part of a "narcissistic personality disorder" similar to that of many film actors or professional athletes.

The description was provided by Dr. Park E. Dietz, a psychiatrist for the prosecution. Dietz quoted the defendant as saying, "Actually, I feel good because I accomplished everything on a grand scale."

Hinckley had a "long-standing interest in becoming famous without working," according to Dietz, and this became a key point in the prosecution's case. It provided a motive for the shootings. The shootings were presented as calculated, practiced and prepared, in short, the product of a rational mind.

Hinckley was not so much sick but a spoiled child who had been "evading responsibility all his life," the prosecutors charged.

In presenting the arguments, the prosecution pointed out Hinckley's keen interest in prior assassinations and other widely publicized crimes, his practice with the gun and choice of exploding bullets for the attack. Such deliberate preparation was a sign of sanity, it said.

Chief prosecutor Roger Adelman admitted that Hinckley exhibited mental problems. He was "a sad, depressed person," he said, but that did not prevent him from knowing right from wrong, or being able to conform his behavior to the law.

He was responsible legally for his actions, the prosecution said and he should pay for them.

Hinckley's defense, headed by Vincent H. Fuller of Washington, D.C., said Hinckley lacked remorse because he was unaware the deed was wrong; therefore, he could not be held responsible for it.

The defendant's feelings at the time were like those of "a little boy with a gun" who had done something naughty, Dr. Thomas C. Goldman testified May 24. Hinckley "feels as if he hadn't done anything all that terrible," he said.

In reality, the defense contended, Hinckley was schizophrenic and compelled by delusions. One was that by attempting the assassination he would gain the attention and love of Jodie Foster, a teen-age actress whose image was lodged in his illusion.

Hinckley saw her in the movie *Taxi Driver* at least 15 times, it was said, and he identified with the taxi driver, a loner who went on a murderous rampage to rescue a girl (Foster) from a house of prostitution.

Hinckley "felt like he was acting out a movie script" in the shooting attack, Dr. David Baer testified. He was striving for a "magical union with Jodie Foster," Dr. William Carpenter Jr. said.

In Carpenter's opinion, Hinckley suffered from "process schizophrenia," a severe and potentially incurable, mental illness.

In short, said Fuller, Hinckley was "a totally irrational individual, driven and motivated by his own world, locked in his own mind." He could not be responsible for his conduct and he had no ability to conform with law, the defense said.

During the trial, Hinckley lapsed into erratic behavior several times. Once, he walked out of the trial without asking permission. Miss Foster was testifying at the time, via videotape, that she had had no relationship with him.

Another time, Hinckley blurted out, "You're wrong" to a prison psychiatrist, who said the assassination attempt had not been undertaken to win Foster's love.

The next day, June 16, Hinckley broke

into tears when his defense called his pursuit of Foster "pathetic" and "delusional."

Would restrict insanity defenses. President Reagan Sept. 13 sent Congress legislation that he said would "simplify the justice system and make it more likely that those who commit crimes pay a price." He called the proposal the Criminal Justice Reform Act of 1982.

The proposed legislation would limit the use of the insanity defense and the "exclusionary rule" in federal criminal cases. It would also reduce the opportunities for persons convicted in state courts to appeal their cases to federal courts.

Reagan's proposal would shift the emphasis in federal cases involving insanity pleas to questions of whether the accused knew what he or she was doing when committing the crime, and whether the person intended to commit the act. Current standards generally focused on whether the defendant realized the wrongfulness of the crime and whether the person acted as the result of an irresistible impulse.

Associate Attorney General Rudolph Giuliani described persons likely to be acquitted under the new plan as those who "had the mental age of a two-year-old," or who "believed they were shooting at a tree when in fact they were shooting at a human being."

Under the proposal, mental illness would be a consideration when a convicted person was being sentenced.

Psychiatrists review insanity plea. The American Psychiatric Association Jan. 19, 1983, issued a position paper in defense of the insanity plea in criminal trials. However, the organization recommended that rules surrounding the plea be tightened.

The paper had been prompted by the controversy generated by the trial of John W. Hinckley Jr., who had shot and wounded President Reagan and three others in March 1981. Hinckley was found not guilty by reason of insanity in June 1982 and was subsequently committed to a mental hospital.

The public had reacted to the verdict with widespread calls for the abolition of the insanity plea.

The APA, which represented over 27,000 psychiatrists, said it was "extremely skeptical" about efforts to replace the insanity verdict with a "guilty but mentally ill" verdict. (The organization took no position in the Hinckley case.)

The group suggested that the courts had placed too great a burden on the psychiatrist called to testify in such cases, and that the insanity plea had blurred the distinctions between legal and medical concepts.

"We believe that neither the law, the public, psychiatry, nor the victims of violence have been well served by the general approach and reform of the last 10 years, which has obscured the quasi-criminal nature of the insanity defense," the paper stated ". . . Insanity is a legal and not a medical concept; responsibility is a moral and not a medical concept."

The organization defended the plea on the ground that "punishment for wrongful deeds should be predicated upon moral responsibility." Persons who committed crimes without fully comprehending their actions, the APA suggested, should not be treated in the same manner as those who understood their actions.

The APA recommended that:

Insanity acquittals should be reserved for defendants diagnosed as "psychotic," rather than those with less serious "antisocial personality disorders." (The APA defined a psychotic as someone so out of touch with reality he was "unable to appreciate the wrongfulness of his conduct.")

Defendants with antisocial personality disorders should be held "accountable for their behavior." (Such a person, according to the APA, understood his actions but might be unconcerned about their consequences.)

Psychiatric testimony should be limited to such areas of competence as a defendant's motivation or mental state.

Persons judged "not guilty by reason of

insanity" should not be released without careful consideration by state or federal authorities. The paper admitted that psychiatrists were unable to predict the "dangerousness" of such persons.

The organization also conceded that "psychiatric evidence" was "usually not sufficiently clear-cut to prove or disprove many legal facts 'beyond a reasonable doubt.' "

Index

A

Abbott Laboratories—71, 122
Abel v. Eli Lilly Co.—144
Abortion and abortion laws—3-
66; antiabortion proposals
rejected—35; basic controversy—3-4; congressional
views and actions—32-38, 49-
52; court actions—12-32, 38-
48; definition—4; funding
controversy—18-22, 23-25, 31-
32; political parties and—53-
56; religious views—56-60;
rights of fetus—32; right to
life proposals to amend con-
stitution—32-38; state actions
—4-12, 38-42, *see also* specific
state name
Abzug, (former) Rep. Bella—16,
33-35
ACTION—23
Adelman, Roger—187
Administrative Procedures
Act—112
Agarwol, Bela—125
Agarwol, Durga—125
Agarwol, Pravat—125
A.H. Robins Company—82
Akron Center v. Akron—26, 46
Akron Decision—46
Akron v. Akron Center—26, 46
Alabama: human
experimentation—136-137
Alan Guttmacher Institute—20,
66, 69
Alaska: abortion—10
Alsop, Judge Donald—21
American Bar Association—12,
96

American Chemical
Society—113-114
American Civil Liberties Union
(ACLU)—31, 35, 48, 130
American College of
Obstetricians and
Gynecologists—47-49
American Cyanamid—86
*American Cyanamid v. Oil,
Chemical and Atomic
Workers' International
Union*—86
American Federation of Labor-
Congress of Industrial
Organizations
(AFL-CIO)—163
American Jewish Congress—51
American Law Institute—15
American Life Lobby—48
American Medical Association
(AMA)—12, 59, 79, 94, 95-96,
108, 154, 170-171
American Orthopsychiatric
Association—165
American Psychiatric
Association—50, 188
American Public Health
Association—60-61
Amniocentesis—50, 89
Amygdalin—*see* Laetrile
Anders v. Floyd—45
Appropriations Bill: 1979—24;
1980—32
Aprindine—149
Armstrong, Paul W.—102
Army, Department of
(U.S.)—139-140
Army of God—64
Artificial hearts—126-128
Artificial insemination—124

Ashcroft, John—27
*Ashcroft v. Planned
Parenthood*—26, 46
Askew, Gov. Reubin—9
Atiyeh, Gov. Vic—159
Atomic Energy Commission
(AEC)—141-142
Ayerst Laboratories—159

B

Baden, Dr. Michael—101-102
Baer, David—187
Baird, William R.—57, 68
Baker, Howard H., Jr.—36, 38
Ball, Dr. Phillip—78
Bangor, Maine: town
meeting—23
Baptists: reaction to
abortion—158
Bargmann, Eve—164
Barrett, Elizabeth—35
Barter, Dr. Robert H.—12
Barth, Dale—118
Bartlett, Dewey F.—32
Baucus, Sen. Max—31, 36, 52,
53
Bayh, Sen. Birch—35
Beal v. Doe—19
Becke v. Swartz—90
Beecher, Dr. Henry K.—99
Belin, David W.—137
Bell, Attorney General
Griffin—22
Bellot v. Baird—39
Bennett, Robert W.—29
Bennet v. Graves—89
Bennet, Wallace F.—32
Benshoof, Janet—48

Benzene (carcinogen)—161
Bergstreser v. Michelle—91
Berman v. Allen—90
Bevilaqua, Bishop Anthony—59
Bhattacharya, Dr.
  Saroj K.—125
Bioethics—2
Birth issues: abortion—*See*
  under "A"; control and family
  planning—*See* Contraception;
  defects—89-91; illegitimacy,
  rise of—65; preconception
  injury—91-92; rate decline—
  93; selective birth—110-111;
  surrogate mothers—92;
  wrongful birth—83, 89-91;
  wrongful life—83, 89-91;
Black, Justice Hugo L.—11
Blackmun, Justice Harry A.—
  11, 14, 15, 20, 26, 42, 44, 69
Black Women Organized for
  Action—39
Blaur, Harold—140
Bleich, Rabbi J. David—33
Block, John R.—121
Boone v. Mullendore—90
Borelli, Dr. Anthony P.—99
Bork, Robert H.—51
Bowman, Ralph S.—154
Boyle, Dr. Joseph F.—50
Bradford, Robert—154
Brady, James S.—186-187
Brain Death (legal
  definition)—94
Breitel, Charles B.—7
Brennan, Justice William—
  11, 20, 26, 30, 68, 70, 163
Brickner, Rabbi Balfour—33
Bridgton Hospital—39
Broaddus, William G.—27
Brown, Gov. Edmund G.—100
Brown, John—120, 125-126
Brown, Leslie—120, 125-126
Brown, Dr. Norman K.—109
Bryant, William—185-186
Buckley, Sen. James L.—32, 34
Burger, Chief Justice Warren—
  11, 15, 25-26, 28, 29, 30, 42,
  70, 163
Burgess, Anna—83
Burnett, Arthur L.—195
Burns, Gov. John A.—4
Byrn, Prof. Robert M.—7

BZ (3-Quinuclidinyl
  benzilate)—140

C

Califano, Joseph A.—19, 23, 27,
  118
California: birthrate—9-10;
  death issue and Natural Death
  Act—100; right to die—100
Canadian Food and Drug—132
Cancer: DES issue—143-147;
  diagnosis freely given—165;
  Laetrile controversy—151-158;
  other carcinogens—161; *see
  also* Food & Drug
  Administration
Candura, Rosaria—101
Capron, Alexander
  Morgan—96-97
*Carey v. Population Services
  International*—70
Carey, Walter Burton, 3d—
  94-95
Carpenter, Dr. William,
  Jr.—187
Carroll, Rev. Charles
  Patrick—16
Carter, Jimmy—19, 21, 24, 25,
  32, 54, 61
Catholic Conference, U.S.—32,
  57
Catholics—*See* Roman
  Catholics
Census Bureau, U.S.—73
Center for Constitutional Rights
  in New York City—29
Center for Disease Control,
  U.S.—65
Central Intelligence Agency
  (CIA)—137-138
Chlormadinone acetate—80
Church, Sen. Frank—96
Clarie, District Judge T.
  Emmet—9, 91
Clark, Barney B.—127-128
Cleveland—46
Cloning—128
Club of Rome—72-73
Coalition for a National
  Population Policy—72
Coats, Andy—56

Cobb, Capt. W.C.—76
Coburn, Daniel R.—103
Cohen, George H.—163
Collester, Donald G., Jr.—102
Commissioned Corps of the
  U.S. Public Health
  Service—52
Community Services
  Administration—23
Congress (U.S.): abortion—32-
  38, 49-52; behavior
  modification—139; birth
  control—78-79; death—93,
  100; DES action—143-147;
  drugs and drug abuse—151-
  158; genetic research—113-
  114; human experimentation
  —129-142; Laetrile
  controversy—151-158; mental
  health—185-189; unnecessary
  surgery—172-177
Connecticut: abortion—9, 43
Connel, Dr. Elizabeth—78
Conroy, Edward T.—56
Consent, informed—129
Consumer Product Safety
  Commission (CPSC)—
  162-164
Contraception: condoms—69;
  Congress, U.S.—78-79;
  controversy—67; dangers of—
  81-82; IUD—82; pill, the—76-
  82; population policy and
  birth rate—72-75; religious
  views—75-76, *see also*
  religious denominations by
  name; restraints on, voided—
  70; sterilization—84-87; zero
  population growth theory—72
Conviod—76
Cooke, Terence Cardinal—5,
  30, 48
Copland, Rhonda—29
Corday, Dr. Eliot—93
Cord Laboratories—159
Costanza, Margaret—61
Cost Benefit Standard—159,
  162
Council for International
  Organizations of Medical
  Science—94
Court actions: abortions—32-38,
  49-52; birth control—67-87;

death (mercy killing)—108-112; drugs and drug abuse—151-158; federal funds—27-29; Laetrile—151-158; mental health—184-188
Cousins, Most Rev. William E.—7
Cox, Archibald—51
Cox, William—23
C-Quens—79
Cranston, Sen. Alan—72
Criminal Justice Reform Act—188
Crisp, Mary D.—55
Curran, Gary—48
Curtis, Carl T.—32

D

Dalkon Shield (IUD)—81-82
Danforth v. Planned Parenthood—31
Davi, Richard—5
Davis, Dr. Hugh J.—78
Davis, Kingsley—9
Death and dying—93-112; definition ambiguous—93-96; euthanasia—108-112; right to die—96-108; Uniform Determination of Death Act—96
Deemer, Connie L.—82
Defective neonates—110-117
Defense of Life, Ad Hoc Committee for the—53
Delaware Euthanasia Education Council—107
Delaware: right to die—107
Dellums, Rep. Ronald V.—33
Del Zio, Doris—124-125
Democratic Party—54
DepoProvera—82-83
DES (diethylstilbesterol)—143, 144-147
De Vries, Dr. William C.—127-128
Dietz, Dr. Park E.—187
Dilation and curettage (D&C)—22
District of Columbia: abortion—11
DNA (deoxyribonucleic

acid)—113-119
DNA Research Bill—119
Doe v. Bridgton Hospital Association Inc.—39
Doe v. Irwin—70
Donnelly, Dr. Joseph P.—16
Dooling, Judge John F., Jr.—18, 21, 22, 27, 28, 29-30, 44
Dorsen, Norman—35
Douglas, Rosalie—92
Douglas, Justice William—9, 11, 68
Downey, Rep. Thomas J.—140
Down's Syndrome—90
Drinan, Robert F.—56
Drobuline—149
Drugs and drug abuse: behavior modification—165; cancer—143, 151-158; DES action—144-147; Gerovital—158; government experimentation—139-142; Thalidomide—5, 157; tranquilizers—157; uncertified drugs—159
Durand, Gilbert—34
Du Val, Dr. Merlin K.—136

E

East, Sen. John P.—48, 49, 50-51, 52
Eaton, Rev. David—68
Edelin, Dr. Kenneth C.—38
Edwards, Dr. Charles C.—77, 79, 159
Edwards, Dr. Robert G.—123
Efstratiadis, Argiris—114
Eichner v. Dillon—107
Eisenhower, Milton S.—72
Eli Lilly and Company—79, 122, 143, 146, 148, 149
Enovid—76
Environmental Protection Agency—118
Epitrate—159
Equal Rights Amendment—55
Erlichman, John D.—7
Ethics—96, 130, 165-183
Euthanasia—108-112
Evans, James—185
Experimentation, human—129-142

F

Falwell, Rev. Jerry—60
Family Life Division—57
Family Planning Bill: 1971—67
Family Planning (defined)—67
Family Planning Services and Population Research Act—72
Fatteh, Dr. Abullah—94
Federal aid ban—27
Federalism, New—182-184
Federal Trade Commission—25
Fennelly, Dr. Joseph F.—103
Ferre, Gov. Luis A.—75
Ferrino v. Eli Lilly—145
Fetal right to sue—91-92
Finch, Robert H.—79
Finesilver, Judge Sherman G.—148
Flannery, Judge Thomas A.—71
Florez, Luis de—139
Florida: abortion—9
Food and Drug Administration, U.S.—76-77, 79, 126, 127, 130, 131, 133, 144, 150, 153-154, 156, 159, 160, 163
Ford, Betty—34
Ford, Gerald—18, 34, 53, 54
Formaldehyde—164
Formaldehyde Institute—164
Foster, Jodie—187
Fountain, L.H.—149
Foy, Dr. Laurance F., Jr.—98-99
Frank, Rep. Barney—55
Frederickson, Donald S.—117
Freedom of Choice in Cancer Therapy, Committee for—154
Freedom of Information Act—142
Fuller, Vincent H.—185, 187

G

Gallese, Liz Roman—130
Gallup Poll—13, 58, 62, 65
Garn, Sen. Jake—51
Gary Northwest Indiana Womens Service v. Boren—43
G.D. Searle and Company—76-77

Geis, Prof. Gilbert—3
Gemma, Pette B.—51
General Electric—123
Genetech—120
Genetic research—113, 114-115
Gerovital—158
Gerster, Dr. Carolyn—51
Gesell, Judge Gerhard A.—11, 84
Gibson, Cambell—74
Giminez, Jimeno Enrique—39
Giulani, Rudolf—188
Goldman, Dr. Thomas C.—187
Goldstein, Dr. Naomi—50
Goodman, Howard M.—118
Gorbach, Dr. Sherwood—119
Gordon Conference on Nucleic Acids—120
Gottlieb, Sidney—138
Government Accounting Office (GAO)—131, 132, 133
Grady, Judge John—27, 30
Great Lakes Family Planning Coalition—62
Greeley, Rev. Andrew—75
Green, Chad—155, 156-157
Guardianship of Tulley—87
Guttmacher, Dr. Alan F.—15, 79

H

Hammurabi's Code of Laws—1
Harris, Dr. David—6
Harris, Patricia Roberts—31
Harris Poll—61
Harris v. McRae—17, 28
Hatch, Sen. Orrin G.—35, 36, 48, 49, 52
Hatfield, Mark—32
Hawaii—4
Hayakawa, Sen. S.I.—38
Health and Human Services Dept.—70, 71, 134, 149, 163, 182
Health Education and Welfare—17, 21, 23, 29, 79, 86, 117, 118, 134
Health Research Group—146, 164
Heart, artificial—126-128
Heflin, Sen. Howell—52

Heller, Jean—65
Helms, Sen. Jesse A.—32, 35, 36, 38, 48, 49
Helms, Richard—139
Hensley, Dr. Michael—149
Hepatitis—136
Hertz, Dr. Roy—68, 78
Hinckley, John W., Jr.—185, 188
Hippocratic Oath—1
Hodgson, Dr. Jane—11
Hoffmann-La Roche—122
Holland, James G.—165
Holton, Gov. Linwood—8
Holtzman, Elizabeth—24
Hope Clinic for Women—63
Horton, Rep. Frank—72
Hughes, Harold—32
Humane Vita—76
Human experimentation—136-142
Human Life Amendment—34
Human Resources Research Organization—165
Hume, Dr. David—94
Hunerwadel v. Baird—42
Hutcheson, Dr. Robert, Jr.—83
Hyde Amendment—18, 21, 24, 27, 30, 49, 50, 51
Hyde, Rep. Henry J.—18, 21, 22, 27, 28, 29, 30, 42, 49, 50, 51
Hysterectomies—179

I

Illegitimacy—17
Illinois: abortion—11
Indiana: abortion—45
Infant care—111-112
Informed consent—136, 165-166
In re Hayes—87
In re Penny—87
In re Storer—107
Insanity defense—185-189
International Federation of Catholic Medical Associations—5
International Playtex-Esmarc Inc.—148
International Population and Urban Research Center—9
In the Matter of Moe—86

In the Matter of Spring—106
Intrauterine devices (IUD)—81-82

J

Jaffe, Frederick S.—62
Jain, Dr. Anrudh K.—80-81
Javed, Dr. Arshad—103
Jefferson, Dr. Mildred—49
Jehovah's Witnesses—97
Jepsen, Sen. Roger W.—48
Jewish Theological Seminary—51
Jiminez, Rosie—62
John Birch Society—7
John F. Kennedy Hospital v. Heston—97
John Paul II—59
Johnson and Johnson—80
Johnson, Douglas—48

K

Kafatos, Dr. Fotis—114
Kapiolani Maternity and Gynecological Hospital—4
Karbon v. Guerinot—90
Kassouf, Dr. Edmund—78
Kasten Liability Bill—150
Kasten, Robert W.—150
Keating, Rep. William J.—16-17
Kefauver-Harris Amendment—131
Kehm, Michael—148
Kehm, Patricia—148
Kenly, Dr. James B.—125
Kennedy, Donald—152
Kennedy, Sen. Edward M.—2, 54, 117, 119, 129
Kennedy, John F.—151
Kentucky: abortion—40
Kerenye, Dr. Thomas D.—110
Khorana, Dr. Har Gobind—113
King, Gov. Edward J.—31
Kistner, Dr. Robert W.—78-79
Koop, Dr. C. Everett—52, 112
Krebiozen—158
Krebs, Dr. Ernst T.—151-152
Krol, John Cardinal—3, 15
Krugman, Saul—136
Kuchera, Dr. Lucile K.—81

L

Lady Jane v. Maher—43
Laetrile—143, 151-158
Lampshire, Deletha—148
Landsman, Stephen—27
Lane, Grace R.—101
Lane v. Candura—100
Laparoscopy—124
Lashbrook, Robert V.—138
League of Women Voters—164
Leahy, Sen. Patrick—35
Lederle Laboratories—132
Lee, Rex E.—26, 48
Lefkowitz, Louis—117
Liacos, Justice Liacos—105
Linden Laboratories—159
Lower, Dr. Richard—94
LSD (lysergic acid
  diethylamide)—137, 139, 140
Lumbard, Judge Edward J.—9
Lynchburg Training School and
  Hospital—85

M

Maher v. Doe—20
Mandel, Gov. Marvin—10
Maniatis, Dr. Thomas—114
Mansour, Sister Agnes
  Mary—59
Marbury v. Madison—26
March for Life—62
March of Dimes—65
Margolis, Lawrence—186
Marijuana—158-159
Marks, Dr. Lawrence—133-134
Marshall, Justice Thurgood—9,
  11, 20, 26, 28, 68, 86, 146, 156
Marston, John H.—124
Martinez, Most Rev. Luis
  Aponte—75
Maryland—10, 56
Massachusetts: abortion—10,
  31, 32, 45; contraception—68;
  Laetrile—109
Massachusetts Institute of
  Technology—72-73, 113
Mathias, Charles McC., Jr.—56
Maxam, Dr. Allen—114
McCreer, General Wade H.—28
McGuire, Judge James P.—39
McHugh, Msgr. James T.—51

McNeal, Barbara—33
Meadows, Dennis L.—73
Medeiros, Humberto Cardinal—
  33, 56
Medicaid—17, 18, 19, 27, 28, 29,
  182, 184
Medical ethics—170-184
Medicare—182-184
Medroxyprogesterone—80
Memorial Sloan-Kettering
  Cancer Center—153
Menffels, Willebrocher A.—128
Merck, Sharpe and Dohme—
  132
Merkel, Rep. Kenneth—7
Methodists—58
Michaels, George M.—5
Michigan—8
Miller, Gov. Keith—10
Miller v. Zbaraz—28, 29
Mink, Patsy—146
Minnesota—11
Missouri—47
M.K. Kellog Foundation—69
Modicon—80
Moertel, Dr. Charles G.—157
Mondale, Walter F.—1-2
Moral Majority—63
Morgan, Dr. Karl Z.—177
Morgun, Dr. Arthur E.—97
"Morning-after" pill—81
Morse, Dr. Robert—103
Moss, John E.—172
Moynihan, Sen. Daniel
  Patrick—37
Mueller, Dr. Robert—110
Muir, Judge Robert—103
Mulhauser, Karen—24, 62

N

Nader, Ralph—146, 163
Narcotics and Dangerous Drugs,
  Bureau of—140
National Abortion Rights
  League—23, 24, 53, 62, 65
National Academy of Sciences—
  49, 60, 115
National Aeronautics and Space
  Administration (NASA)—
  141-142
National Center for Health
  Statistics—73-74

National Committee for Human
  Life Amendment—23
National Conference of Catholic
  Bishops—35
National Conference of
  Commissions on Uniform
  State Laws—12
National Council of Catholic
  Bishops—56
National Family Planning and
  Reproductive Health
  Association—71
National Family Planning
  Forum—62
National Family Planning
  Foundation—61
National Federation of Catholic
  Physicians—12
National Institute of Health—
  116, 119, 131
National Labor Relations
  Board—23
National Opinion Research
  Center—65
National Organization for the
  Reform of Marijuana
  Laws—158
National Organization for
  Women—62
National Pro Life Political
  Action Committee—57
National Research Act—134
National Right to Life
  Committee—35, 63
Nelson, Sen. Gaylord—78,
  140-141
Nerve gas—140
Newcomb Hospital—39
New Jersey: abortion—8, 31
Newman, Judge John O.—9
New Right—48
New York City Health and
  Hospitals Corp.—18
New York Department of
  Health—71
New York State: abortion—5-7;
  contraception—69; mental
  health—140; right to die—107
New York State Psychiatric
  Institute—140
Nickles, Don—56
Nixon, Richard M.—6, 12, 14,
  15, 34

O

Oak Ridge Cancer
    Center—141-142
Occupational Safety and Health
    Administration (OSHA)—23,
    161-162
Ochs, Carol—91
O'Connor, Justice Sandra
    Day—48, 49, 60, 63
Office of Budget
    Management—164
Office of Population Affairs—67
Oil, Chemical and Atomic
    Workers' International
    Union—87
Oklahoma: abortion—56;
    Laetrile—148
Olson, Alice—138
Olson, Frank R.—137
One Nation Under God
    Coalition—60
Operation Avalanche—34
Oraflex—148-149
Ornex—159
O'Rourke, Rev. Joseph—57
Orth Pharmaceutical
    Corporation—80
Oversight and Investigations
    Subcommittee of the House
    Interstate and Foreign
    Commerce Committee—172
Oxprenolol hydrochloride—132

P

Packwood, Sen. Robert W.—19,
    31, 36, 38, 48
Papola, Dr. Gino—12
Parents Aid Society—57
Parker, Barrington D.—186
Park v. Chessin—90-91
Paul VI—57
Payton v. Abbot
    Laboratory—147
Pediatrics, American Academy
    of—111
Pennhurst State School v.
    Haldoman—170
Pennsylvania: abortion—10, 44
Peterson, Dr. Chase—128
Peterson, Fay—163

Pitchford, Maria Elaine—40
Pius XII—99
Planned Parenthood Federation
    of America—21, 27, 30, 47,
    61, 69, 70, 71, 78, 81
Planned Parenthood Inc.—16,
    18
Planned Parenthood of Missouri
    v. Danfourth—42
Planned Parenthood Physicians,
    American Association of—68
Planned Parenthood v.
    Ashcroft—48
Plunkett, Judge J. Jerome—11
Plutonium test—141
Poelker, John H.—20
Poelker v. Doe—20
Pomeroy, Karen Ann—95
Population Council—62, 80
Population Growth and the
    American Future, Commis-
    sion on—13-14
Powell, Justice Lewis F., Jr.—
    15, 20, 26, 28, 30, 46, 86, 162
President's Commission for the
    Study of Ethical Problems in
    Medicine and Biomedical
    Research—95, 171
Privitera v. California—156
Procter & Gamble—147-148
Product Liability Bill—150-151
Project Sanguine—141
Prostaglandin F2 Alpha—68
Provest—79
Proxmire, Sen. William—19-20
Psychosis—188-189

Q

Quakers—57
Queen's Medical Center—5
Quern v. Zbaraz—27
Quinlan, Joseph—101-104
Quinlan, Julia—101-104
Quinlan, Karen Anne—100-105
Quirico, Francis J.—32, 107

R

Rabbinical Council of America
    and Orthodox Judaism—33
Rados, William—126
Randell, Robert—158

Reagan, Ronald—36, 38, 48,
    171, 182-184, 185
Reasonable practitioners—166
Rehnquist, Justice William H.—
    14, 15, 28, 29, 30, 42, 44,
    63, 70
Reid, Judge Clarence A., Jr.—8
Religious Roundtable—60
Republican Party—55-56
Ribicoff, Sen. Abraham A.—130
Richardson, John A.—154
Richardson, Marcus—38
Ridings, Dorothy—64
Right to Choose v. Byrne—31
Right to Life amendment—33
Robaczynski, Mary Rose—109
Robboy, Dr. Stanley—147
Robinson, Rev. James—40
Rockefeller, Gov. Nelson A.—5,
    6, 34
Roe v. Wade—3, 14-17, 18, 26,
    46, 47, 49
Roger, Paul—119
Roman Catholics: abortion—
    4-5, 24, 32-38, 56-57;
    contraception—67, 75-76;
    euthanasia—110
Roncallo, Rep. Angelo D.—16
Rosenberg, Howard—142
Rosenblum, Victor G.—29
Roussin, Rev. John C.—57
Royal College of General
    Practitioners—77
Ruether, Dr. Rosemary
    Radford—51
Russo, Sen. Marty—51
Rutter, William—118
Ruwet, Col. Vincent—137
Ryan, Dr. George M.—49

S

Saccharin—164
Sackett, Dr. Walter W.—9, 100
Saikewicz and Spring—86
Saikewicz, Joseph—101, 106
Sanger, Fred—118
Schreiber, Sidney M.—38
Schroeder v. Perkel—90
Schweiker, Richard S.—70, 149,
    150, 169, 182
Second opinion—178
Segedy, Alan G.—26

Senate, U.S.: abortion—13; amendment—32; the pill—78-81
Sendel v. Abbott Laboratories—122
Sequential pills—80
Sessa, Dr. Grazia—114
Severns, Mary Reeser—107
Severns v. Wilmington Medical Center, Inc.—107
Sewell, Dr. David—94
Shannon, Rep. James M.—56
Shapp, Milton J.—10
Sherlock v. Stillwater Clinic—90
Shumway, Dr. Norman—94
Siegel, Rabbi Seymour—51
Siegman, Rabbi Henry—51
Sim, Dr. Van M.—79
Simopoulous, Dr. Chris—48
Simopoulos v. Virginia—46, 48
Smith, Kline and French Laboratories—159
Smith, William French—186
Social Security Act—19
Sorkin v. Lee—89
Speakes, Larry—38
Sperling, Philip—165
Spitler, Linda Kay—85
Spring, Earle—106
Squibb and Sons, R.—133
Steinem, Gloria—62
Sterilization—83-87
Stevens, John Paul—26, 27, 29
Stilbine—146
Stokes, Louis—22
Stump, Judge Harold—85
Stump v. Sparkman—85
Superintendent of Belchertown State School v. Saikewicz—101, 106
Supreme Court: abortion—12, 46-49; birth and birth control—93-112; death—97; drugs and drug abuse—156
Surgery and surgeons: liability—91; unnecessary—172-177
Surrogate mothers—92
Susman, Frank—27
Syphilis: human experimentation—136
Szoka, Archbishop Edmund—59

T

Taeker, Conrad F.—72
Taft, Sen. Robert, Jr.—72
Tampon liability—147
Taylor, Rev. Eamon—57
Tay Sachs disease—65
Ten Million, Committee of—34
Tennessee Health Dept.—83
Texas—8
Texas Heart Institute—126
Thompson, Donavan J.—109
Thrombophlebitis—77
Todd, Malcolm C.—108
Toxic Shock Syndrome—147
Travis, Alice—33
Triglycerides—141
Tris—162
Tucker, Bruce O.—94
Tydings, Sen. Joseph D.—68, 72

U

Udall, Rep. Morris—72
Uncertified drugs—159
UNESCO—94
United Nations Population Division—13
United Press International—14
University of Utah Medical Center—127
Upjohn Company—79, 83, 122
U.S. v. Rutherford—156
U.S. v. Zbaraz—28, 29

V

Vasectomy, failure of—84
Vatican: abortion—59; birth control—76; euthanasia—109-110
Vermont: abortion—7
Virginia: abortion—8, 43, 48; involuntary sterilization—85
Vuitch, Dr. Milan—11

W

Waddill, Dr. William, Jr.—39
Watson, Dr. James D.—1
Waxman, Henry D.—71
Weddington, Sarah—50, 55

Weicker, Sen. Lowell P., Jr.—37, 38
Wensel, William—29
Werber, Henry F.—71
Westoff, Charles F.—73, 75
White, Justice Byron R.—11, 14, 15, 29, 30, 42, 44, 69, 85
Williams v. Zbaraz—27, 28
Willke, Dr. J.C.—63
Wilson, Rep. Charles—32
Wimmershoff-Caplan, Sue—33
Wisconsin: abortion—7; birth control—68
Wisconsin Citizens Concerned for the Unborn—7
Wisner, Frank—139
Women's abortion rights—41
Women's Caucus of the California Democractic Council—33
Women's Groups v. Amendments—33-34
Women's Lobby—57
World Health Organization—4
Wright, James—24
Wright, Judge J. Skelly—97
Wrongful birth and wrongful life (defined)—89

X

X-Rays—177-178

Y

Yano, Sen. Vincent H.—4-5
Yoon, Dr. In Bal—84
Young, Milton R.—32
Young, Sen. Robert A.—51

Z

Zero Population Growth Inc.—62
Zero population growth (theory)—16, 72
Zevallos, Dr. Hector—63
Zoser—1
Zwach, Rep. John M.—33
Zygmaniak, George—108
Zygmaniak, Lester—108